SPIDER-MAN 2099

WRITER
PETER DAVID

ARTIST, #1-4
WILL SLINEY

PENCILER, #5
RICK LEONARDI

INKER, #5
LIVESAY

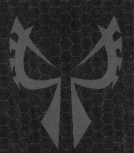

COLOR ARTIST
ANTONIO FABELA

LETTERER
VC'S JOE CARAMAGNA

COVER ART
SIMONE BIANCHI (#1),
ALEXANDER LOZANO (#2)
AND **FRANCESCO MATTINA** (#3-5)

EDITOR
ELLIE PYLE

SENIOR EDITOR
NICK LOWE

Collection Editor: Jennifer Grünwald • Assistant Editor: Sarah Brunstad • Associate Managing Editor: Alex Starbuck
Editor, Special Projects: Mark D. Beazley • Senior Editor, Special Projects: Jeff Youngquist
SVP Print, Sales & Marketing: David Gabriel • Book Design: Jeff Powell

Editor in Chief: Axel Alonso • Chief Creative Officer: Joe Quesada • Publisher: Dan Buckley • Executive Producer: Alan Fine

PIDER-MAN 2099 VOL. 1: OUT OF TIME. Contains material originally published in magazine form as SPIDER-MAN 2099 #1-5 and AMAZING SPIDER-MAN #1. First printing 2015. ISBN# 978-0-7851-9079-0. Published by IARVEL WORLDWIDE, INC., a subsidiary of MARVEL ENTERTAINMENT, LLC. OFFICE OF PUBLICATION: 135 West 50th Street, New York, NY 10020. **Printed in Canada.** ALAN FINE, EVP - Office of the President, Marvel Worldwide, Inc. nd EVP & CMO Marvel Characters B.V.; DAN BUCKLEY, Publisher & President - Print, Animation & Digital Divisions; JOE QUESADA, Chief Creative Officer; TOM BREVOORT, SVP of Publishing; DAVID BOGART, SVP of Operations & rocurement, Publishing; C.B. CEBULSKI, SVP of Creator & Content Development; DAVID GABRIEL, SVP Print, Sales & Marketing; JIM O'KEEFE, VP of Operations & Logistics; DAN CARR, Executive Director of Publishing Technology; USAN CRESPI, Editorial Operations Manager; ALEX MORALES, Publishing Operations Manager; STAN LEE, Chairman Emeritus. For information regarding advertising in Marvel Comics or on Marvel.com, please contact Niza isla, Director of Marvel Partnerships, at ndisla@marvel.com. For Marvel subscription inquiries, please call 800-217-9158. **Manufactured between 12/12/2014 and 1/19/2015 by SOLISCO PRINTERS, SCOTT, QC, CANADA.**

0 9 8 7 6 5 4 3 2 1

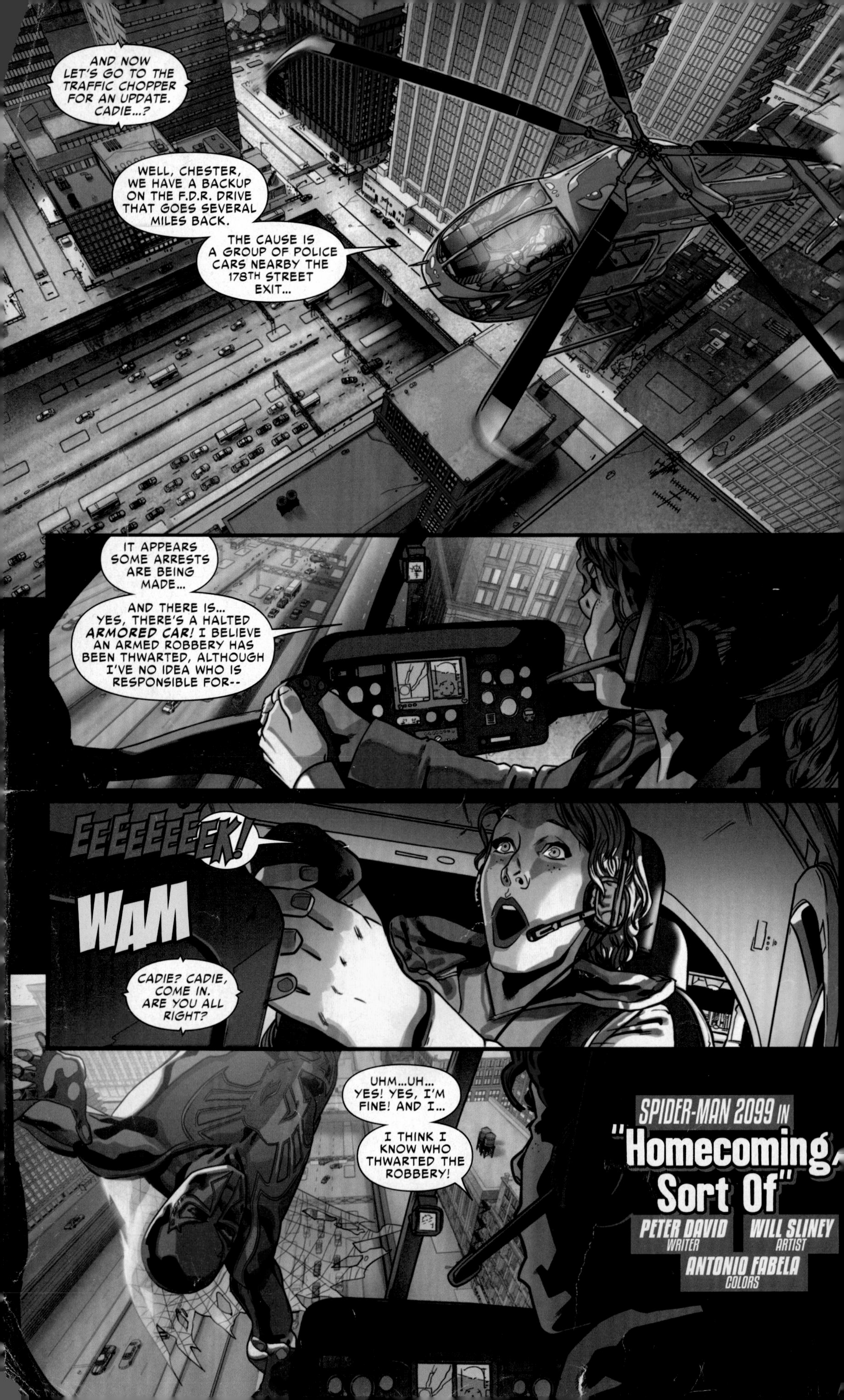
AND NOW LET'S GO TO THE TRAFFIC CHOPPER FOR AN UPDATE. CADIE...?
WELL, CHESTER, WE HAVE A BACKUP ON THE F.D.R. DRIVE THAT GOES SEVERAL MILES BACK.
THE CAUSE IS A GROUP OF POLICE CARS NEARBY THE 178TH STREET EXIT...
IT APPEARS SOME ARRESTS ARE BEING MADE...
AND THERE IS... YES, THERE'S A HALTED ARMORED CAR! I BELIEVE AN ARMED ROBBERY HAS BEEN THWARTED, ALTHOUGH I'VE NO IDEA WHO IS RESPONSIBLE FOR--
EEEEEEEEK!
WAM
CADIE? CADIE, COME IN. ARE YOU ALL RIGHT?
UHM...UH... YES! YES, I'M FINE! AND I...
I THINK I KNOW WHO THWARTED THE ROBBERY!
SPIDER-MAN 2099 IN
"Homecoming, Sort Of"
PETER DAVID WRITER
WILL SLINEY ARTIST
ANTONIO FABELA COLORS

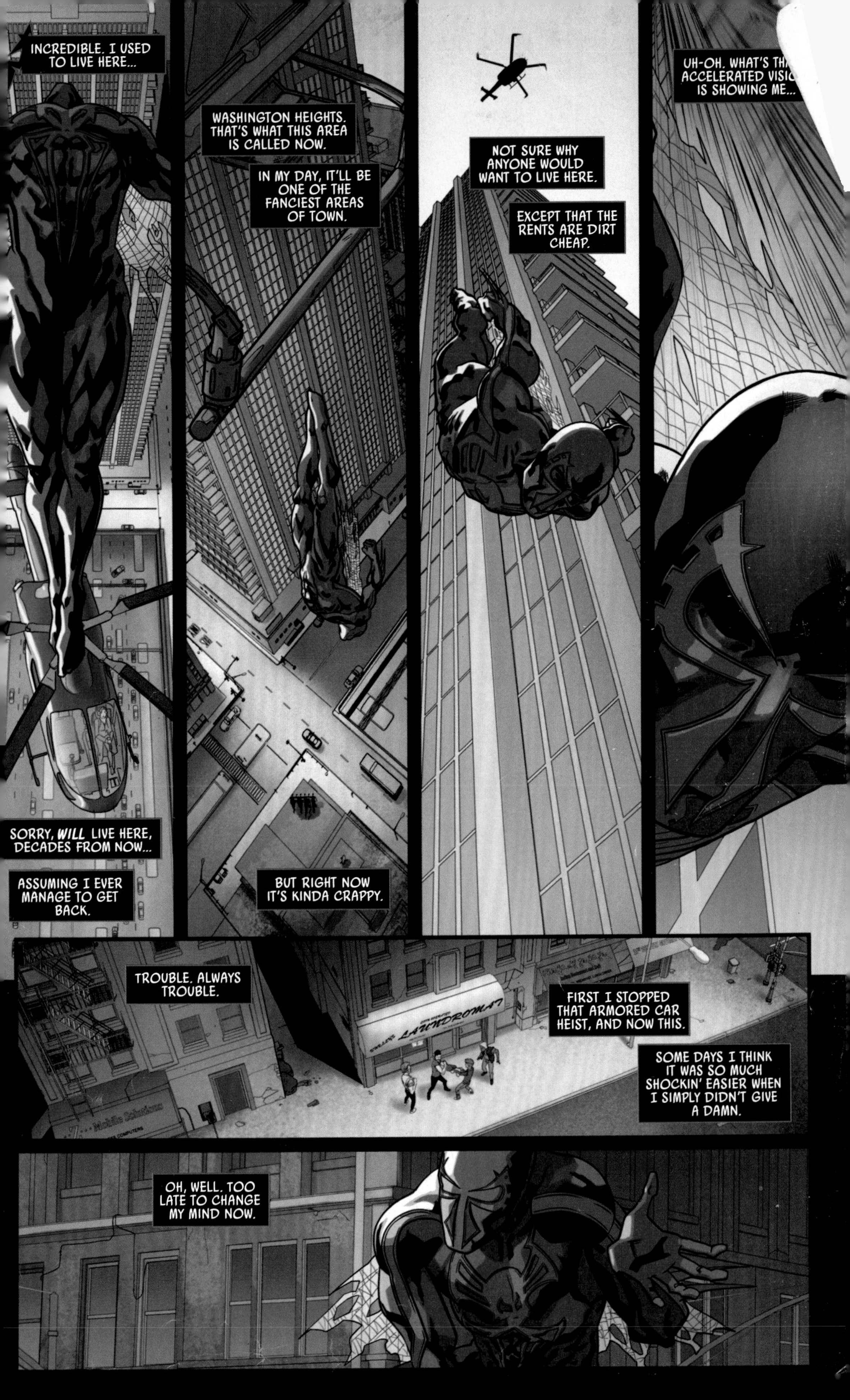

INCREDIBLE. I USED TO LIVE HERE...
SORRY, WILL LIVE HERE, DECADES FROM NOW...
ASSUMING I EVER MANAGE TO GET BACK.
WASHINGTON HEIGHTS. THAT'S WHAT THIS AREA IS CALLED NOW.
IN MY DAY, IT'LL BE ONE OF THE FANCIEST AREAS OF TOWN.
BUT RIGHT NOW IT'S KINDA CRAPPY.
NOT SURE WHY ANYONE WOULD WANT TO LIVE HERE.
EXCEPT THAT THE RENTS ARE DIRT CHEAP.
UH-OH. WHAT'S TH ACCELERATED VISI IS SHOWING ME...
TROUBLE. ALWAYS TROUBLE.
LAUNDROMAT
FIRST I STOPPED THAT ARMORED CAR HEIST, AND NOW THIS.
SOME DAYS I THINK IT WAS SO MUCH SHOCKIN' EASIER WHEN I SIMPLY DIDN'T GIVE A DAMN.
OH, WELL. TOO LATE TO CHANGE MY MIND NOW.

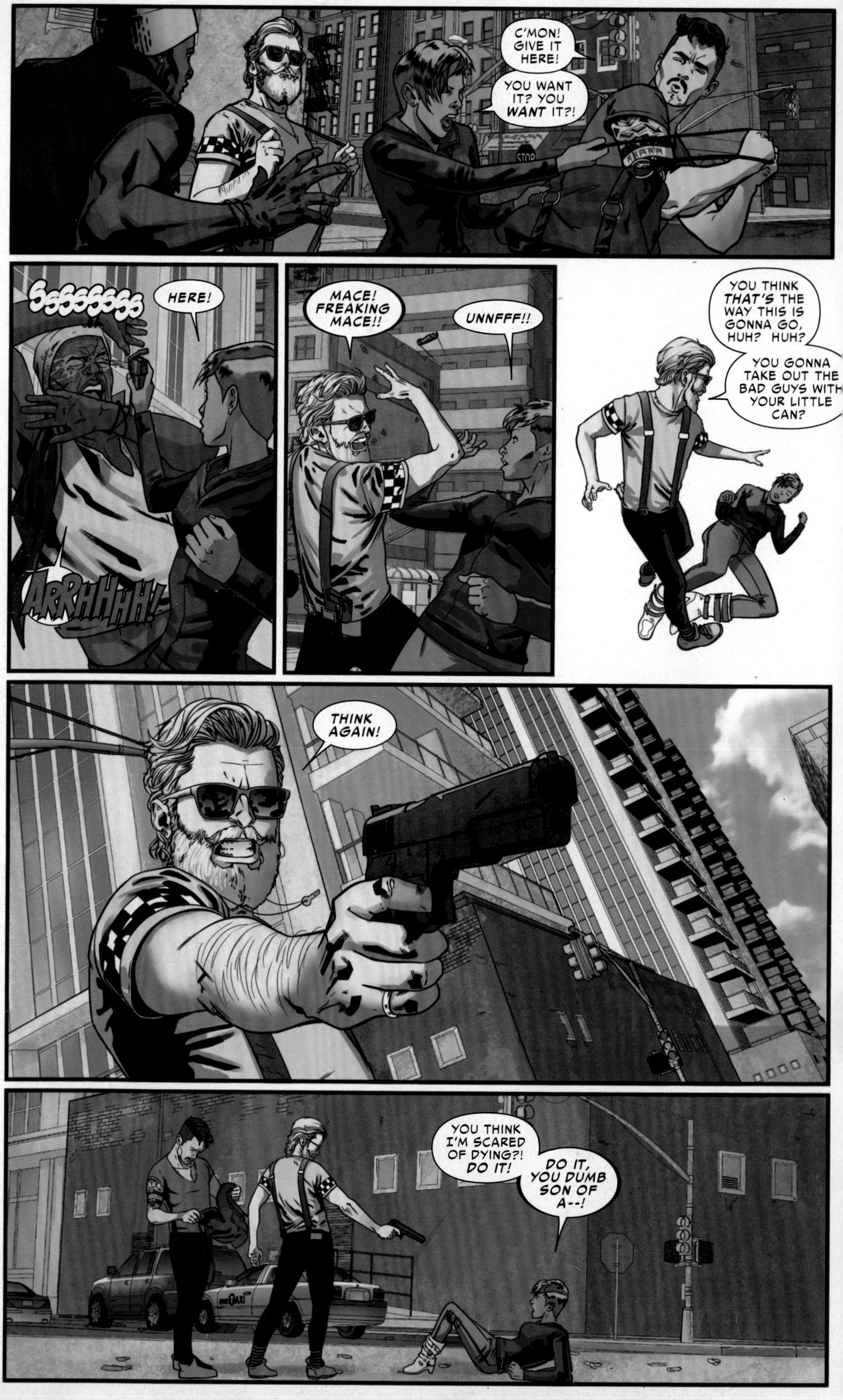
C'MON! GIVE IT HERE!
YOU WANT IT? YOU WANT IT?!
SSSSSSSS
HERE!
ARRHHHH!
MACE! FREAKING MACE!!
UNNFFF!!
YOU THINK THAT'S THE WAY THIS IS GONNA GO, HUH? HUH?
YOU GONNA TAKE OUT THE BAD GUYS WITH YOUR LITTLE CAN?
THINK AGAIN!
YOU THINK I'M SCARED OF DYING?! DO IT!
DO IT, YOU DUMB SON OF A--!

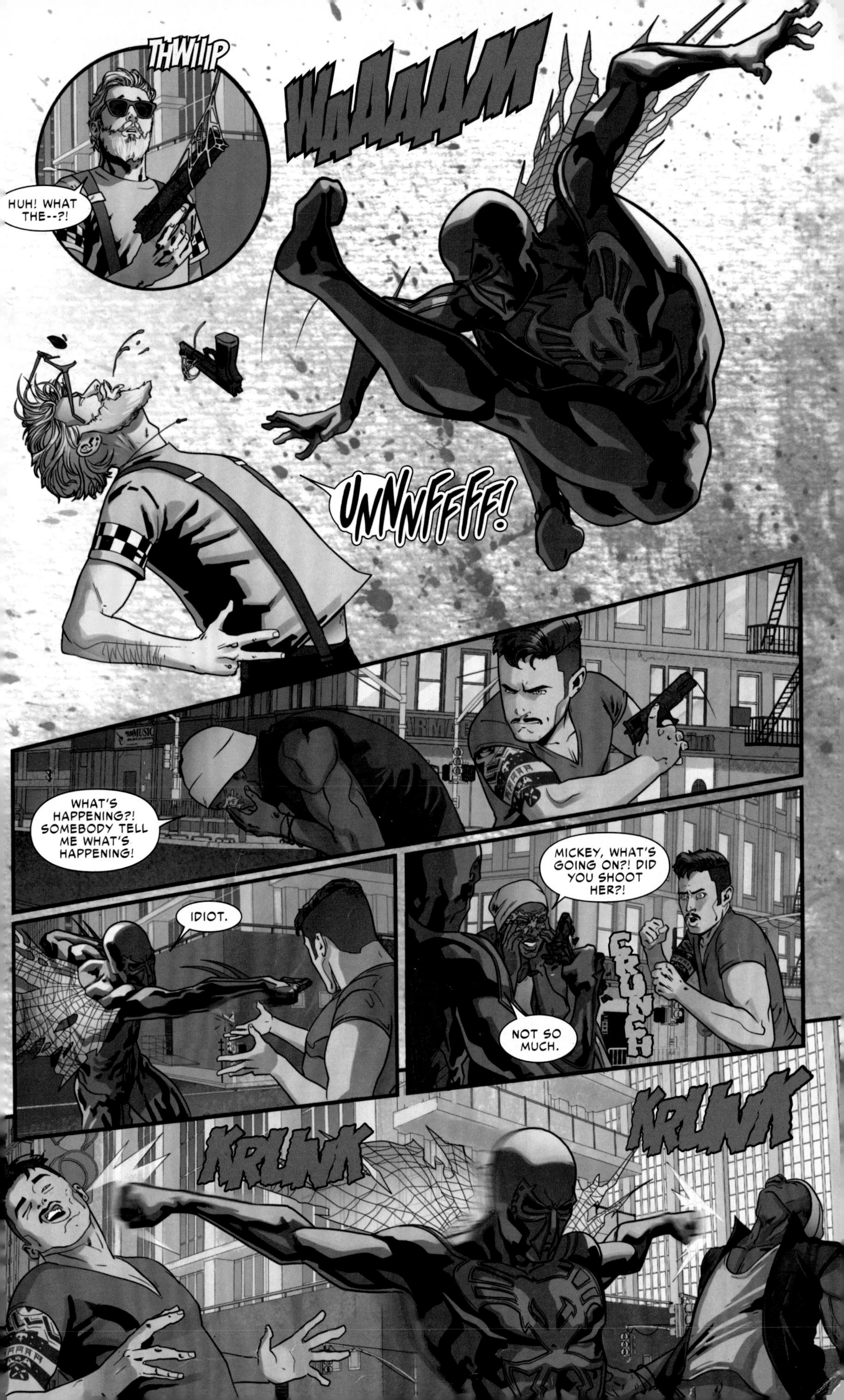
THWIIP
HUH! WHAT THE--?!
WAAAAAM
UNNNFFFF!
WHAT'S HAPPENING?! SOMEBODY TELL ME WHAT'S HAPPENING!
MICKEY, WHAT'S GOING ON?! DID YOU SHOOT HER?!
IDIOT.
NOT SO MUCH.
CRUNCH
KRUNK
KRUNK

YOU CAN CALL THE POLICE ANYTIME YOU W--

HUH?

WAAAP

YOU DUMB CLUCK!

DID I SHOUT FOR HELP? *DID* I? DID I WANT YOU TO BUTT IN?

NO, I DIDN'T! SO HOW ABOUT NEXT TIME YOU *ASK* IF THE PERSON YOU'VE DECIDED TO SAVE WANTS YOU TO SHOVE YOUR MASKED NOSE INTO HER BUSINESS!

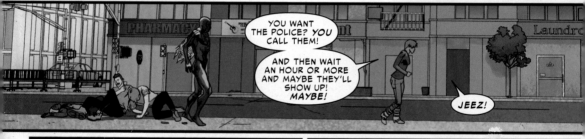

YOU WANT THE POLICE? *YOU* CALL THEM!

AND THEN WAIT AN HOUR OR MORE AND MAYBE THEY'LL SHOW UP! *MAYBE!*

JEEZ!

WHAT THE SHOCK IS WRONG WITH PEOPLE IN THIS DECADE?

WELL, IF Y'ASK ME--

WAAM

HMMM...

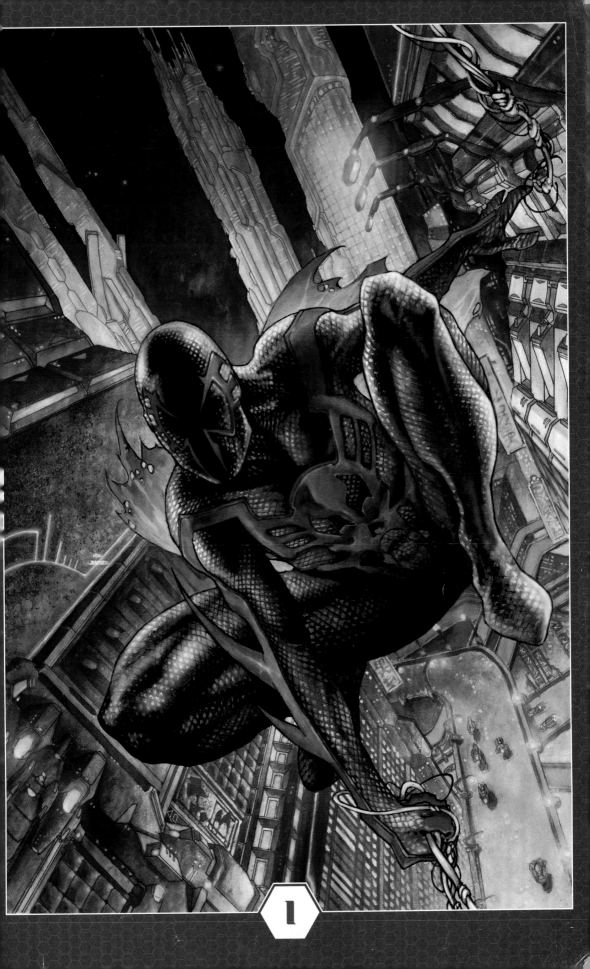

1

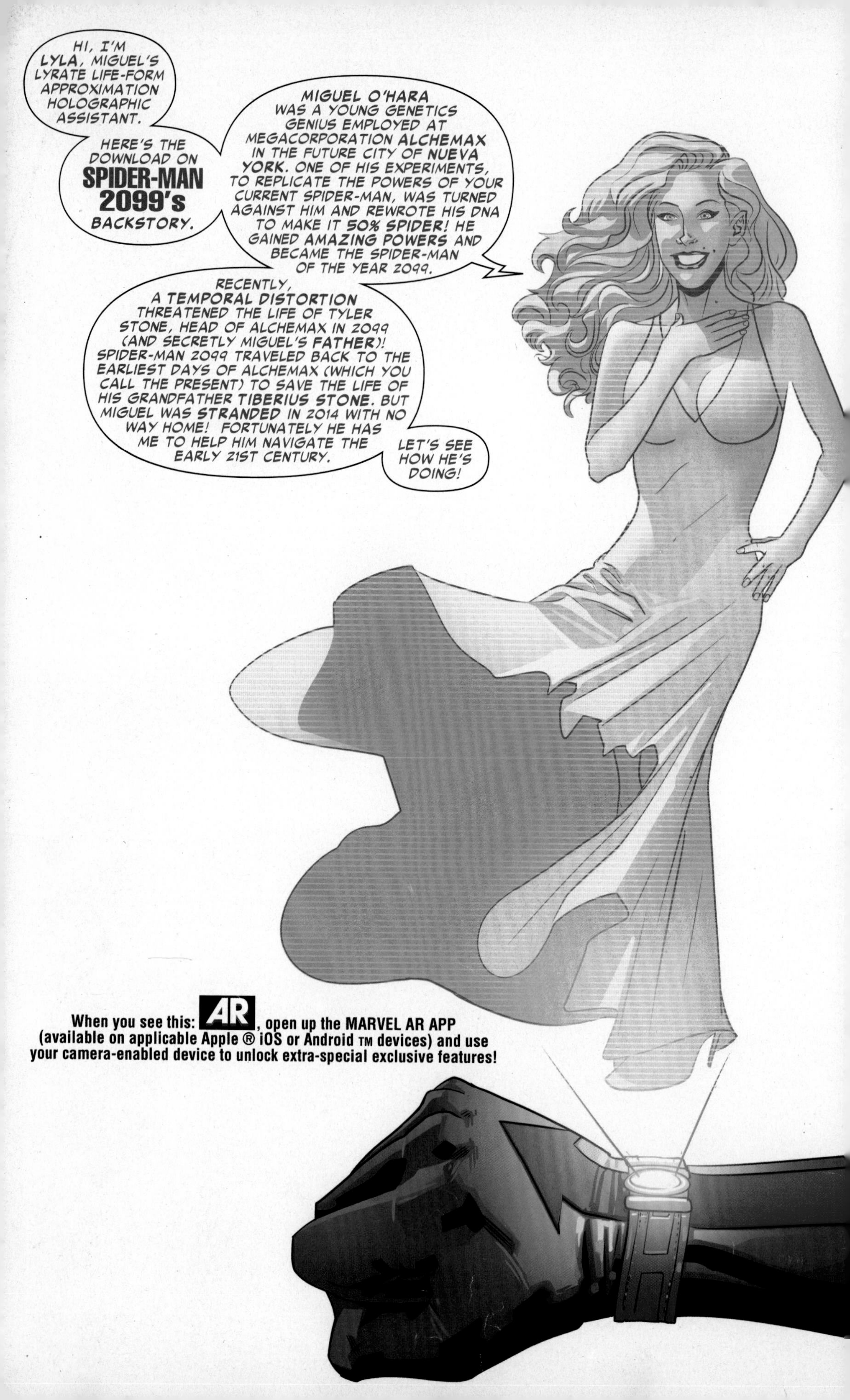
HI, I'M LYLA, MIGUEL'S LYRATE LIFE-FORM APPROXIMATION HOLOGRAPHIC ASSISTANT.
HERE'S THE DOWNLOAD ON SPIDER-MAN 2099's BACKSTORY.
MIGUEL O'HARA WAS A YOUNG GENETICS GENIUS EMPLOYED AT MEGACORPORATION ALCHEMAX IN THE FUTURE CITY OF NUEVA YORK. ONE OF HIS EXPERIMENTS, TO REPLICATE THE POWERS OF YOUR CURRENT SPIDER-MAN, WAS TURNED AGAINST HIM AND REWROTE HIS DNA TO MAKE IT 50% SPIDER! HE GAINED AMAZING POWERS AND BECAME THE SPIDER-MAN OF THE YEAR 2099.
RECENTLY, A TEMPORAL DISTORTION THREATENED THE LIFE OF TYLER STONE, HEAD OF ALCHEMAX IN 2099 (AND SECRETLY MIGUEL'S FATHER)! SPIDER-MAN 2099 TRAVELED BACK TO THE EARLIEST DAYS OF ALCHEMAX (WHICH YOU CALL THE PRESENT) TO SAVE THE LIFE OF HIS GRANDFATHER TIBERIUS STONE. BUT MIGUEL WAS STRANDED IN 2014 WITH NO WAY HOME! FORTUNATELY HE HAS ME TO HELP HIM NAVIGATE THE EARLY 21ST CENTURY.
LET'S SEE HOW HE'S DOING!

When you see this: AR, open up the MARVEL AR APP (available on applicable Apple ® iOS or Android ™ devices) and use your camera-enabled device to unlock extra-special exclusive features!

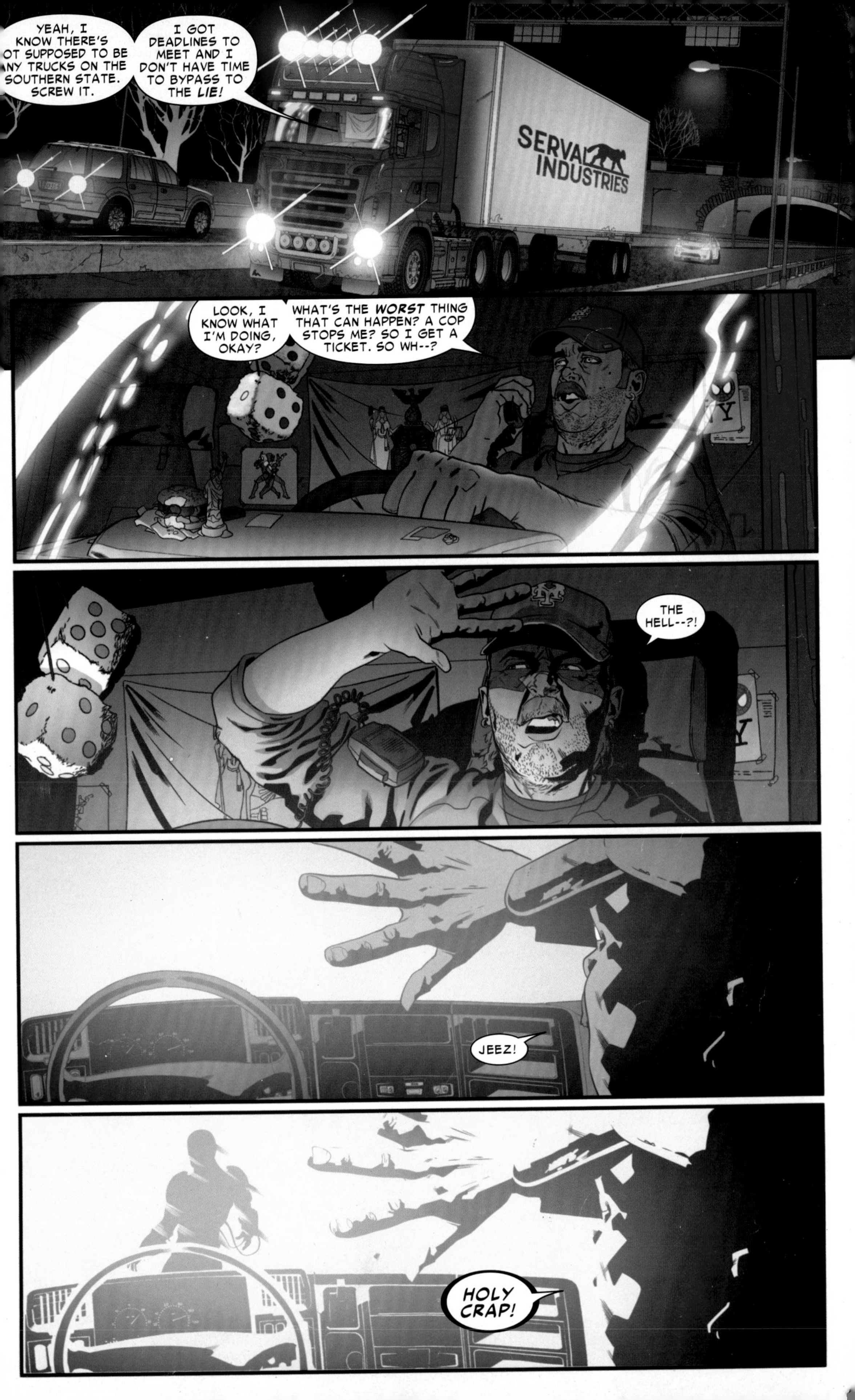
YEAH, I KNOW THERE'S OT SUPPOSED TO BE NY TRUCKS ON THE SOUTHERN STATE. SCREW IT.
I GOT DEADLINES TO MEET AND I DON'T HAVE TIME TO BYPASS TO THE LIE!
SERVAL INDUSTRIES
LOOK, I KNOW WHAT I'M DOING, OKAY?
WHAT'S THE WORST THING THAT CAN HAPPEN? A COP STOPS ME? SO I GET A TICKET. SO WH--?
THE HELL--?!
JEEZ!
HOLY CRAP!

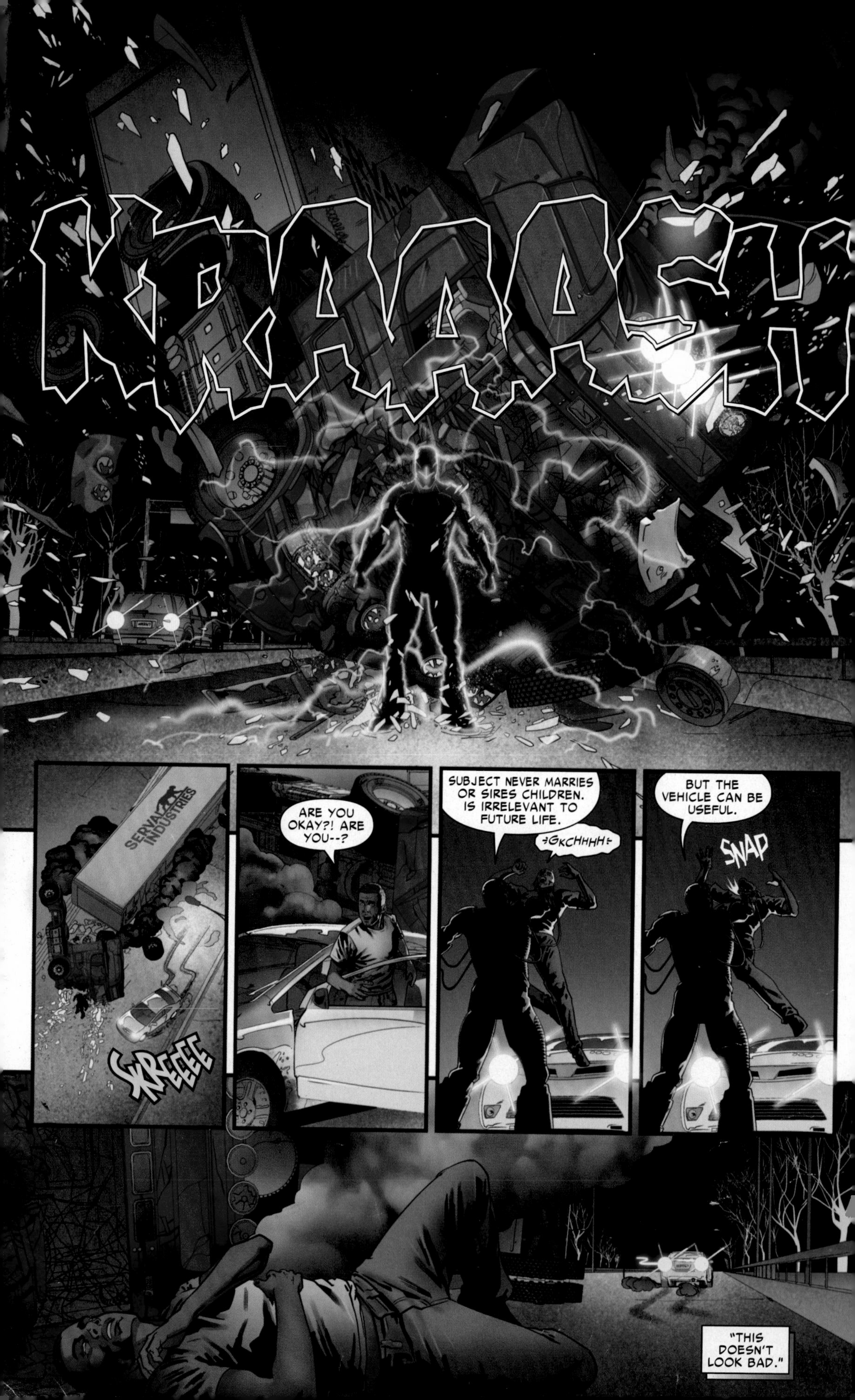
KRAAASH
SERVAL INDUSTRIES
SKREEEE
ARE YOU OKAY?! ARE YOU--?
SUBJECT NEVER MARRIES OR SIRES CHILDREN. IS IRRELEVANT TO FUTURE LIFE.
GKCHHHH
BUT THE VEHICLE CAN BE USEFUL.
SNAP
"THIS DOESN'T LOOK BAD."

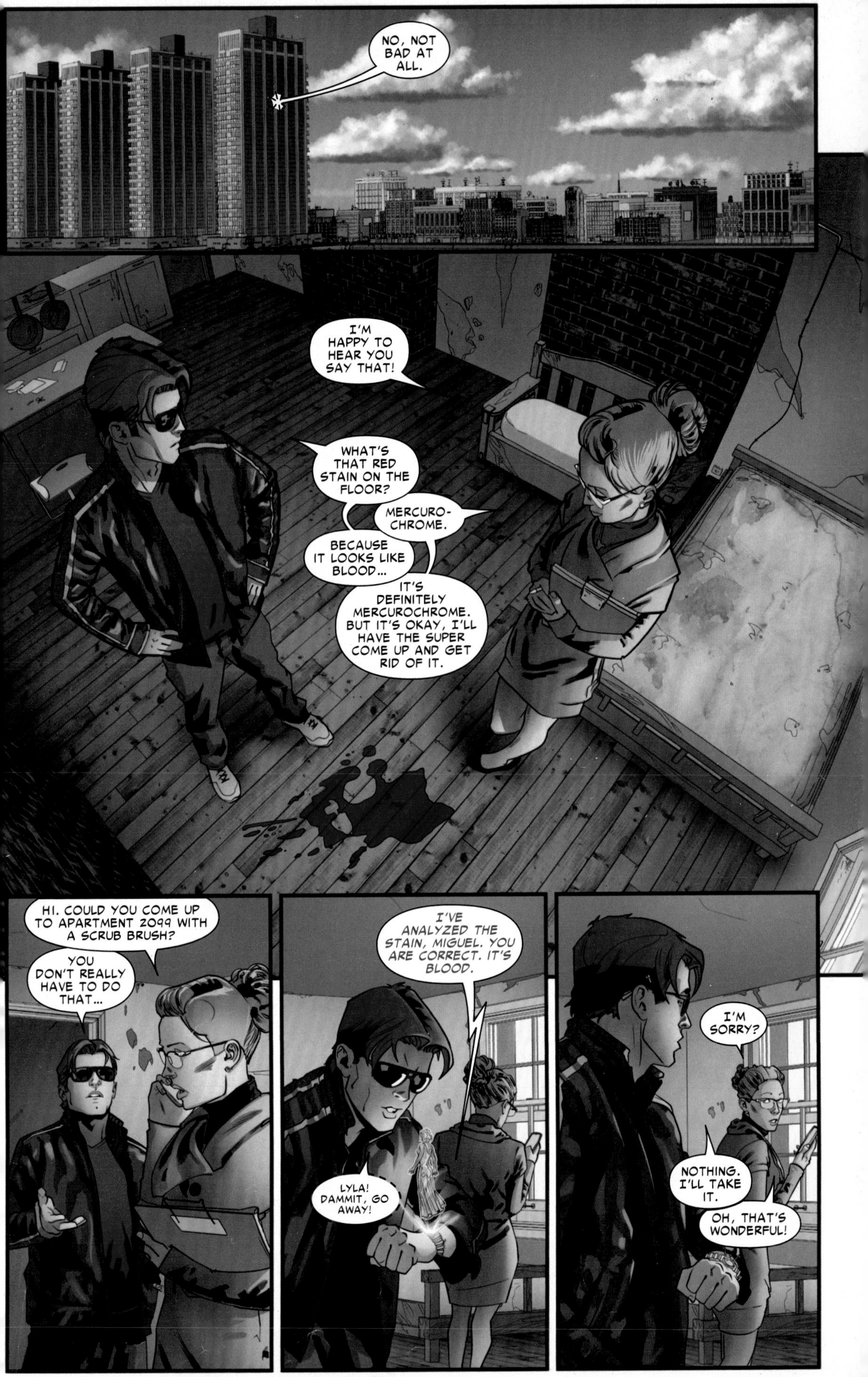
NO, NOT BAD AT ALL.
I'M HAPPY TO HEAR YOU SAY THAT!
WHAT'S THAT RED STAIN ON THE FLOOR?
MERCURO-CHROME.
BECAUSE IT LOOKS LIKE BLOOD...
IT'S DEFINITELY MERCUROCHROME. BUT IT'S OKAY, I'LL HAVE THE SUPER COME UP AND GET RID OF IT.
HI. COULD YOU COME UP TO APARTMENT 2099 WITH A SCRUB BRUSH?
YOU DON'T REALLY HAVE TO DO THAT...
I'VE ANALYZED THE STAIN, MIGUEL. YOU ARE CORRECT. IT'S BLOOD.
LYLA! DAMMIT, GO AWAY!
I'M SORRY?
NOTHING. I'LL TAKE IT.
OH, THAT'S WONDERFUL!

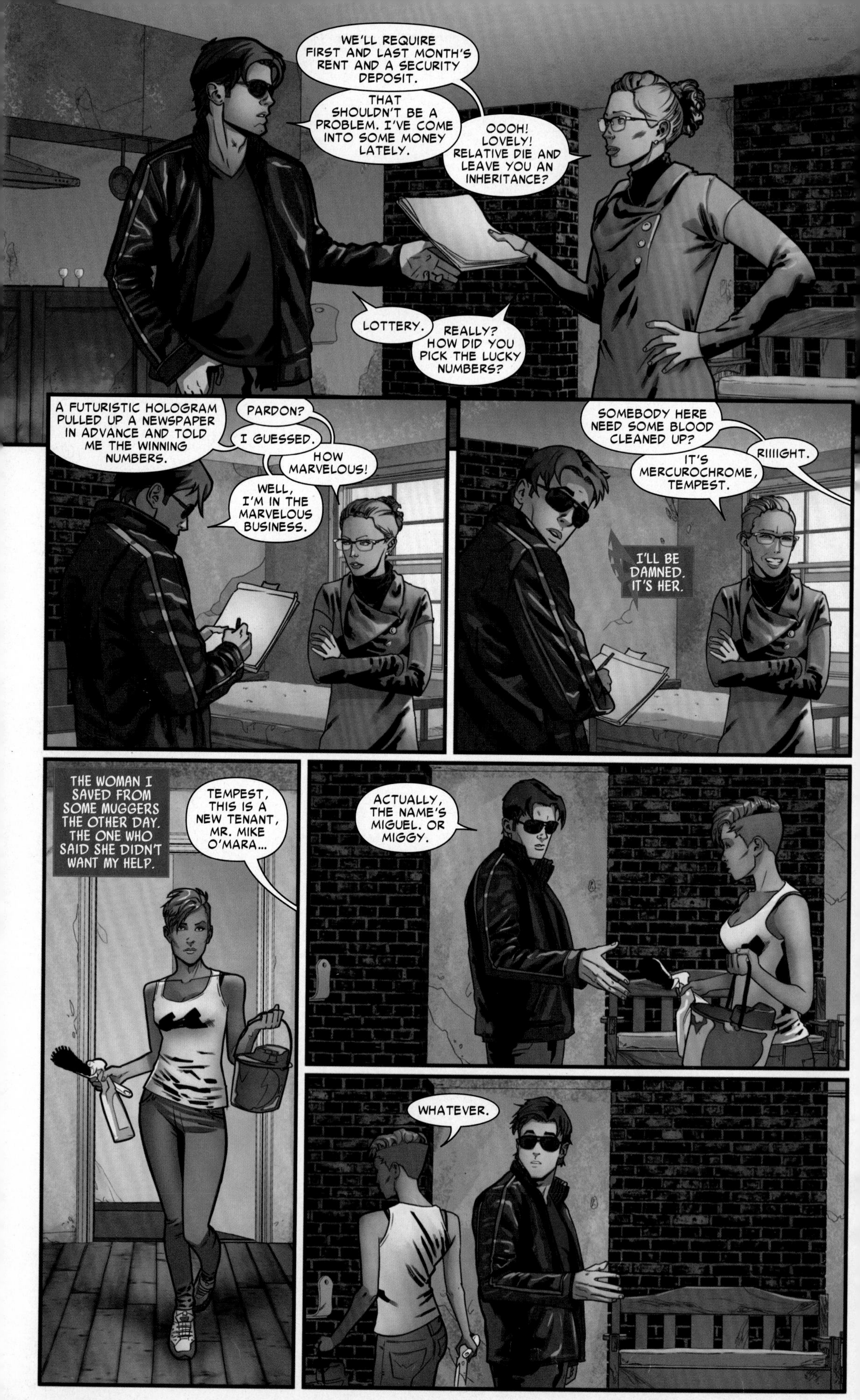
WE'LL REQUIRE FIRST AND LAST MONTH'S RENT AND A SECURITY DEPOSIT.
THAT SHOULDN'T BE A PROBLEM. I'VE COME INTO SOME MONEY LATELY.
OOOH! LOVELY! RELATIVE DIE AND LEAVE YOU AN INHERITANCE?
LOTTERY.
REALLY? HOW DID YOU PICK THE LUCKY NUMBERS?
A FUTURISTIC HOLOGRAM PULLED UP A NEWSPAPER IN ADVANCE AND TOLD ME THE WINNING NUMBERS.
PARDON?
I GUESSED.
HOW MARVELOUS!
WELL, I'M IN THE MARVELOUS BUSINESS.
SOMEBODY HERE NEED SOME BLOOD CLEANED UP?
RIIIIGHT.
IT'S MERCUROCHROME, TEMPEST.
I'LL BE DAMNED. IT'S HER.
THE WOMAN I SAVED FROM SOME MUGGERS THE OTHER DAY. THE ONE WHO SAID SHE DIDN'T WANT MY HELP.
TEMPEST, THIS IS A NEW TENANT, MR. MIKE O'MARA...
ACTUALLY, THE NAME'S MIGUEL. OR MIGGY.
WHATEVER.

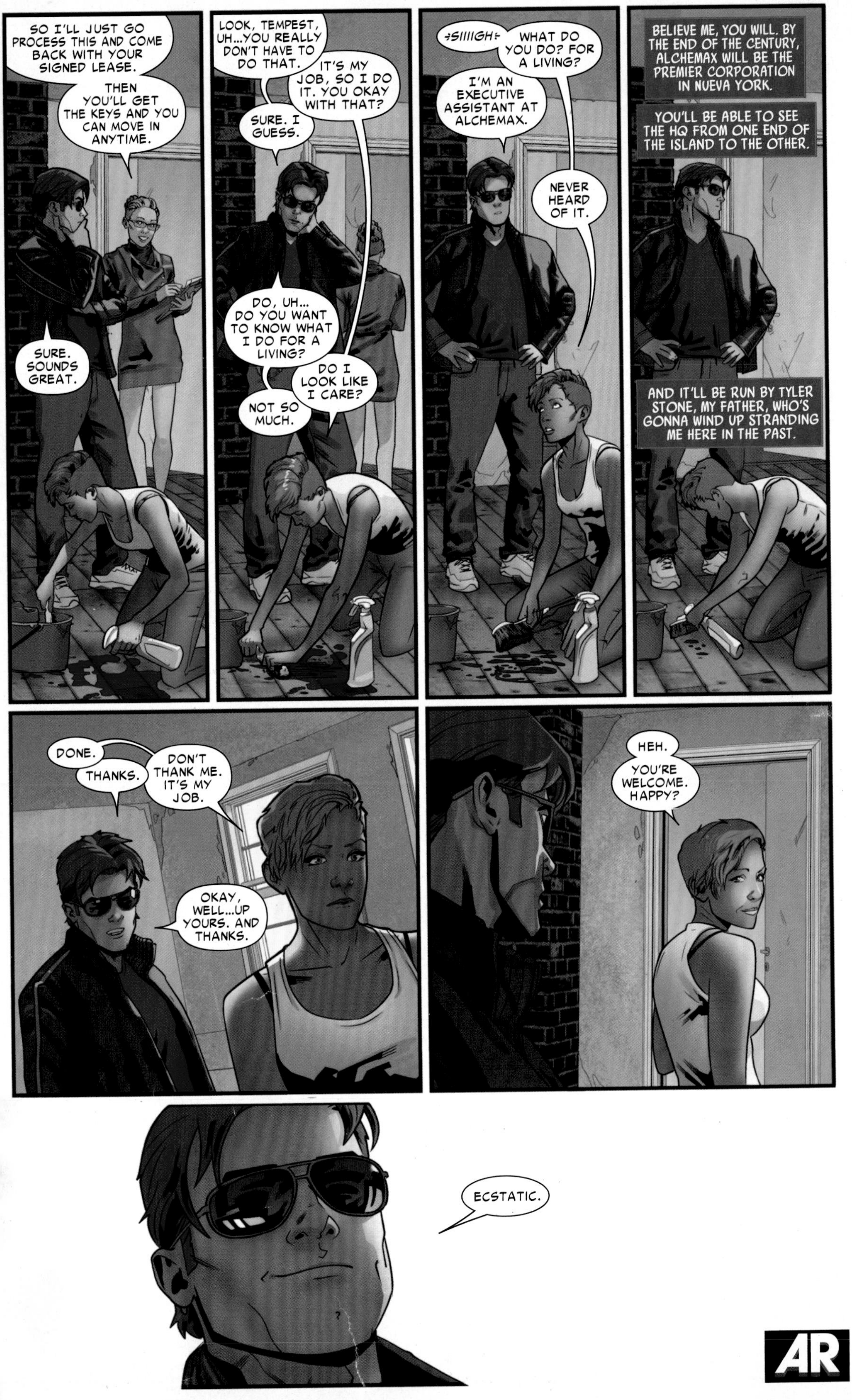

SO I'LL JUST GO PROCESS THIS AND COME BACK WITH YOUR SIGNED LEASE.
THEN YOU'LL GET THE KEYS AND YOU CAN MOVE IN ANYTIME.
SURE. SOUNDS GREAT.
LOOK, TEMPEST, UH...YOU REALLY DON'T HAVE TO DO THAT.
IT'S MY JOB, SO I DO IT. YOU OKAY WITH THAT?
SURE. I GUESS.
DO, UH... DO YOU WANT TO KNOW WHAT I DO FOR A LIVING?
DO I LOOK LIKE I CARE?
NOT SO MUCH.
SIIIIGH
WHAT DO YOU DO? FOR A LIVING?
I'M AN EXECUTIVE ASSISTANT AT ALCHEMAX.
NEVER HEARD OF IT.
BELIEVE ME, YOU WILL. BY THE END OF THE CENTURY, ALCHEMAX WILL BE THE PREMIER CORPORATION IN NUEVA YORK.
YOU'LL BE ABLE TO SEE THE HQ FROM ONE END OF THE ISLAND TO THE OTHER.
AND IT'LL BE RUN BY TYLER STONE, MY FATHER, WHO'S GONNA WIND UP STRANDING ME HERE IN THE PAST.
DONE.
THANKS.
DON'T THANK ME. IT'S MY JOB.
OKAY, WELL...UP YOURS. AND THANKS.
HEH.
YOU'RE WELCOME. HAPPY?
ECSTATIC.
AR

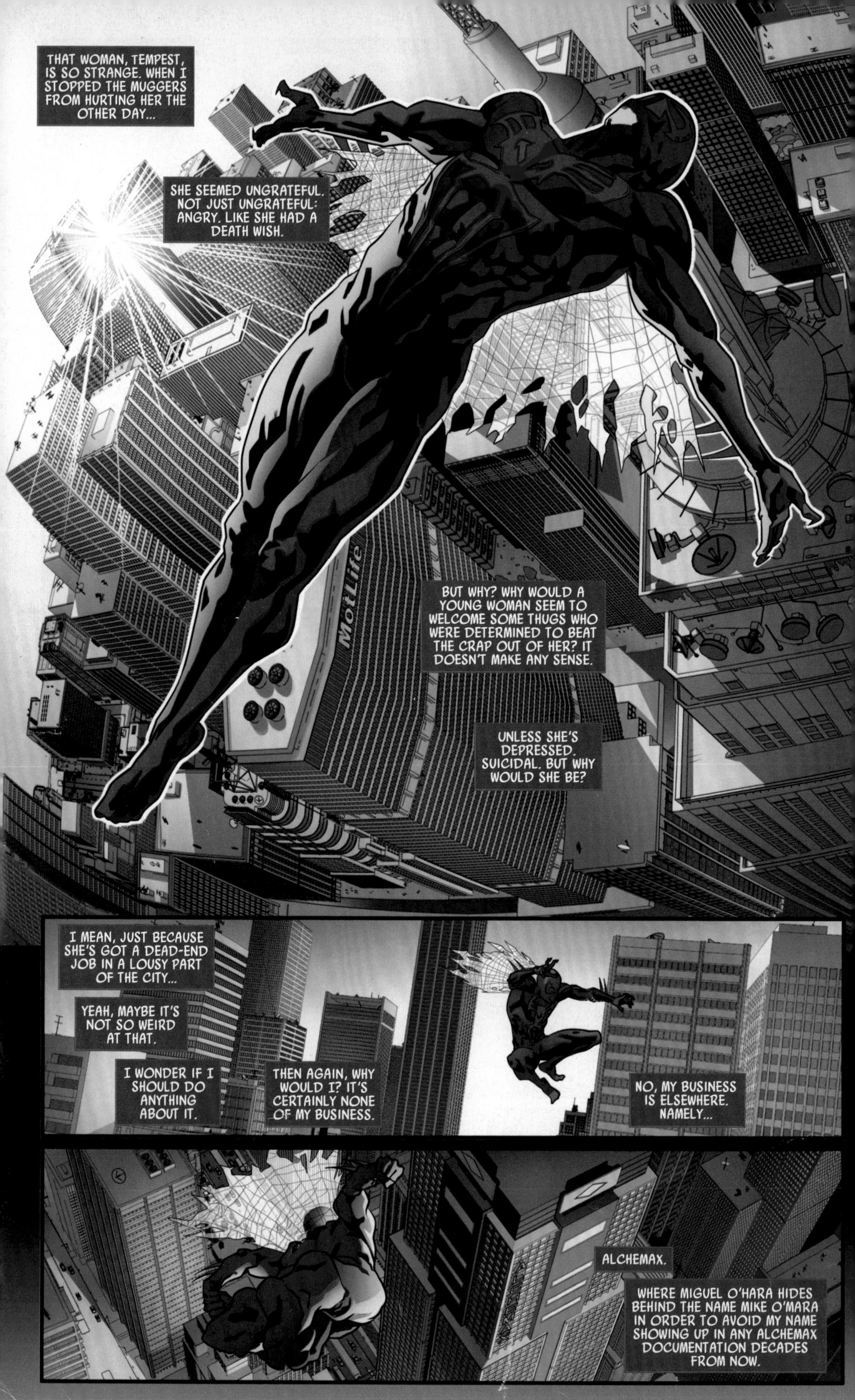
THAT WOMAN, TEMPEST, IS SO STRANGE. WHEN I STOPPED THE MUGGERS FROM HURTING HER THE OTHER DAY...
SHE SEEMED UNGRATEFUL. NOT JUST UNGRATEFUL: ANGRY. LIKE SHE HAD A DEATH WISH.
MetLife
BUT WHY? WHY WOULD A YOUNG WOMAN SEEM TO WELCOME SOME THUGS WHO WERE DETERMINED TO BEAT THE CRAP OUT OF HER? IT DOESN'T MAKE ANY SENSE.
UNLESS SHE'S DEPRESSED. SUICIDAL. BUT WHY WOULD SHE BE?
I MEAN, JUST BECAUSE SHE'S GOT A DEAD-END JOB IN A LOUSY PART OF THE CITY...
YEAH, MAYBE IT'S NOT SO WEIRD AT THAT.
I WONDER IF I SHOULD DO ANYTHING ABOUT IT.
THEN AGAIN, WHY WOULD I? IT'S CERTAINLY NONE OF MY BUSINESS.
NO, MY BUSINESS IS ELSEWHERE. NAMELY...
ALCHEMAX.
WHERE MIGUEL O'HARA HIDES BEHIND THE NAME MIKE O'MARA IN ORDER TO AVOID MY NAME SHOWING UP IN ANY ALCHEMAX DOCUMENTATION DECADES FROM NOW.

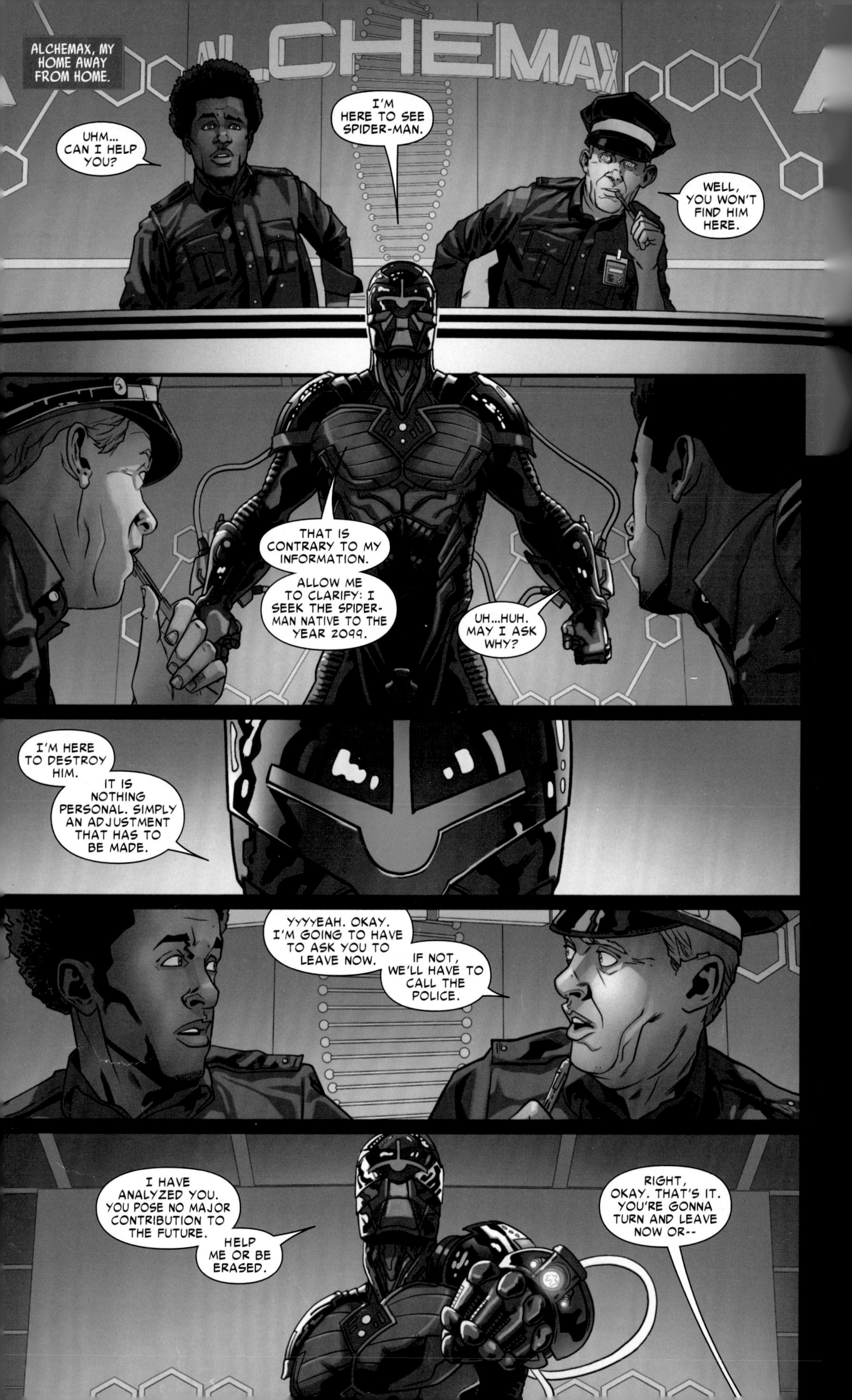

ALCHEMAX, MY HOME AWAY FROM HOME.
UHM... CAN I HELP YOU?
I'M HERE TO SEE SPIDER-MAN.
WELL, YOU WON'T FIND HIM HERE.
THAT IS CONTRARY TO MY INFORMATION.
ALLOW ME TO CLARIFY: I SEEK THE SPIDER-MAN NATIVE TO THE YEAR 2099.
UH...HUH. MAY I ASK WHY?
I'M HERE TO DESTROY HIM.
IT IS NOTHING PERSONAL. SIMPLY AN ADJUSTMENT THAT HAS TO BE MADE.
YYYYEAH. OKAY. I'M GOING TO HAVE TO ASK YOU TO LEAVE NOW.
IF NOT, WE'LL HAVE TO CALL THE POLICE.
I HAVE ANALYZED YOU. YOU POSE NO MAJOR CONTRIBUTION TO THE FUTURE.
HELP ME OR BE ERASED.
RIGHT, OKAY. THAT'S IT. YOU'RE GONNA TURN AND LEAVE NOW OR--

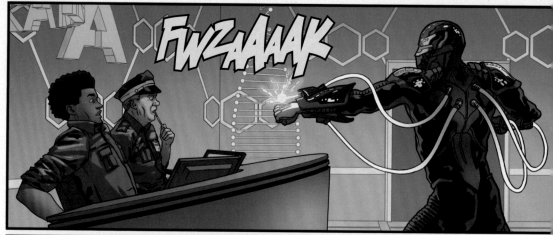

FWZAAAAK

ARRRHHHHH!

YOUR TWINS HAVE NOT BEEN SPAWNED YET.

ONE IS RUN OVER BY A CAR AND KILLED, BUT THE OTHER PERFORMS SERIOUS CANCER RESEARCH.

KILLING YOU WOULD BE DETRIMENTAL TO HUMANITY, BUT YOU CAN BE WOUNDED WITH IMPUNITY. WHERE IS SPIDER-MAN? TELL ME NOW OR--

EIGHTEENTH FLOOR! HE'S ON THE EIGHTEENTH FLOOR!

ELEVATORS ARE TO THE RIGHT!

THANK YOU.

CONDOLENCES ON THE LOSS OF YOUR CHILD IN ELEVEN YEARS.

ALCHEMA

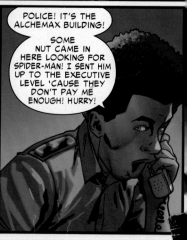

POLICE! IT'S THE ALCHEMAX BUILDING!

SOME NUT CAME IN HERE LOOKING FOR SPIDER-MAN! I SENT HIM UP TO THE EXECUTIVE LEVEL 'CAUSE THEY DON'T PAY ME ENOUGH! HURRY!

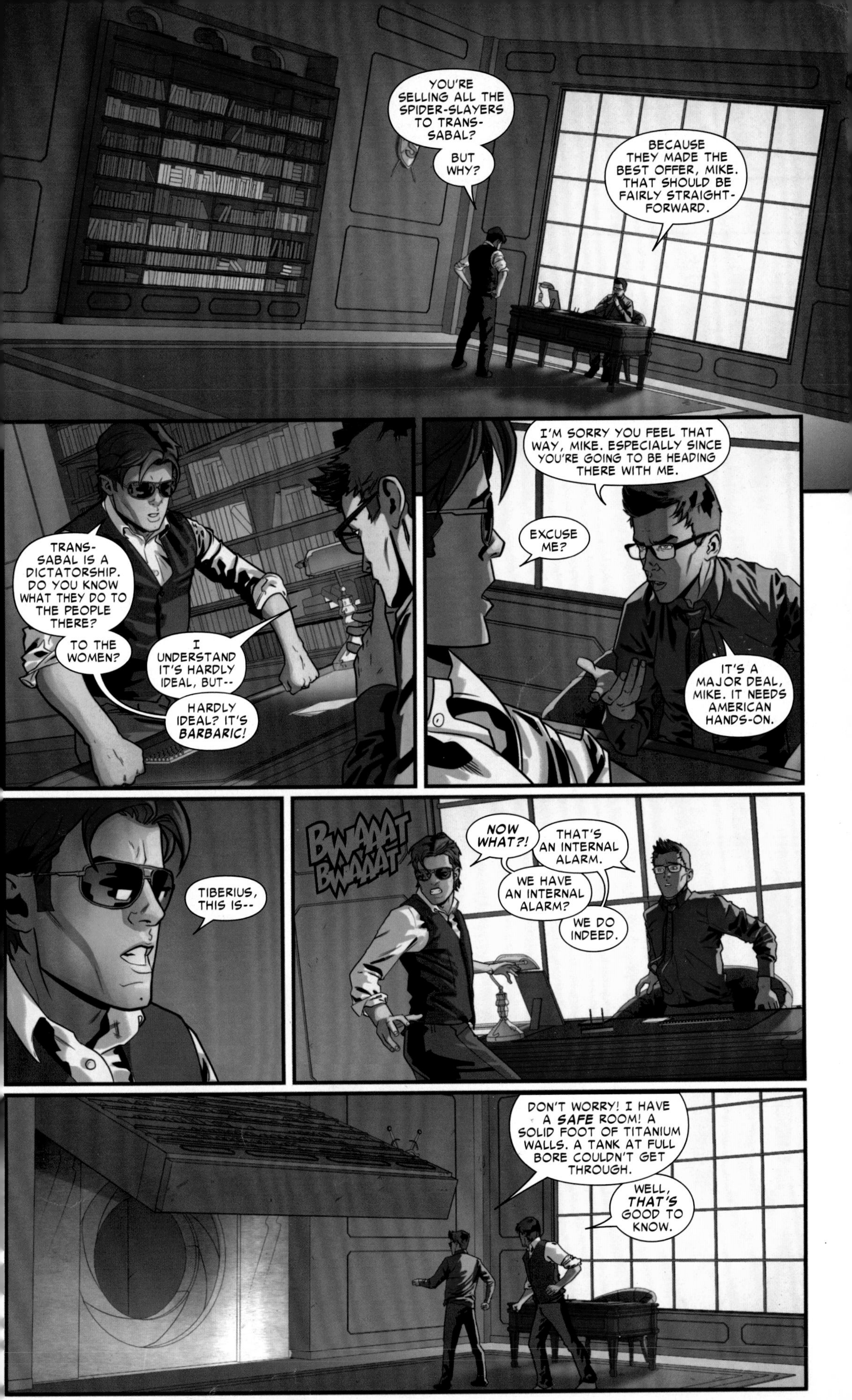
YOU'RE SELLING ALL THE SPIDER-SLAYERS TO TRANS-SABAL?
BUT WHY?
BECAUSE THEY MADE THE BEST OFFER, MIKE. THAT SHOULD BE FAIRLY STRAIGHT-FORWARD.
TRANS-SABAL IS A DICTATORSHIP. DO YOU KNOW WHAT THEY DO TO THE PEOPLE THERE?
TO THE WOMEN?
I UNDERSTAND IT'S HARDLY IDEAL, BUT--
HARDLY IDEAL? IT'S BARBARIC!
I'M SORRY YOU FEEL THAT WAY, MIKE. ESPECIALLY SINCE YOU'RE GOING TO BE HEADING THERE WITH ME.
EXCUSE ME?
IT'S A MAJOR DEAL, MIKE. IT NEEDS AMERICAN HANDS-ON.
TIBERIUS, THIS IS--
BWAAAT BWAAAT
NOW WHAT?!
THAT'S AN INTERNAL ALARM.
WE HAVE AN INTERNAL ALARM?
WE DO INDEED.
DON'T WORRY! I HAVE A SAFE ROOM! A SOLID FOOT OF TITANIUM WALLS. A TANK AT FULL BORE COULDN'T GET THROUGH.
WELL, THAT'S GOOD TO KNOW.

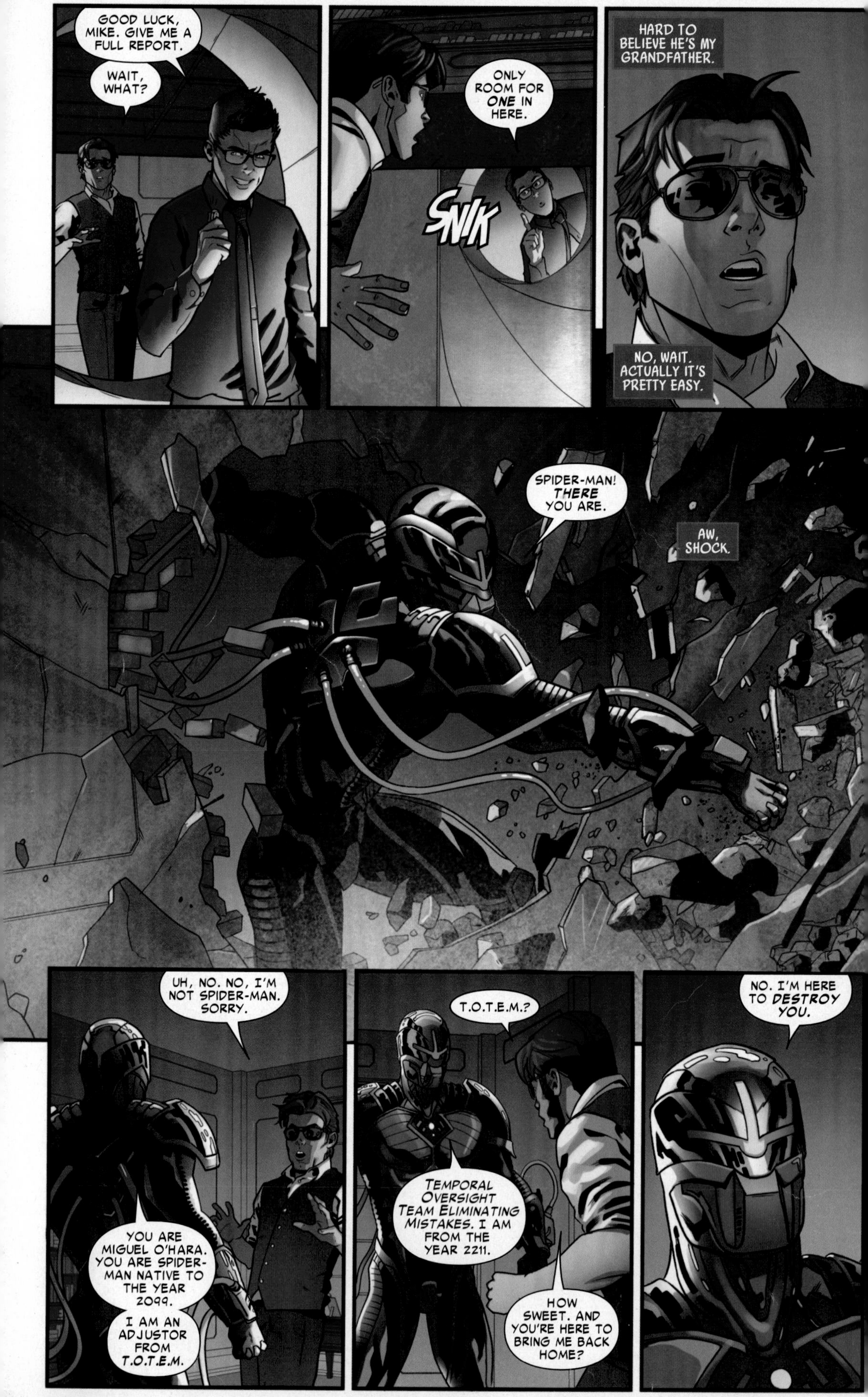
GOOD LUCK, MIKE. GIVE ME A FULL REPORT.
WAIT, WHAT?
ONLY ROOM FOR ONE IN HERE.
SNIK
HARD TO BELIEVE HE'S MY GRANDFATHER.
NO, WAIT. ACTUALLY IT'S PRETTY EASY.
SPIDER-MAN! THERE YOU ARE.
AW, SHOCK.
UH, NO. NO, I'M NOT SPIDER-MAN. SORRY.
YOU ARE MIGUEL O'HARA. YOU ARE SPIDER-MAN NATIVE TO THE YEAR 2099.
I AM AN ADJUSTOR FROM T.O.T.E.M.
T.O.T.E.M.?
TEMPORAL OVERSIGHT TEAM ELIMINATING MISTAKES. I AM FROM THE YEAR 2211.
HOW SWEET. AND YOU'RE HERE TO BRING ME BACK HOME?
NO. I'M HERE TO DESTROY YOU.

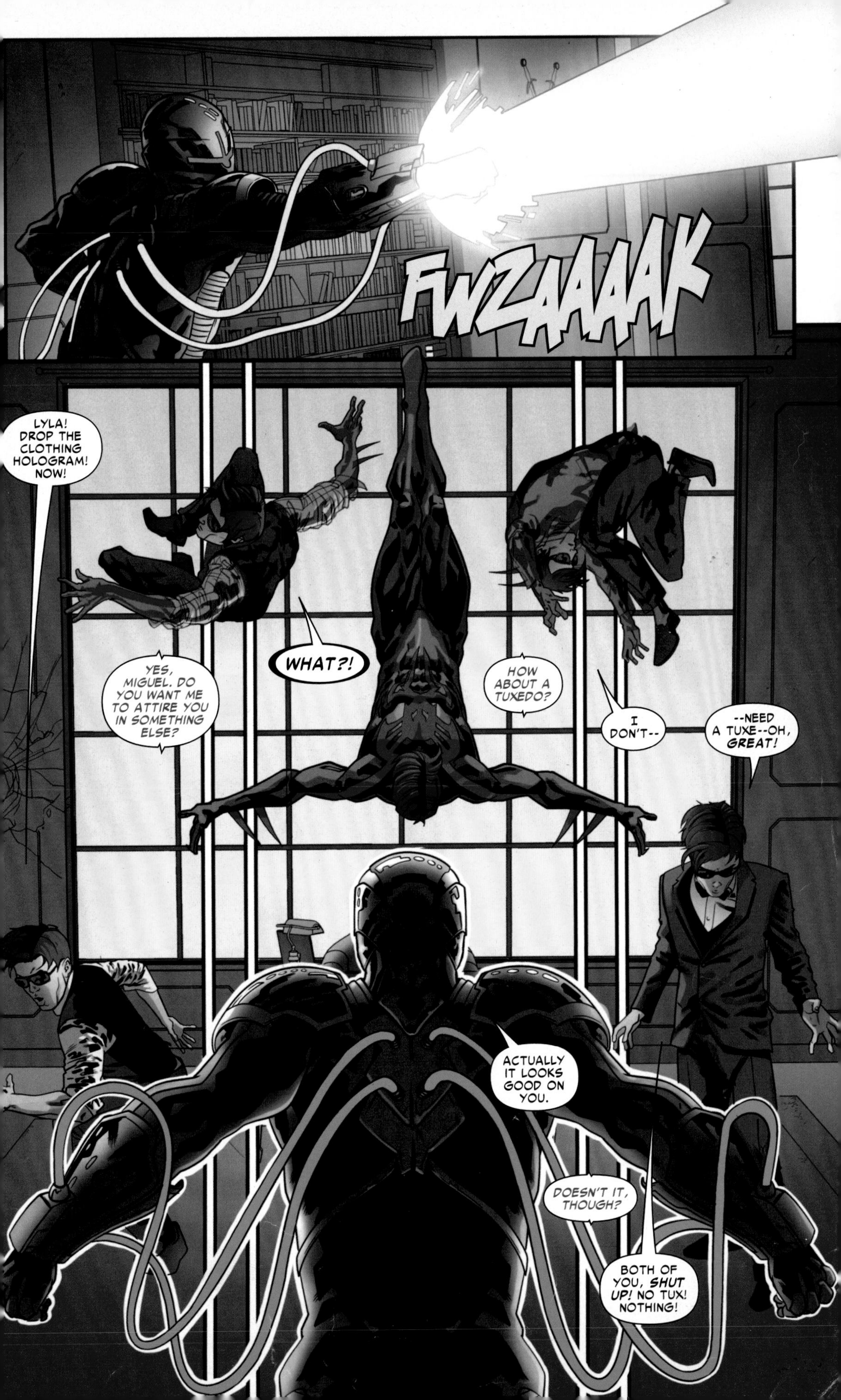
FWZAAAAK
LYLA! DROP THE CLOTHING HOLOGRAM! NOW!
YES, MIGUEL. DO YOU WANT ME TO ATTIRE YOU IN SOMETHING ELSE?
WHAT?!
HOW ABOUT A TUXEDO?
I DON'T--
--NEED A TUXE--OH, GREAT!
ACTUALLY IT LOOKS GOOD ON YOU.
DOESN'T IT, THOUGH?
BOTH OF YOU, SHUT UP! NO TUX! NOTHING!

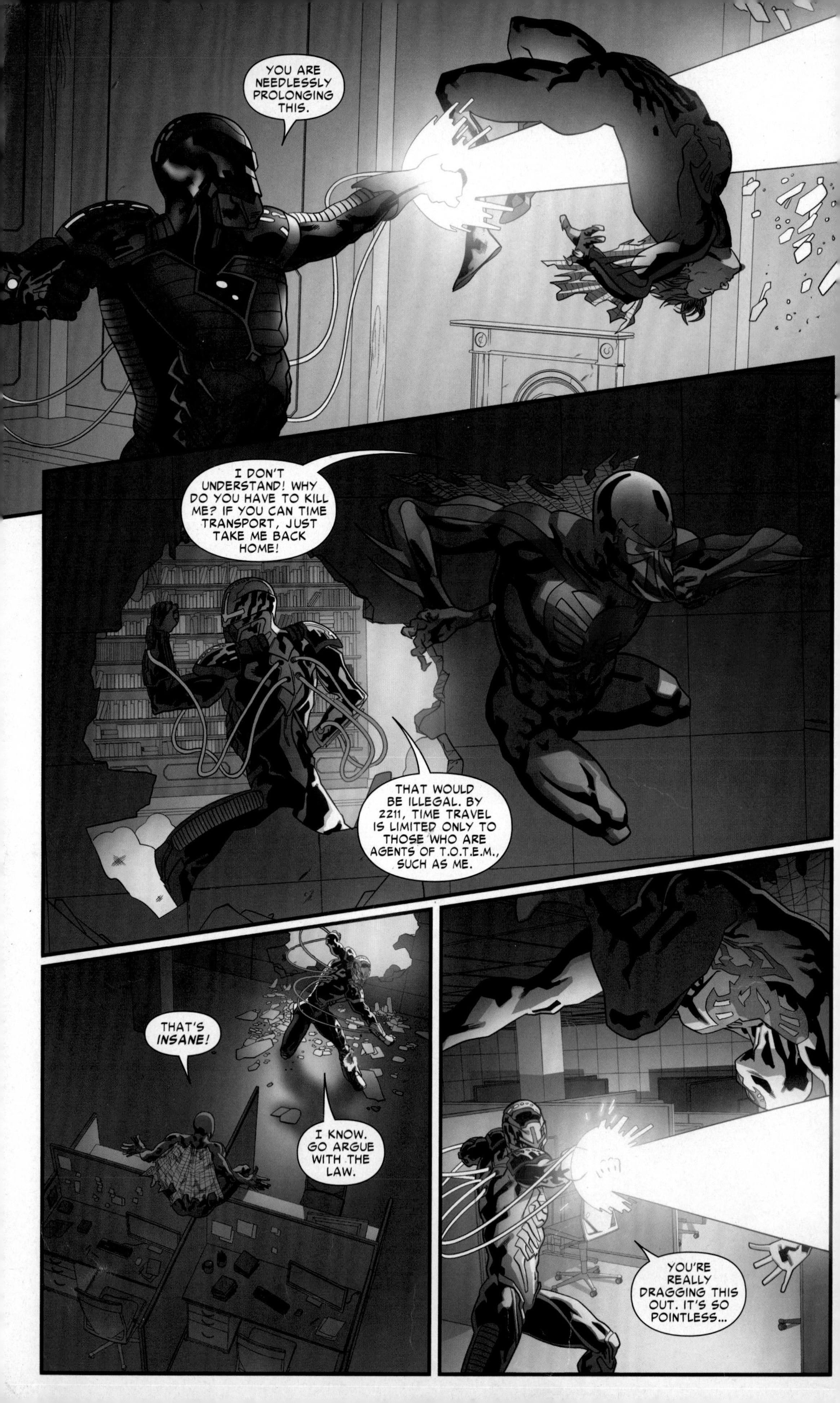

YOU ARE NEEDLESSLY PROLONGING THIS.
I DON'T UNDERSTAND! WHY DO YOU HAVE TO KILL ME? IF YOU CAN TIME TRANSPORT, JUST TAKE ME BACK HOME!
THAT WOULD BE ILLEGAL. BY 2211, TIME TRAVEL IS LIMITED ONLY TO THOSE WHO ARE AGENTS OF T.O.T.E.M., SUCH AS ME.
THAT'S *INSANE!*
I KNOW. GO ARGUE WITH THE LAW.
YOU'RE REALLY DRAGGING THIS OUT. IT'S SO POINTLESS...

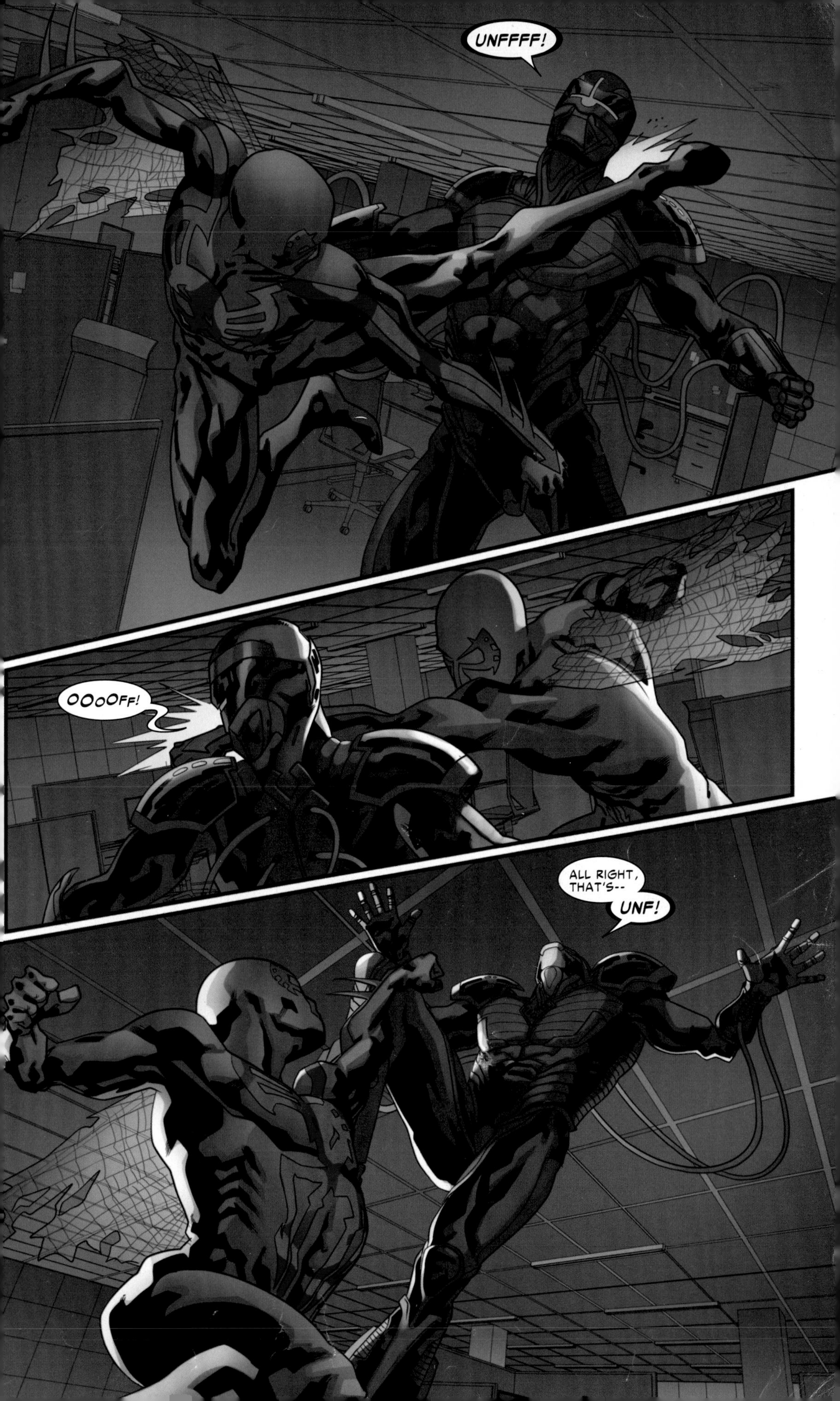
UNFFFF!
OOOOFF!
ALL RIGHT, THAT'S--
UNF!

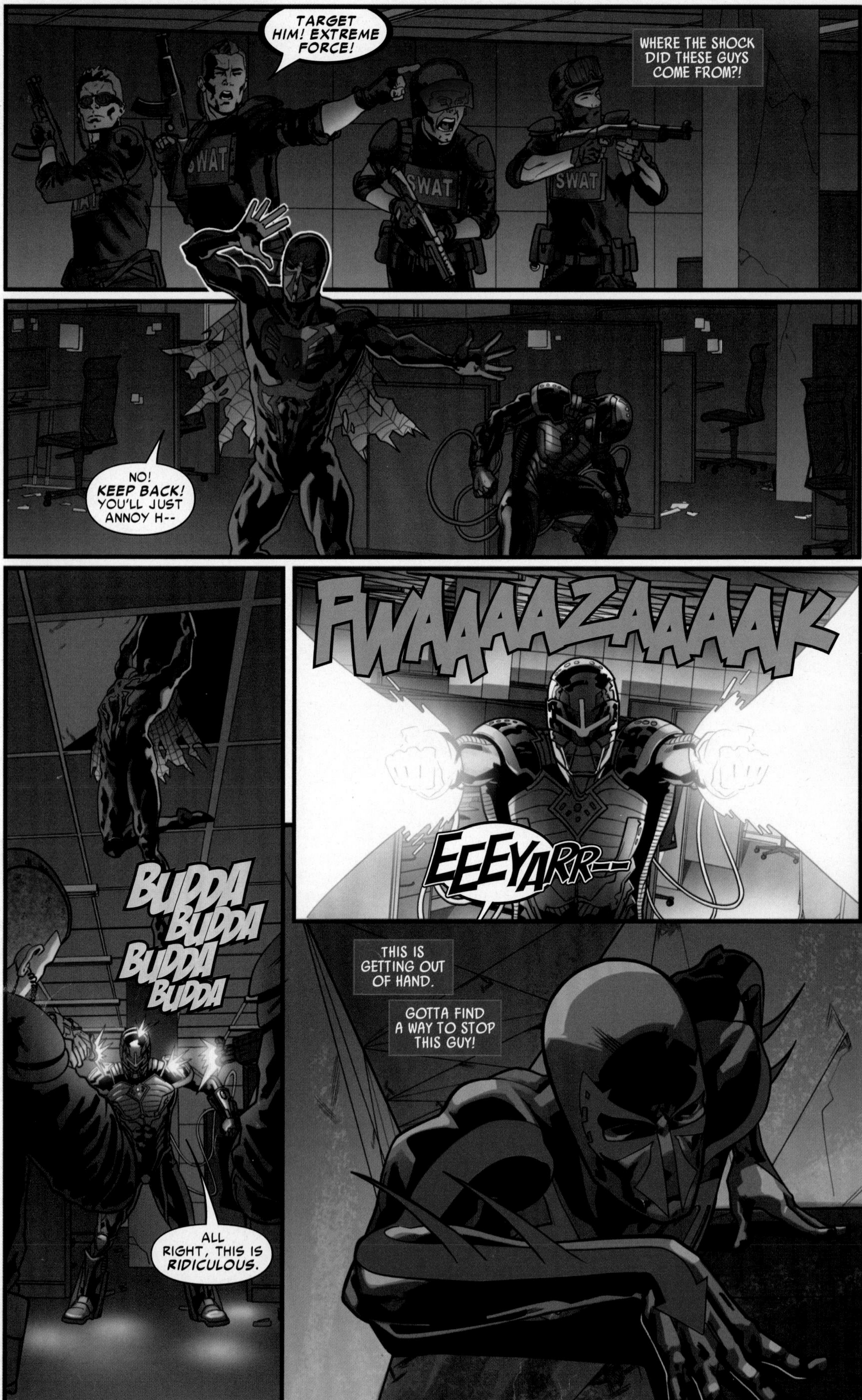
TARGET HIM! EXTREME FORCE!
WHERE THE SHOCK DID THESE GUYS COME FROM?!
SWAT
SWAT
SWAT
NO! KEEP BACK! YOU'LL JUST ANNOY H--
FWAAAAZAAAAK
EEEYARR--
BUDDA BUDDA BUDDA BUDDA
ALL RIGHT, THIS IS RIDICULOUS.
THIS IS GETTING OUT OF HAND.
GOTTA FIND A WAY TO STOP THIS GUY!

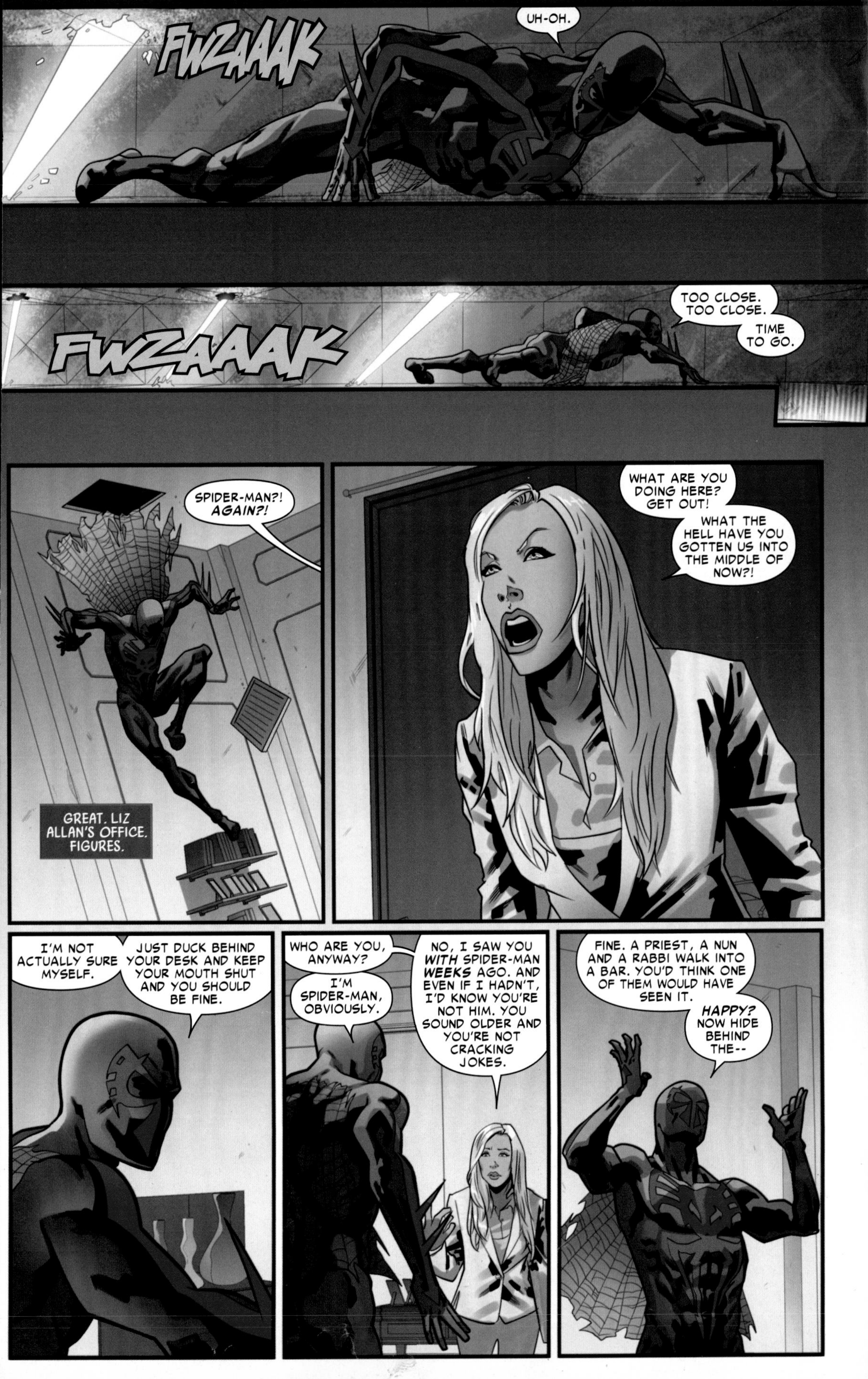
UH-OH.
FWZAAAK
FWZAAAK
TOO CLOSE. TOO CLOSE.
TIME TO GO.
SPIDER-MAN?! AGAIN?!
GREAT. LIZ ALLAN'S OFFICE. FIGURES.
WHAT ARE YOU DOING HERE? GET OUT!
WHAT THE HELL HAVE YOU GOTTEN US INTO THE MIDDLE OF NOW?!
I'M NOT ACTUALLY SURE MYSELF.
JUST DUCK BEHIND YOUR DESK AND KEEP YOUR MOUTH SHUT AND YOU SHOULD BE FINE.
WHO ARE YOU, ANYWAY?
I'M SPIDER-MAN, OBVIOUSLY.
NO, I SAW YOU WITH SPIDER-MAN WEEKS AGO. AND EVEN IF I HADN'T, I'D KNOW YOU'RE NOT HIM. YOU SOUND OLDER AND YOU'RE NOT CRACKING JOKES.
FINE. A PRIEST, A NUN AND A RABBI WALK INTO A BAR. YOU'D THINK ONE OF THEM WOULD HAVE SEEN IT.
HAPPY? NOW HIDE BEHIND THE--

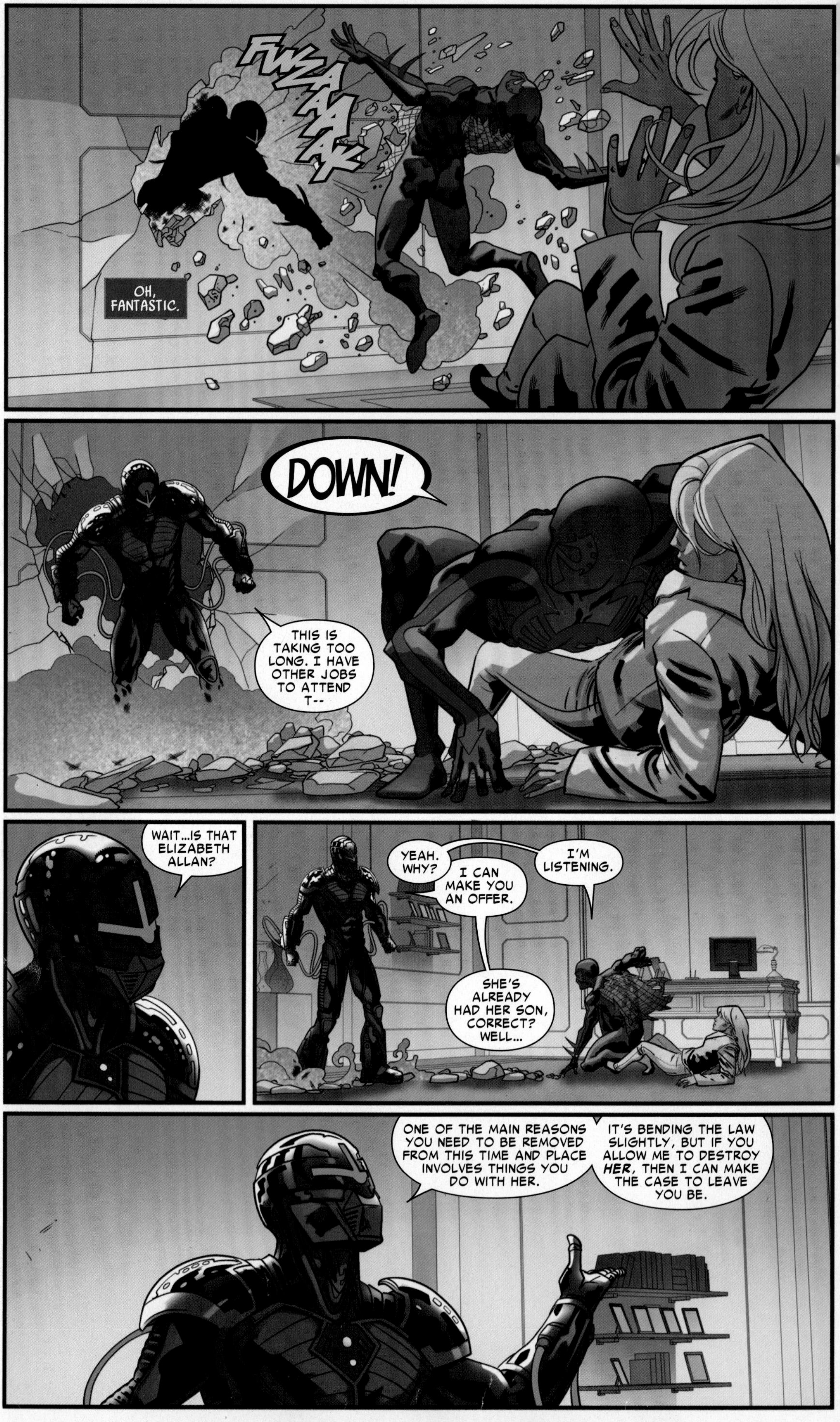
FWAAAAK
OH, FANTASTIC.
DOWN!
THIS IS TAKING TOO LONG. I HAVE OTHER JOBS TO ATTEND T--
WAIT...IS THAT ELIZABETH ALLAN?
YEAH. WHY?
I CAN MAKE YOU AN OFFER.
I'M LISTENING.
SHE'S ALREADY HAD HER SON, CORRECT? WELL...
ONE OF THE MAIN REASONS YOU NEED TO BE REMOVED FROM THIS TIME AND PLACE INVOLVES THINGS YOU DO WITH HER.
IT'S BENDING THE LAW SLIGHTLY, BUT IF YOU ALLOW ME TO DESTROY HER, THEN I CAN MAKE THE CASE TO LEAVE YOU BE.

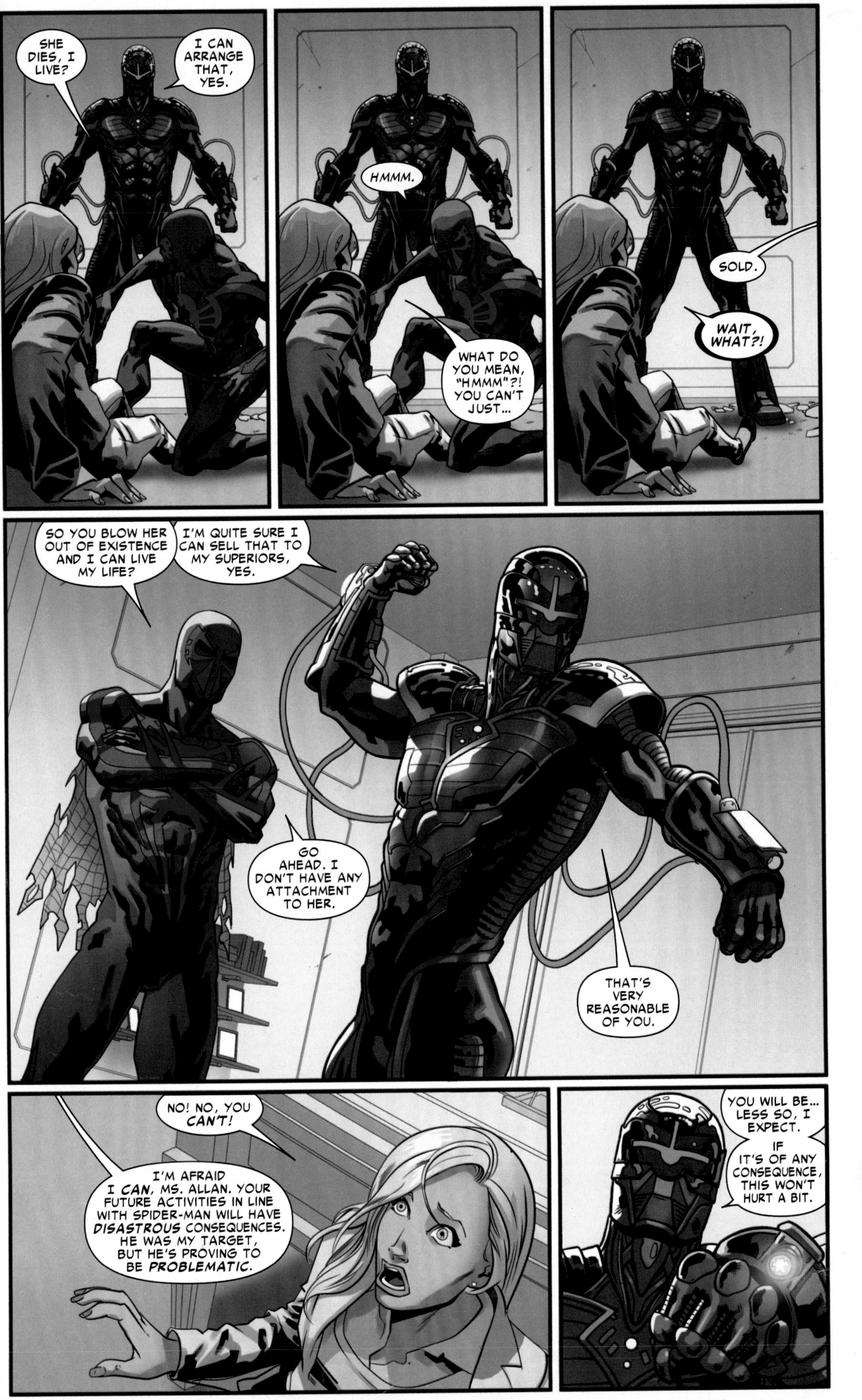
SHE DIES, I LIVE?
I CAN ARRANGE THAT, YES.
HMMM.
WHAT DO YOU MEAN, "HMMM"?! YOU CAN'T JUST...
SOLD.
WAIT, WHAT?!
SO YOU BLOW HER OUT OF EXISTENCE AND I CAN LIVE MY LIFE?
I'M QUITE SURE I CAN SELL THAT TO MY SUPERIORS, YES.
GO AHEAD. I DON'T HAVE ANY ATTACHMENT TO HER.
THAT'S VERY REASONABLE OF YOU.
NO! NO, YOU CAN'T!
I'M AFRAID I CAN, MS. ALLAN. YOUR FUTURE ACTIVITIES IN LINE WITH SPIDER-MAN WILL HAVE DISASTROUS CONSEQUENCES. HE WAS MY TARGET, BUT HE'S PROVING TO BE PROBLEMATIC.
YOU WILL BE... LESS SO, I EXPECT.
IF IT'S OF ANY CONSEQUENCE, THIS WON'T HURT A BIT.

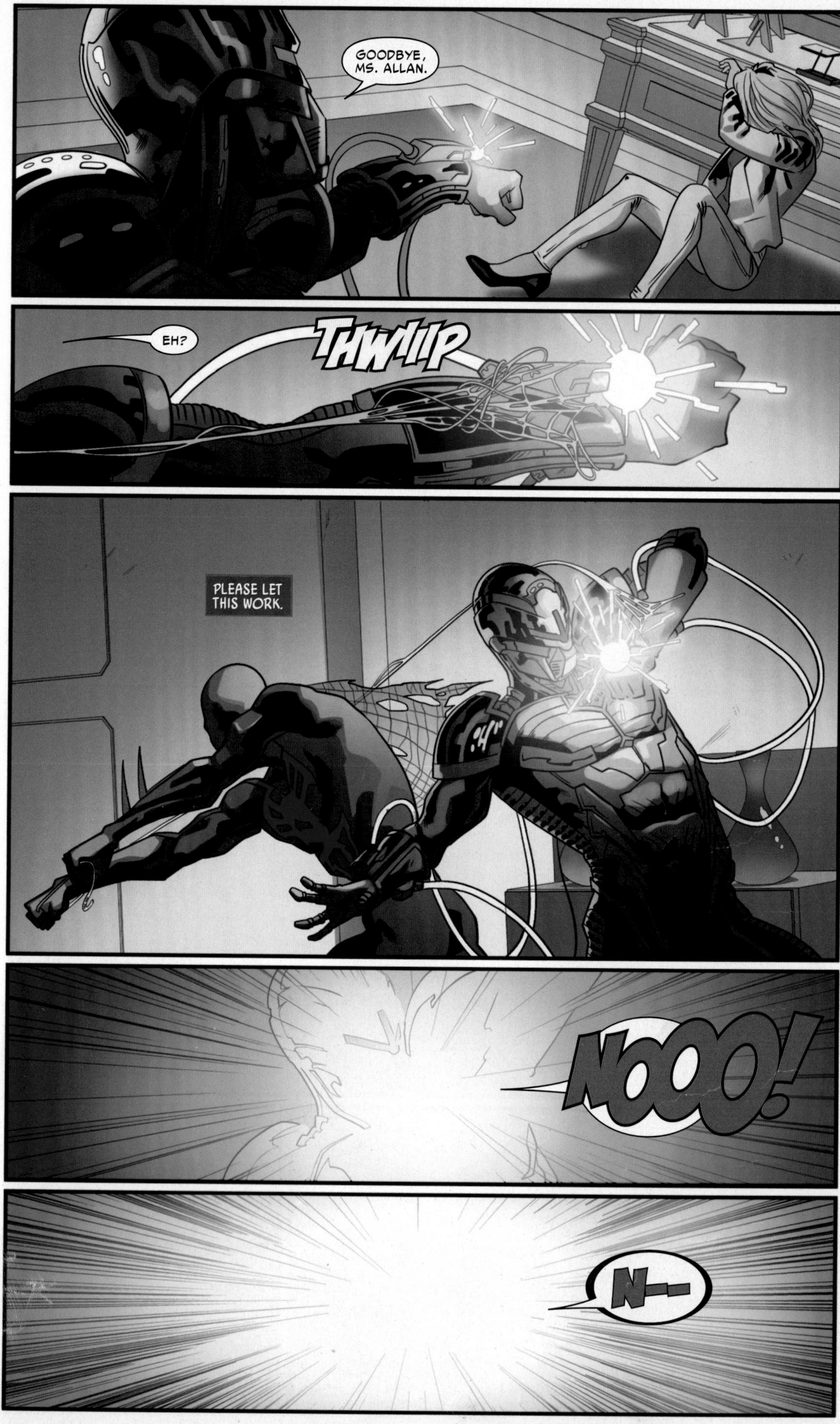
GOODBYE, MS. ALLAN.
EH?
THWIIP
PLEASE LET THIS WORK.
NOOO!
N--

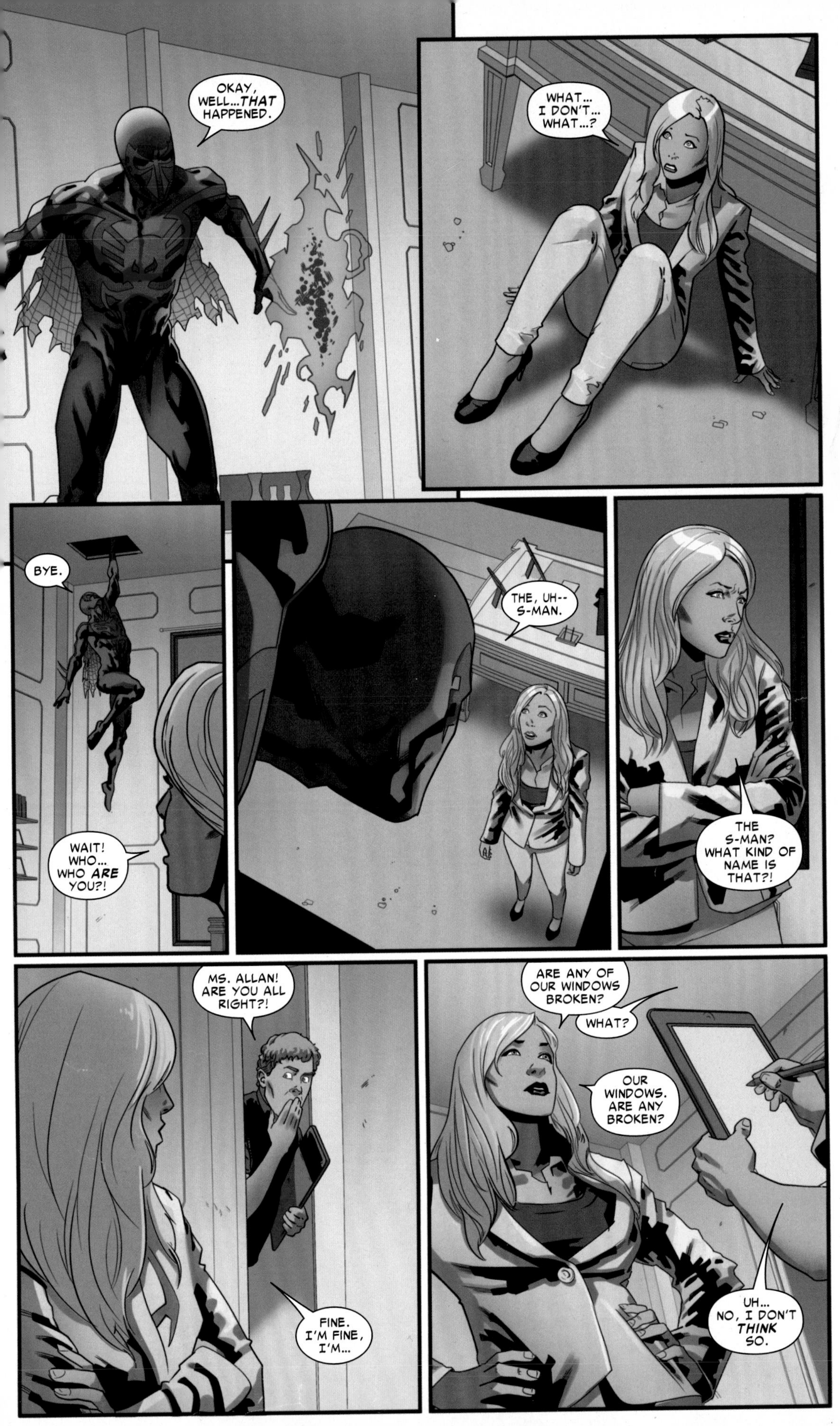
OKAY, WELL...THAT HAPPENED.
WHAT... I DON'T... WHAT...?
BYE.
WAIT! WHO... WHO ARE YOU?!
THE, UH-- S-MAN.
THE S-MAN? WHAT KIND OF NAME IS THAT?!
MS. ALLAN! ARE YOU ALL RIGHT?!
FINE. I'M FINE, I'M...
ARE ANY OF OUR WINDOWS BROKEN?
WHAT?
OUR WINDOWS. ARE ANY BROKEN?
UH... NO, I DON'T THINK SO.

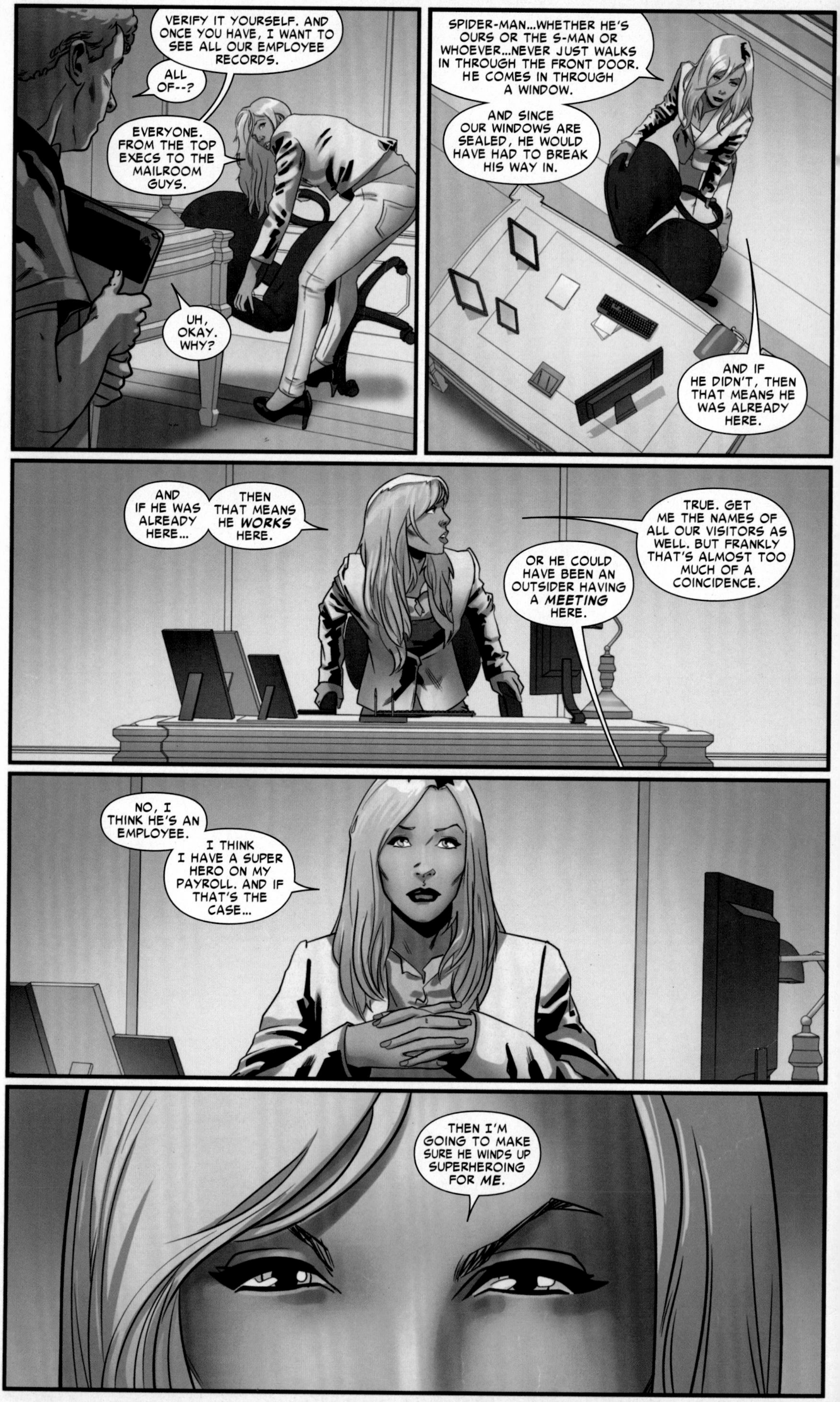
VERIFY IT YOURSELF. AND ONCE YOU HAVE, I WANT TO SEE ALL OUR EMPLOYEE RECORDS.
ALL OF--?
EVERYONE. FROM THE TOP EXECS TO THE MAILROOM GUYS.
UH, OKAY. WHY?
SPIDER-MAN...WHETHER HE'S OURS OR THE S-MAN OR WHOEVER...NEVER JUST WALKS IN THROUGH THE FRONT DOOR. HE COMES IN THROUGH A WINDOW.
AND SINCE OUR WINDOWS ARE SEALED, HE WOULD HAVE HAD TO BREAK HIS WAY IN.
AND IF HE DIDN'T, THEN THAT MEANS HE WAS ALREADY HERE.
AND IF HE WAS ALREADY HERE...
THEN THAT MEANS HE *WORKS* HERE.
OR HE COULD HAVE BEEN AN OUTSIDER HAVING A *MEETING* HERE.
TRUE. GET ME THE NAMES OF ALL OUR VISITORS AS WELL. BUT FRANKLY THAT'S ALMOST TOO MUCH OF A COINCIDENCE.
NO, I THINK HE'S AN EMPLOYEE.
I THINK I HAVE A SUPER HERO ON MY PAYROLL. AND IF THAT'S THE CASE...
THEN I'M GOING TO MAKE SURE HE WINDS UP SUPERHEROING FOR *ME*.

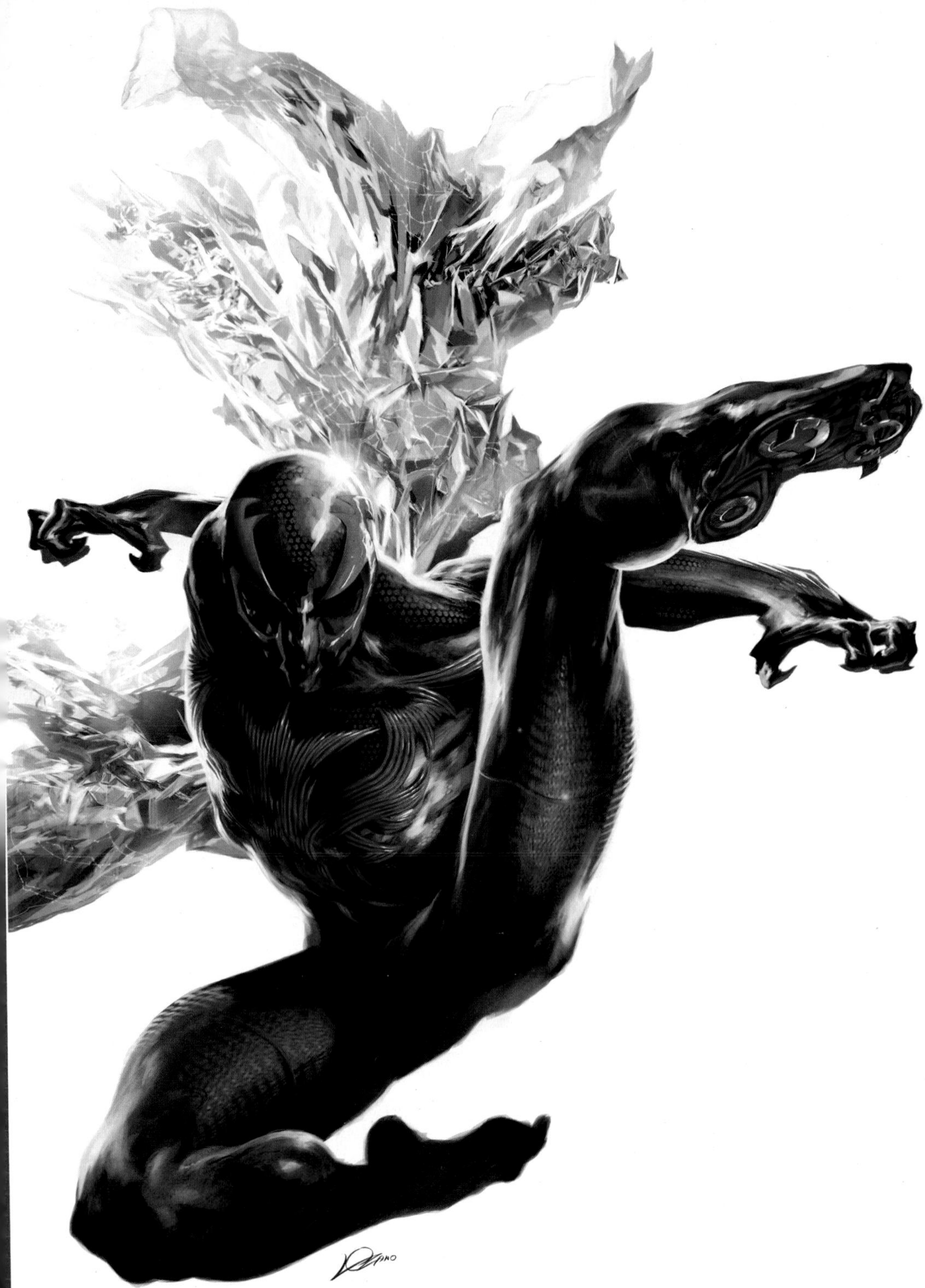

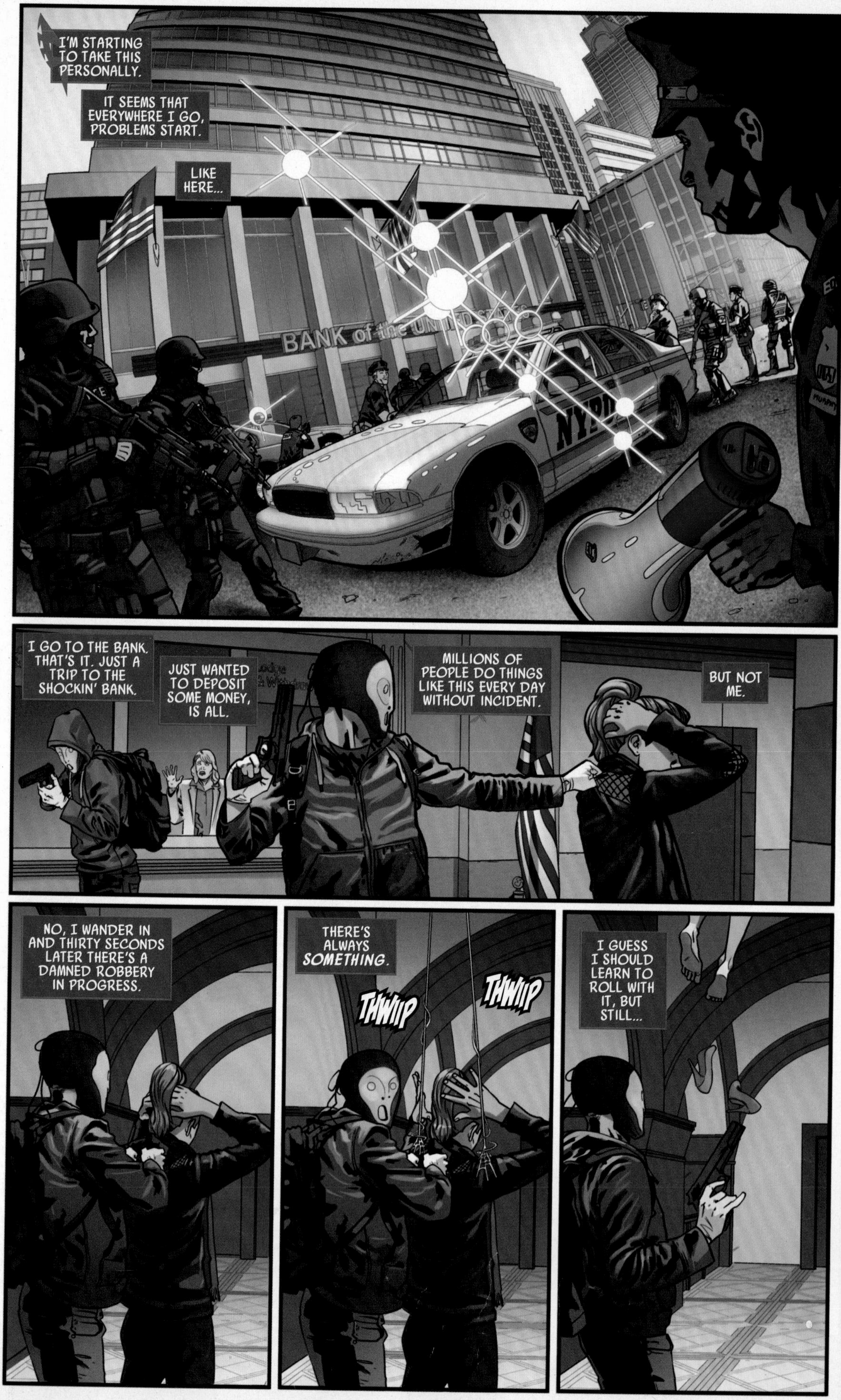
I'M STARTING TO TAKE THIS PERSONALLY.
IT SEEMS THAT EVERYWHERE I GO, PROBLEMS START.
LIKE HERE...
BANK of the UNITED STATES
NYPD
I GO TO THE BANK. THAT'S IT. JUST A TRIP TO THE SHOCKIN' BANK.
JUST WANTED TO DEPOSIT SOME MONEY, IS ALL.
MILLIONS OF PEOPLE DO THINGS LIKE THIS EVERY DAY WITHOUT INCIDENT.
BUT NOT ME.
NO, I WANDER IN AND THIRTY SECONDS LATER THERE'S A DAMNED ROBBERY IN PROGRESS.
THERE'S ALWAYS *SOMETHING*.
THWIIP
THWIIP
I GUESS I SHOULD LEARN TO ROLL WITH IT, BUT STILL...

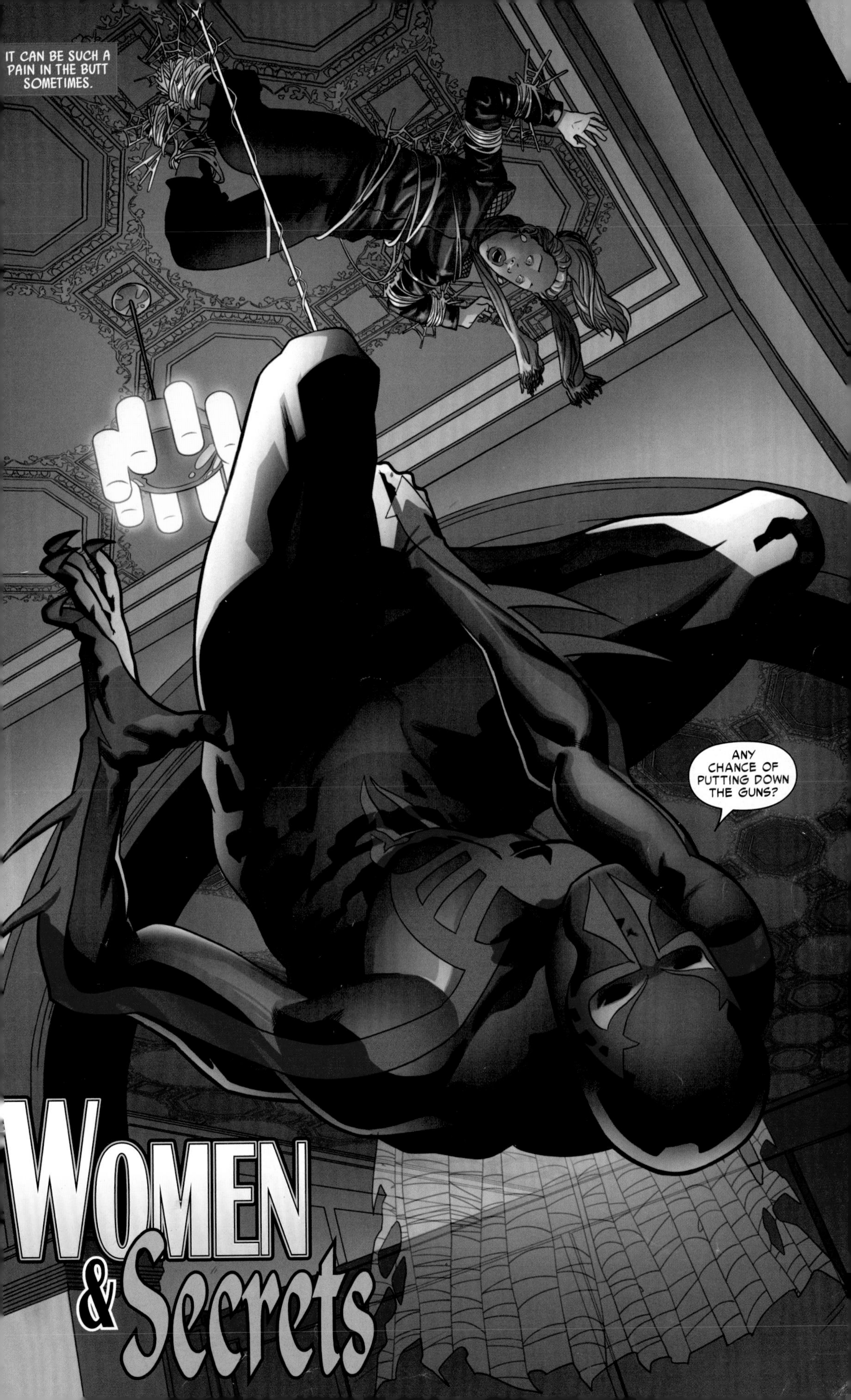
IT CAN BE SUCH A PAIN IN THE BUTT SOMETIMES.
ANY CHANCE OF PUTTING DOWN THE GUNS?
WOMEN & Secrets

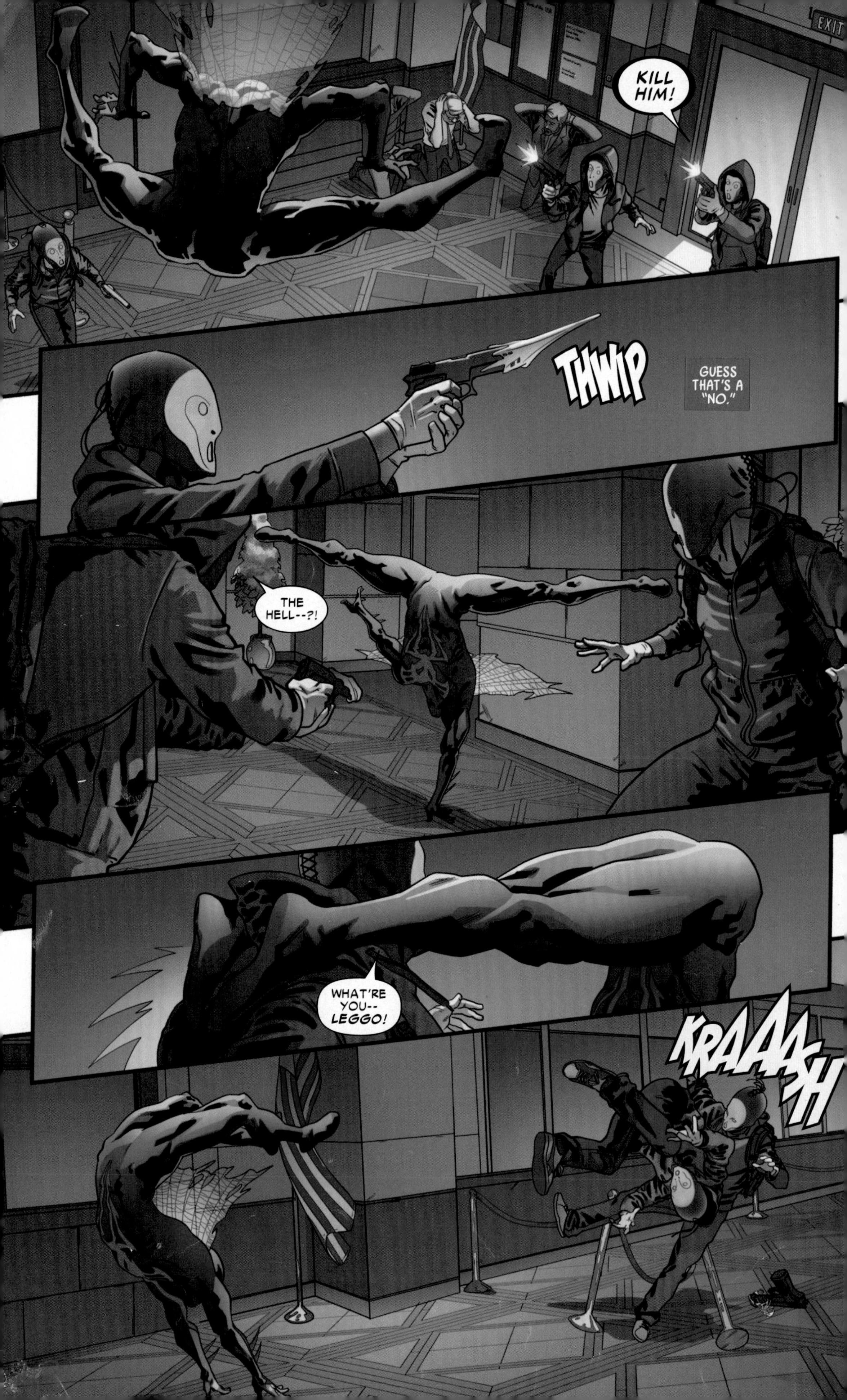
KILL HIM!
THWIP
GUESS THAT'S A "NO."
THE HELL--?!
WHAT'RE YOU-- LEGGO!
KRAAASH

UNHHH...

IT WAS THEIR IDEA. ROBBING THE BANK. TOTALLY THEM.

THEY WERE LIKE, "IT'LL BE EASY," AND I'M LIKE, "BUT GUYS, IT'S BANK ROBBERY! WE SHOULDN'T BE DOING THAT!"

AND THEY'RE LIKE, "TERRY, COME ON, DON'T BE A WUSS." AND I'M LIKE--

POW

SHUT UP.

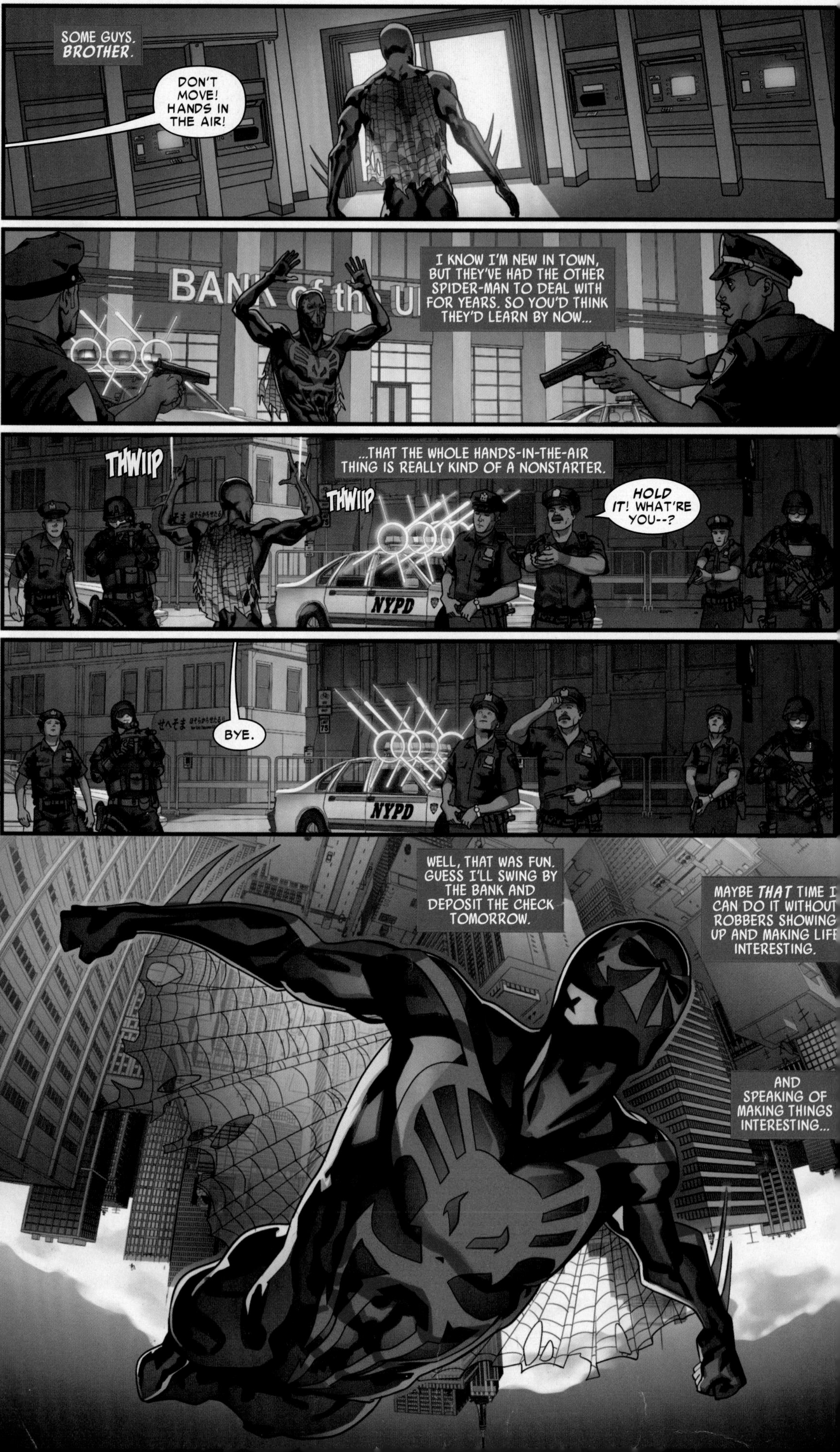
SOME GUYS. BROTHER.
DON'T MOVE! HANDS IN THE AIR!
BANK of the U
I KNOW I'M NEW IN TOWN, BUT THEY'VE HAD THE OTHER SPIDER-MAN TO DEAL WITH FOR YEARS. SO YOU'D THINK THEY'D LEARN BY NOW...
THWIIP
...THAT THE WHOLE HANDS-IN-THE-AIR THING IS REALLY KIND OF A NONSTARTER.
THWIIP
HOLD IT! WHAT'RE YOU--?
NYPD
BYE.
NYPD
WELL, THAT WAS FUN. GUESS I'LL SWING BY THE BANK AND DEPOSIT THE CHECK TOMORROW.
MAYBE THAT TIME I CAN DO IT WITHOUT ROBBERS SHOWING UP AND MAKING LIFE INTERESTING.
AND SPEAKING OF MAKING THINGS INTERESTING...

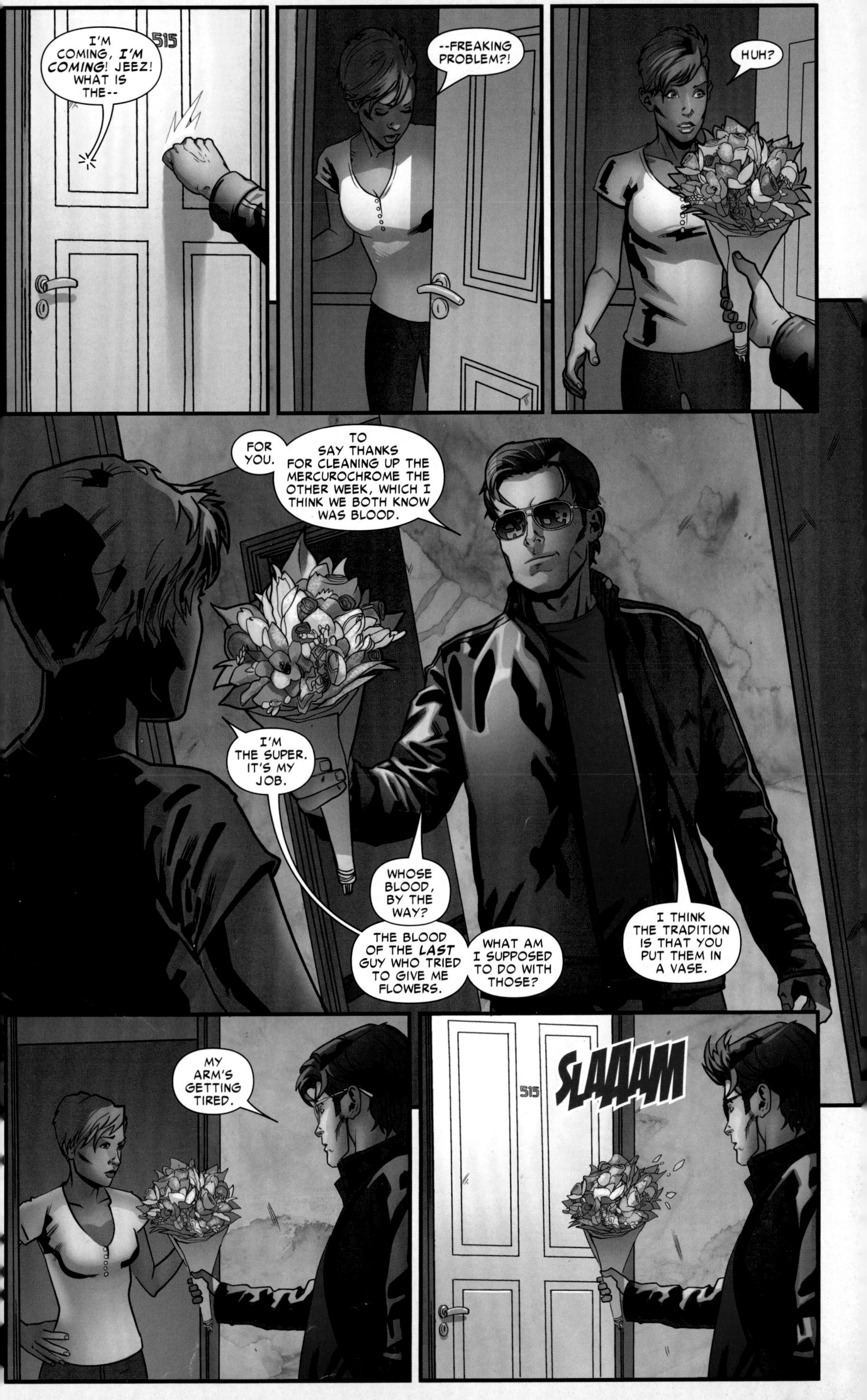

515
I'M COMING, I'M COMING! JEEZ! WHAT IS THE--
--FREAKING PROBLEM?!
HUH?
FOR YOU.
TO SAY THANKS FOR CLEANING UP THE MERCUROCHROME THE OTHER WEEK, WHICH I THINK WE BOTH KNOW WAS BLOOD.
I'M THE SUPER. IT'S MY JOB.
WHOSE BLOOD, BY THE WAY?
THE BLOOD OF THE LAST GUY WHO TRIED TO GIVE ME FLOWERS.
WHAT AM I SUPPOSED TO DO WITH THOSE?
I THINK THE TRADITION IS THAT YOU PUT THEM IN A VASE.
MY ARM'S GETTING TIRED.
515
SLAAAM

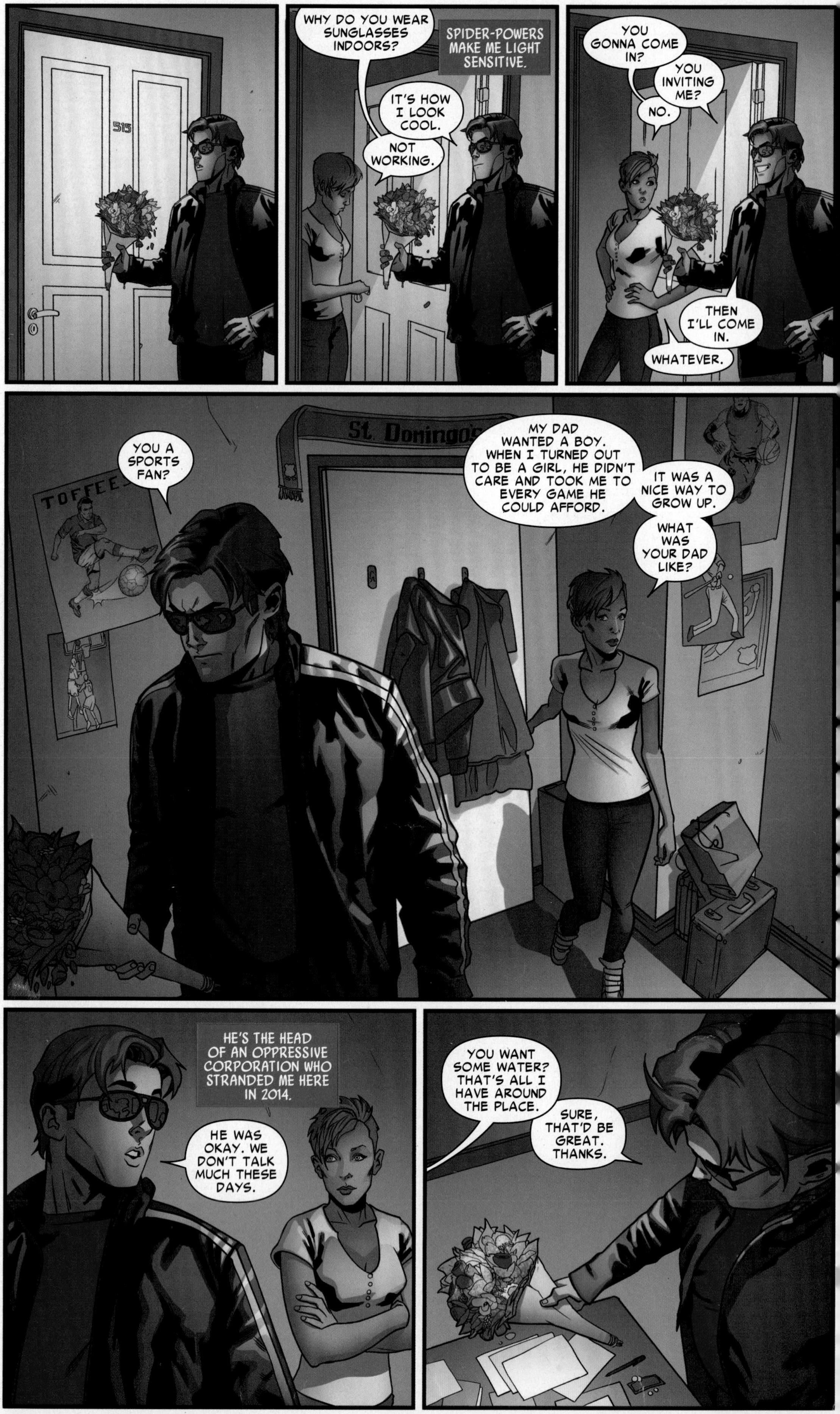
515
WHY DO YOU WEAR SUNGLASSES INDOORS?
SPIDER-POWERS MAKE ME LIGHT SENSITIVE.
IT'S HOW I LOOK COOL.
NOT WORKING.
YOU GONNA COME IN?
YOU INVITING ME?
NO.
THEN I'LL COME IN.
WHATEVER.
St. Domingo's
TOFFEES
YOU A SPORTS FAN?
MY DAD WANTED A BOY. WHEN I TURNED OUT TO BE A GIRL, HE DIDN'T CARE AND TOOK ME TO EVERY GAME HE COULD AFFORD.
IT WAS A NICE WAY TO GROW UP.
WHAT WAS YOUR DAD LIKE?
HE'S THE HEAD OF AN OPPRESSIVE CORPORATION WHO STRANDED ME HERE IN 2014.
HE WAS OKAY. WE DON'T TALK MUCH THESE DAYS.
YOU WANT SOME WATER? THAT'S ALL I HAVE AROUND THE PLACE.
SURE, THAT'D BE GREAT. THANKS.

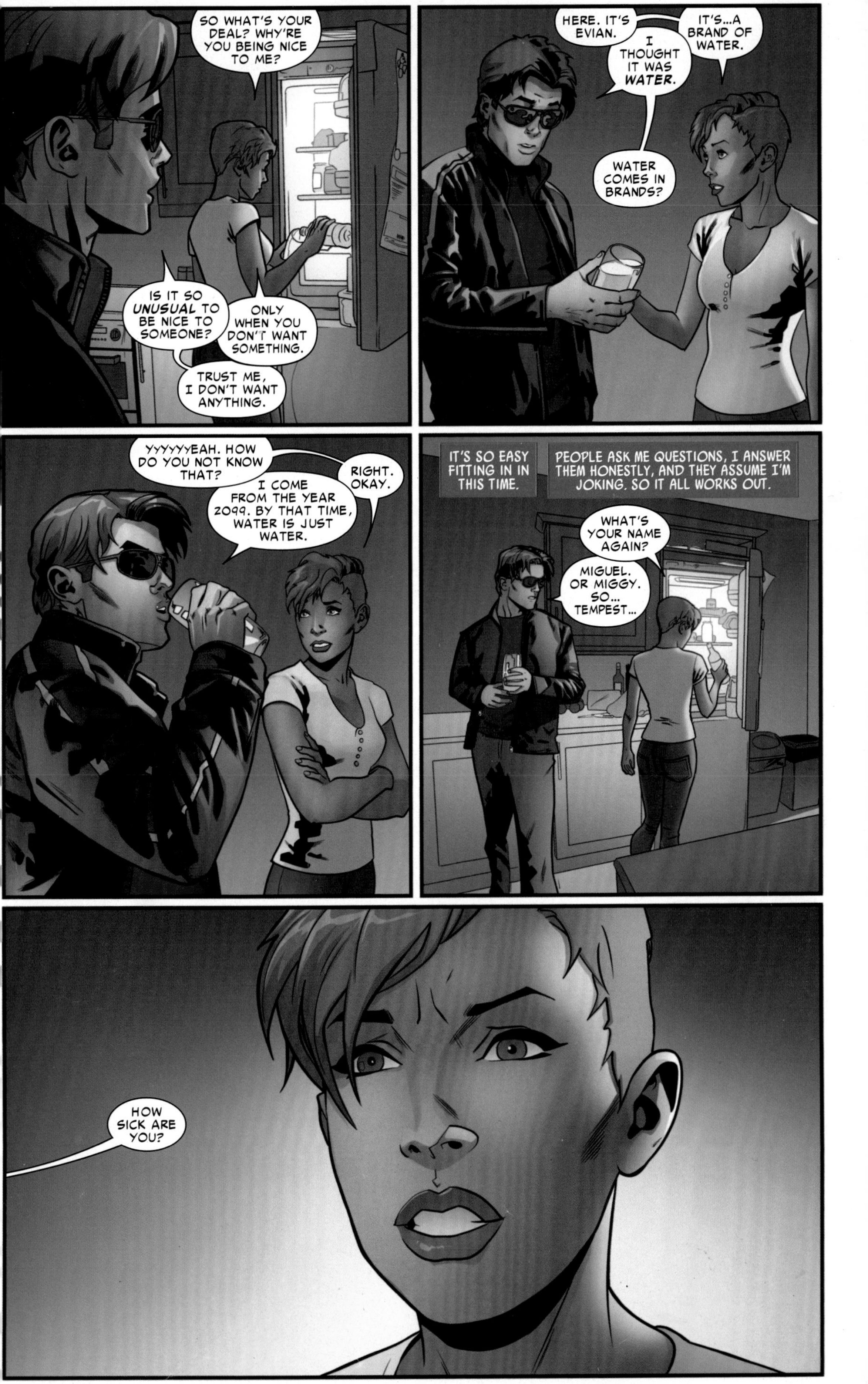
SO WHAT'S YOUR DEAL? WHY'RE YOU BEING NICE TO ME?
IS IT SO UNUSUAL TO BE NICE TO SOMEONE?
ONLY WHEN YOU DON'T WANT SOMETHING.
TRUST ME, I DON'T WANT ANYTHING.
HERE. IT'S EVIAN.
I THOUGHT IT WAS WATER.
IT'S...A BRAND OF WATER.
WATER COMES IN BRANDS?
YYYYYYEAH. HOW DO YOU NOT KNOW THAT?
I COME FROM THE YEAR 2099. BY THAT TIME, WATER IS JUST WATER.
RIGHT. OKAY.
IT'S SO EASY FITTING IN IN THIS TIME.
PEOPLE ASK ME QUESTIONS, I ANSWER THEM HONESTLY, AND THEY ASSUME I'M JOKING. SO IT ALL WORKS OUT.
WHAT'S YOUR NAME AGAIN?
MIGUEL. OR MIGGY. SO... TEMPEST...
HOW SICK ARE YOU?

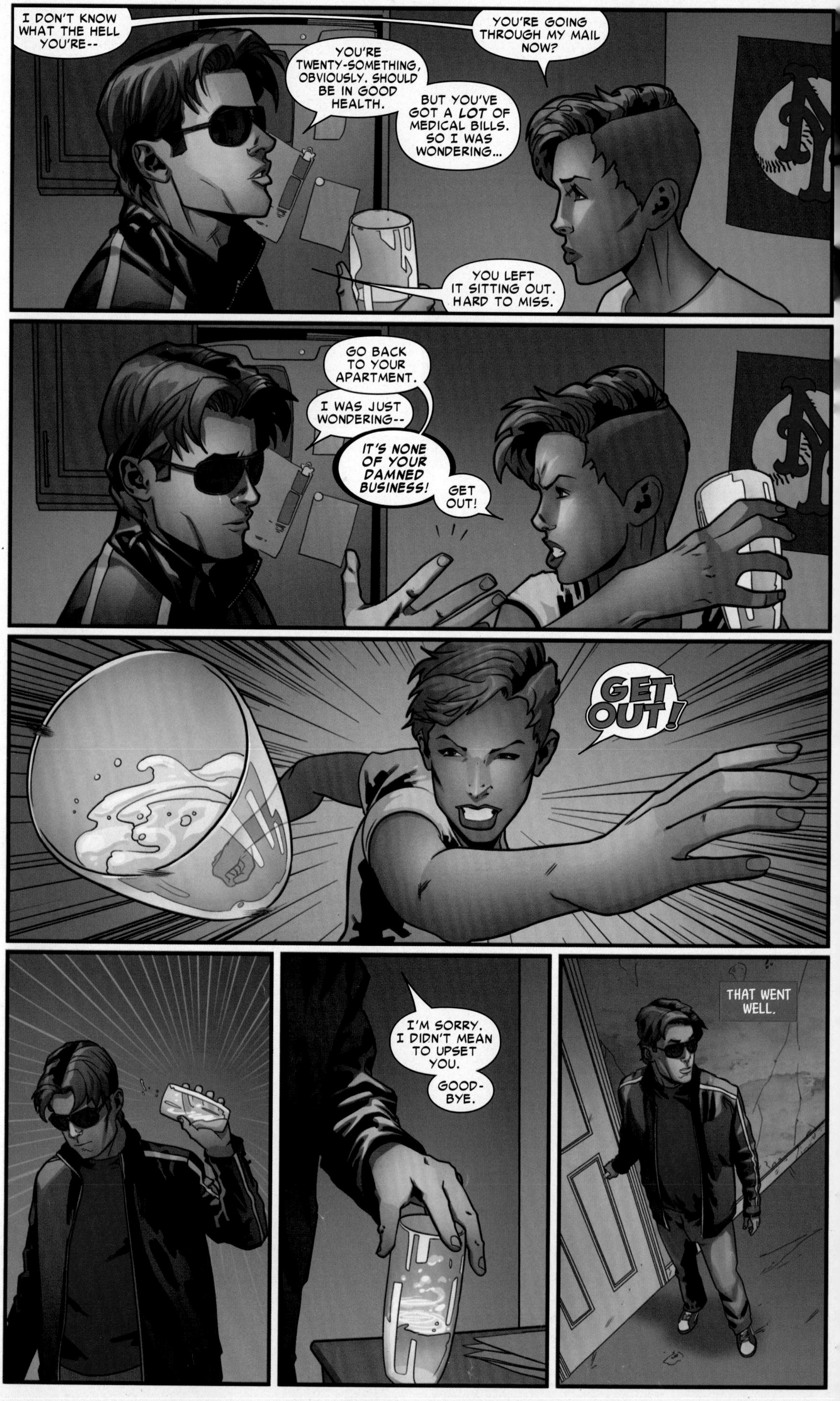
I DON'T KNOW WHAT THE HELL YOU'RE--
YOU'RE GOING THROUGH MY MAIL NOW?
YOU'RE TWENTY-SOMETHING, OBVIOUSLY. SHOULD BE IN GOOD HEALTH.
BUT YOU'VE GOT A *LOT* OF MEDICAL BILLS. SO I WAS WONDERING...
YOU LEFT IT SITTING OUT. HARD TO MISS.
GO BACK TO YOUR APARTMENT.
I WAS JUST WONDERING--
IT'S NONE OF YOUR DAMNED BUSINESS!
GET OUT!
GET OUT!
I'M SORRY. I DIDN'T MEAN TO UPSET YOU.
GOOD-BYE.
THAT WENT WELL.

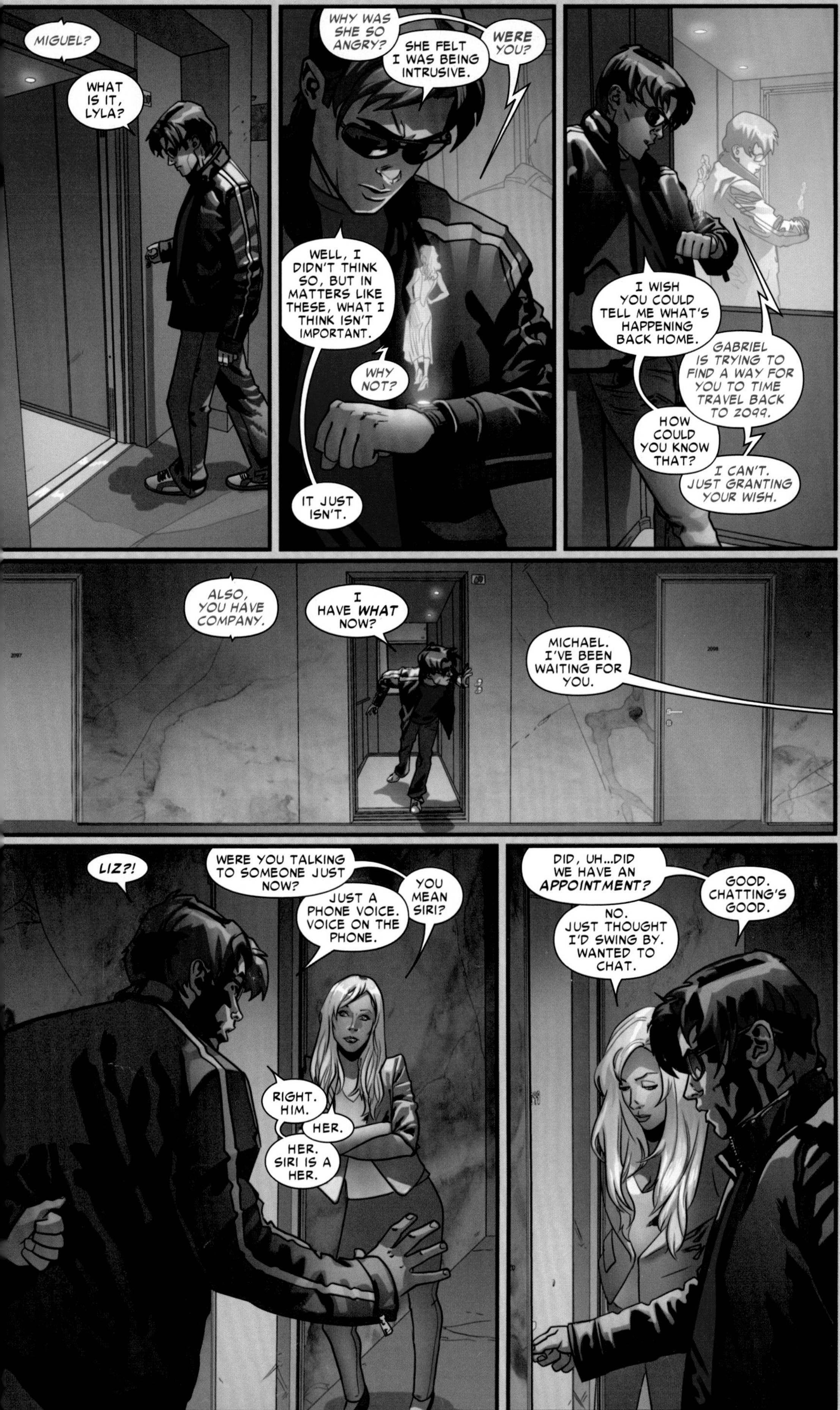
MIGUEL?
WHAT IS IT, LYLA?
WHY WAS SHE SO ANGRY?
SHE FELT I WAS BEING INTRUSIVE.
WERE YOU?
WELL, I DIDN'T THINK SO, BUT IN MATTERS LIKE THESE, WHAT I THINK ISN'T IMPORTANT.
WHY NOT?
IT JUST ISN'T.
I WISH YOU COULD TELL ME WHAT'S HAPPENING BACK HOME.
GABRIEL IS TRYING TO FIND A WAY FOR YOU TO TIME TRAVEL BACK TO 2099.
HOW COULD YOU KNOW THAT?
I CAN'T. JUST GRANTING YOUR WISH.
ALSO, YOU HAVE COMPANY.
I HAVE WHAT NOW?
MICHAEL. I'VE BEEN WAITING FOR YOU.
LIZ?!
WERE YOU TALKING TO SOMEONE JUST NOW?
JUST A PHONE VOICE. VOICE ON THE PHONE.
YOU MEAN SIRI?
RIGHT. HIM.
HER.
HER. SIRI IS A HER.
DID, UH...DID WE HAVE AN APPOINTMENT?
NO. JUST THOUGHT I'D SWING BY. WANTED TO CHAT.
GOOD. CHATTING'S GOOD.

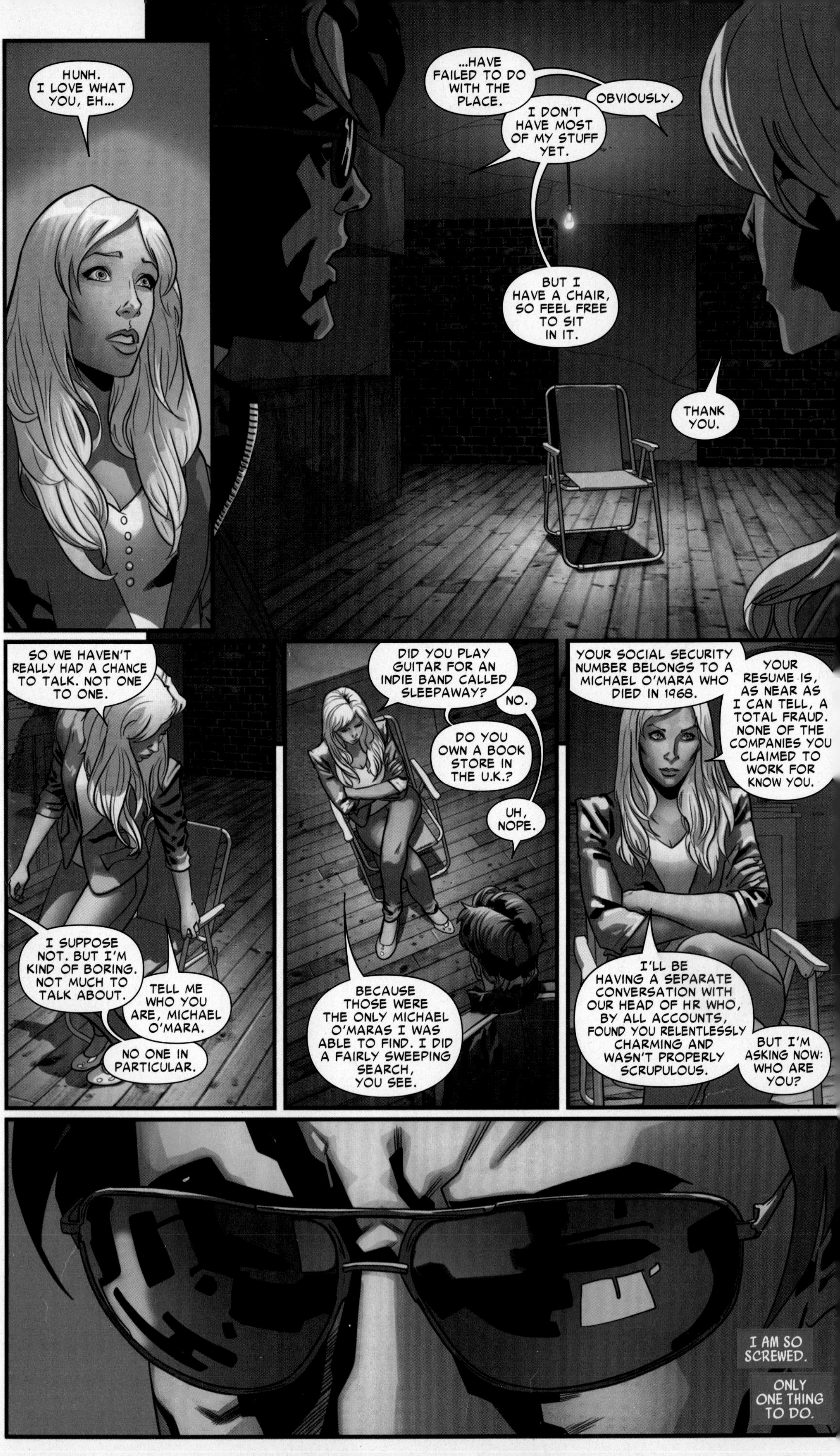
HUNH. I LOVE WHAT YOU, EH...
...HAVE FAILED TO DO WITH THE PLACE.
OBVIOUSLY.
I DON'T HAVE MOST OF MY STUFF YET.
BUT I HAVE A CHAIR, SO FEEL FREE TO SIT IN IT.
THANK YOU.
SO WE HAVEN'T REALLY HAD A CHANCE TO TALK. NOT ONE TO ONE.
I SUPPOSE NOT. BUT I'M KIND OF BORING. NOT MUCH TO TALK ABOUT.
TELL ME WHO YOU ARE, MICHAEL O'MARA.
NO ONE IN PARTICULAR.
DID YOU PLAY GUITAR FOR AN INDIE BAND CALLED SLEEPAWAY?
NO.
DO YOU OWN A BOOK STORE IN THE U.K.?
UH, NOPE.
BECAUSE THOSE WERE THE ONLY MICHAEL O'MARAS I WAS ABLE TO FIND. I DID A FAIRLY SWEEPING SEARCH, YOU SEE.
YOUR SOCIAL SECURITY NUMBER BELONGS TO A MICHAEL O'MARA WHO DIED IN 1968.
YOUR RESUME IS, AS NEAR AS I CAN TELL, A TOTAL FRAUD. NONE OF THE COMPANIES YOU CLAIMED TO WORK FOR KNOW YOU.
I'LL BE HAVING A SEPARATE CONVERSATION WITH OUR HEAD OF HR WHO, BY ALL ACCOUNTS, FOUND YOU RELENTLESSLY CHARMING AND WASN'T PROPERLY SCRUPULOUS.
BUT I'M ASKING NOW: WHO ARE YOU?
I AM SO SCREWED.
ONLY ONE THING TO DO.

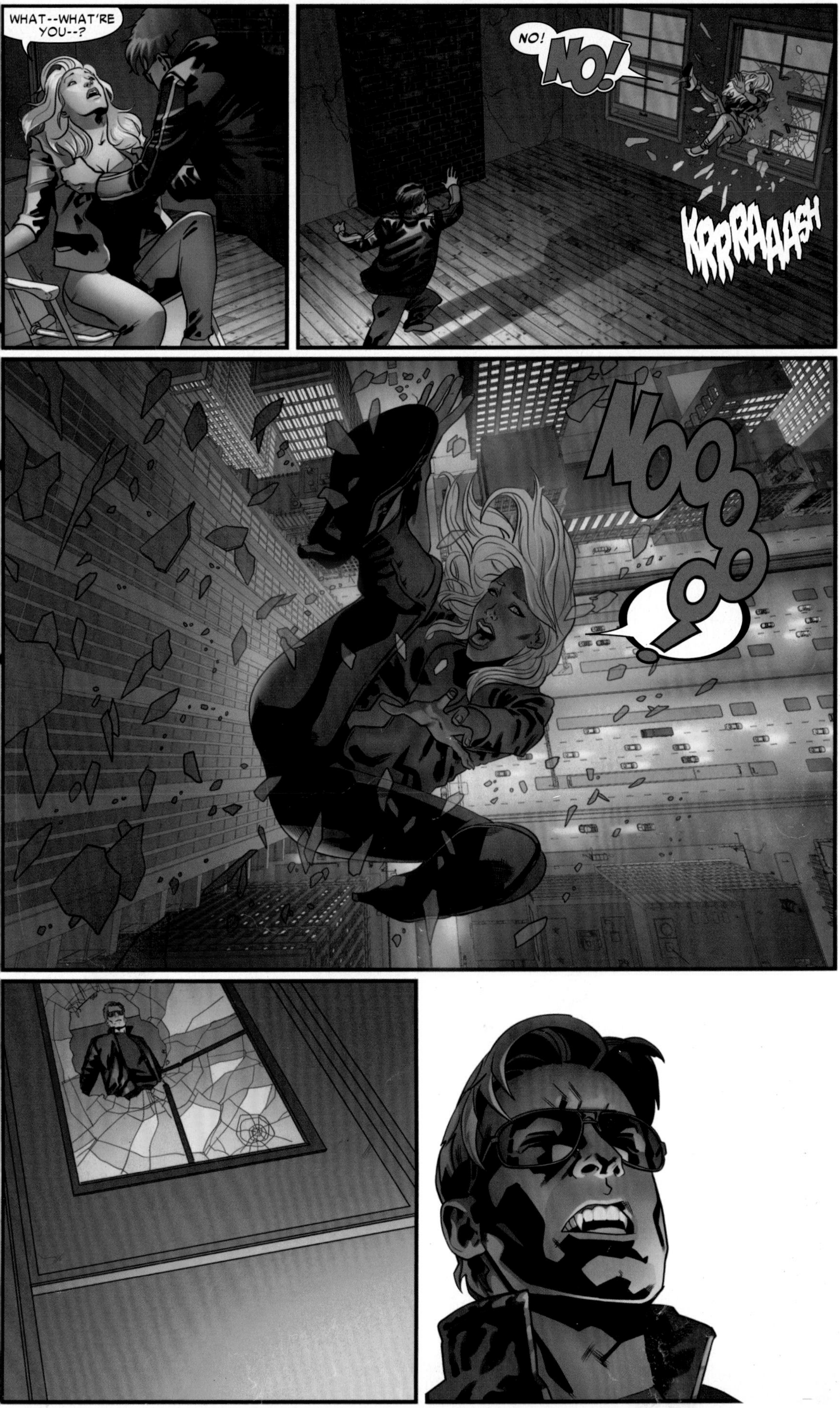
WHAT--WHAT'RE YOU--?
NO! NO!
KRRRAAASH
NOOOOOO!

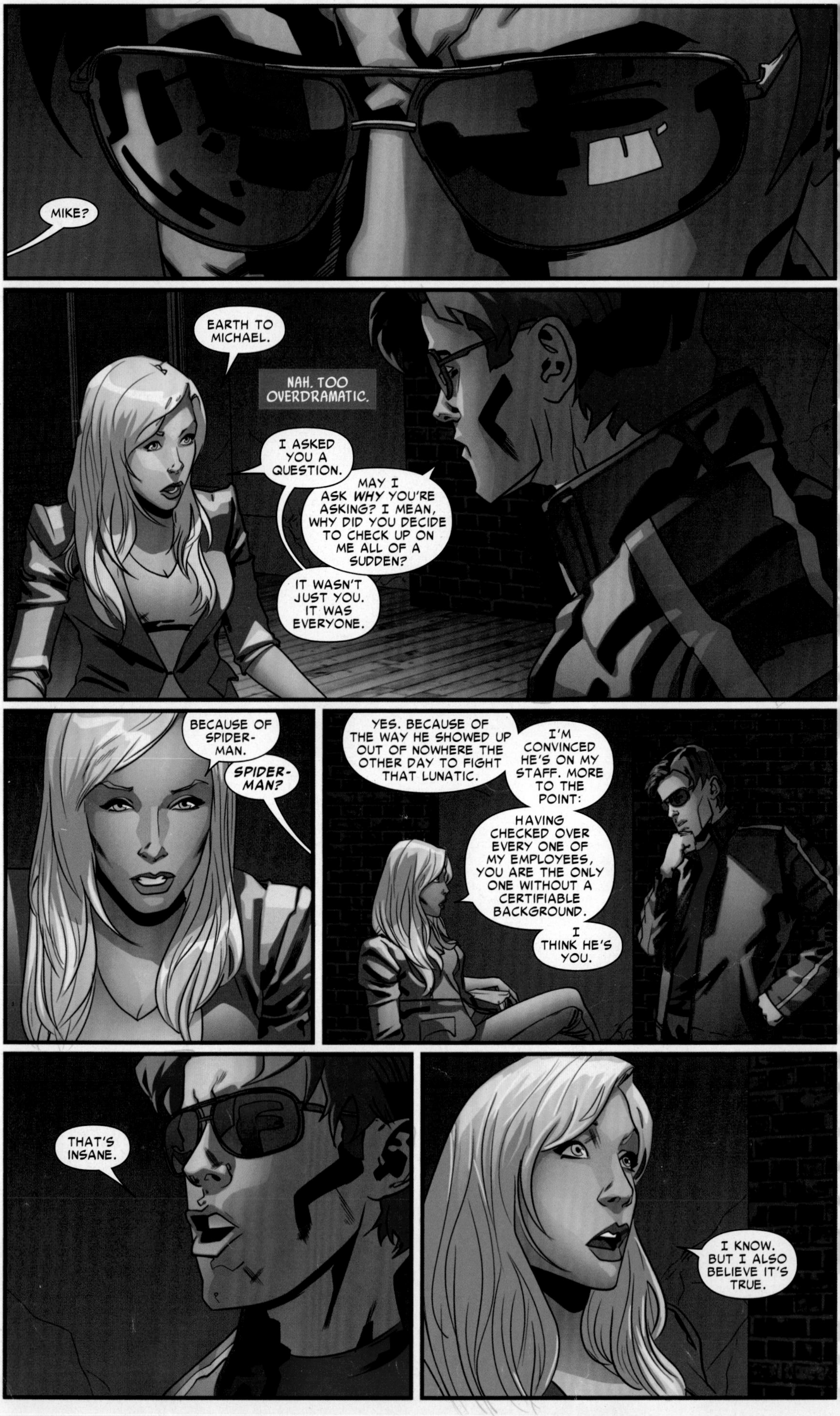
MIKE?
EARTH TO MICHAEL.
NAH. TOO OVERDRAMATIC.
I ASKED YOU A QUESTION.
MAY I ASK WHY YOU'RE ASKING? I MEAN, WHY DID YOU DECIDE TO CHECK UP ON ME ALL OF A SUDDEN?
IT WASN'T JUST YOU. IT WAS EVERYONE.
BECAUSE OF SPIDER-MAN.
SPIDER-MAN?
YES. BECAUSE OF THE WAY HE SHOWED UP OUT OF NOWHERE THE OTHER DAY TO FIGHT THAT LUNATIC.
I'M CONVINCED HE'S ON MY STAFF. MORE TO THE POINT:
HAVING CHECKED OVER EVERY ONE OF MY EMPLOYEES, YOU ARE THE ONLY ONE WITHOUT A CERTIFIABLE BACKGROUND.
I THINK HE'S YOU.
THAT'S INSANE.
I KNOW. BUT I ALSO BELIEVE IT'S TRUE.

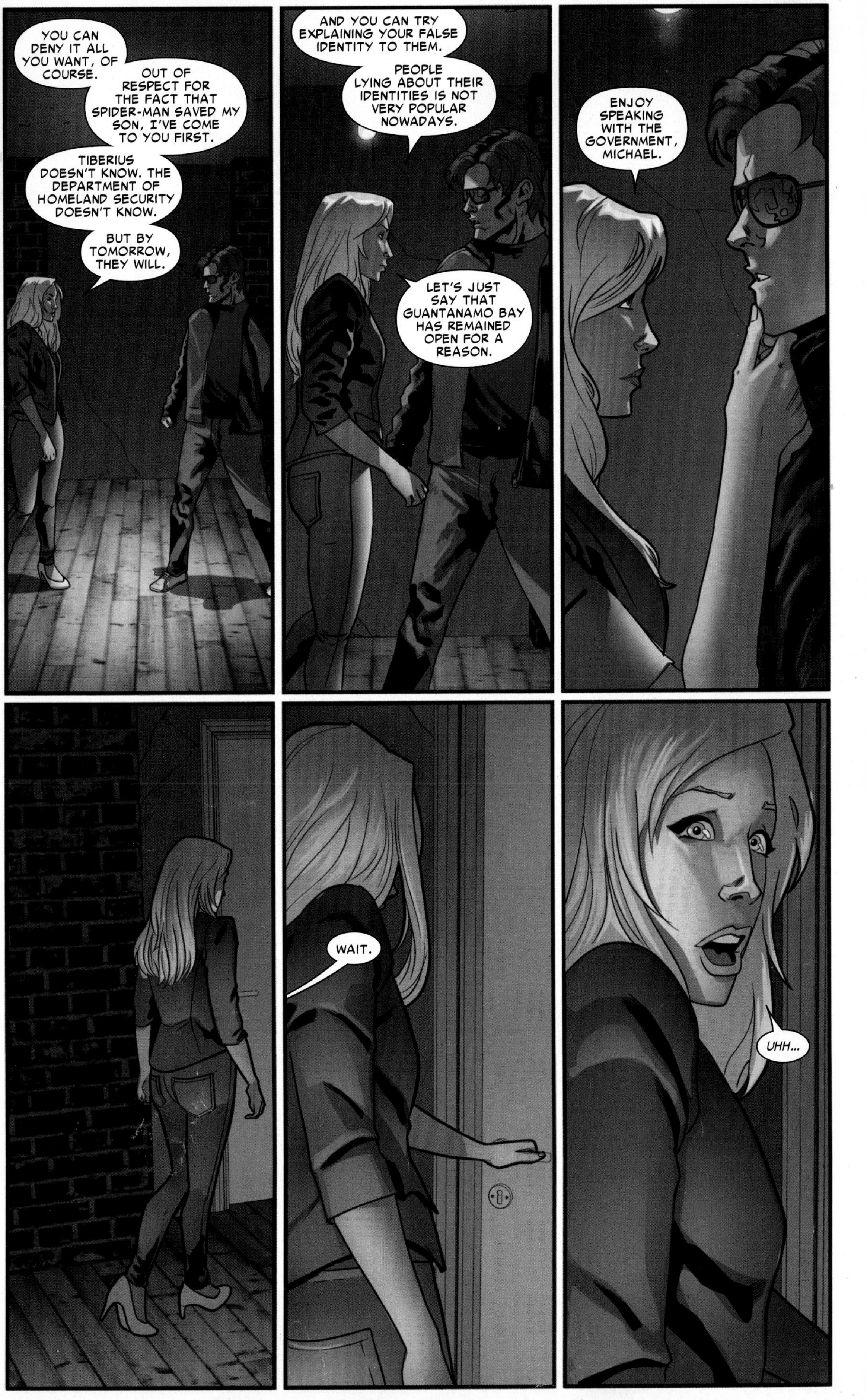

YOU CAN DENY IT ALL YOU WANT, OF COURSE.
OUT OF RESPECT FOR THE FACT THAT SPIDER-MAN SAVED MY SON, I'VE COME TO YOU FIRST.
TIBERIUS DOESN'T KNOW. THE DEPARTMENT OF HOMELAND SECURITY DOESN'T KNOW.
BUT BY TOMORROW, THEY WILL.
AND YOU CAN TRY EXPLAINING YOUR FALSE IDENTITY TO THEM.
PEOPLE LYING ABOUT THEIR IDENTITIES IS NOT VERY POPULAR NOWADAYS.
LET'S JUST SAY THAT GUANTANAMO BAY HAS REMAINED OPEN FOR A REASON.
ENJOY SPEAKING WITH THE GOVERNMENT, MICHAEL.
WAIT.
UHH...

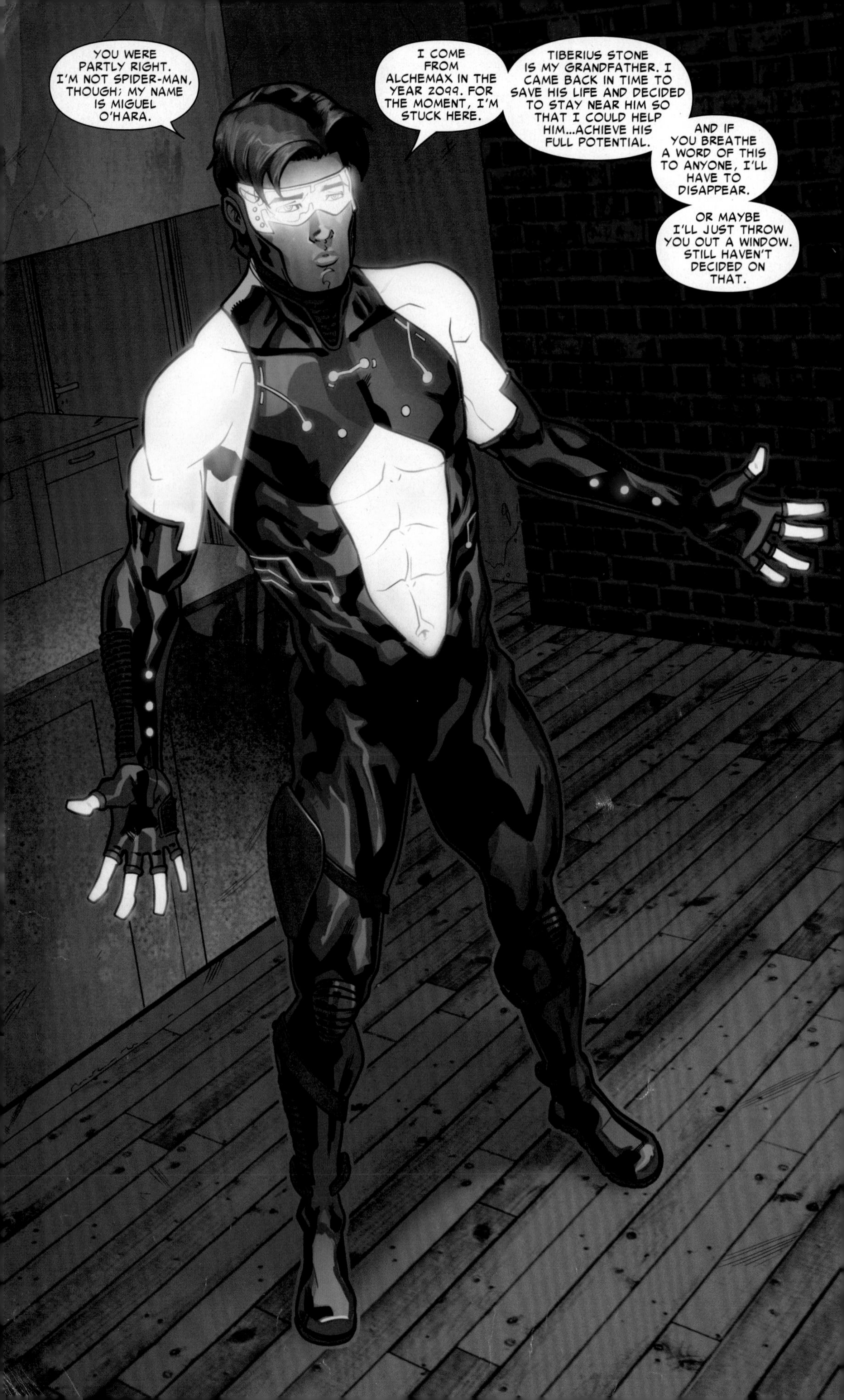
YOU WERE PARTLY RIGHT. I'M NOT SPIDER-MAN, THOUGH; MY NAME IS MIGUEL O'HARA.
I COME FROM ALCHEMAX IN THE YEAR 2099. FOR THE MOMENT, I'M STUCK HERE.
TIBERIUS STONE IS MY GRANDFATHER. I CAME BACK IN TIME TO SAVE HIS LIFE AND DECIDED TO STAY NEAR HIM SO THAT I COULD HELP HIM...ACHIEVE HIS FULL POTENTIAL.
AND IF YOU BREATHE A WORD OF THIS TO ANYONE, I'LL HAVE TO DISAPPEAR.
OR MAYBE I'LL JUST THROW YOU OUT A WINDOW. STILL HAVEN'T DECIDED ON THAT.

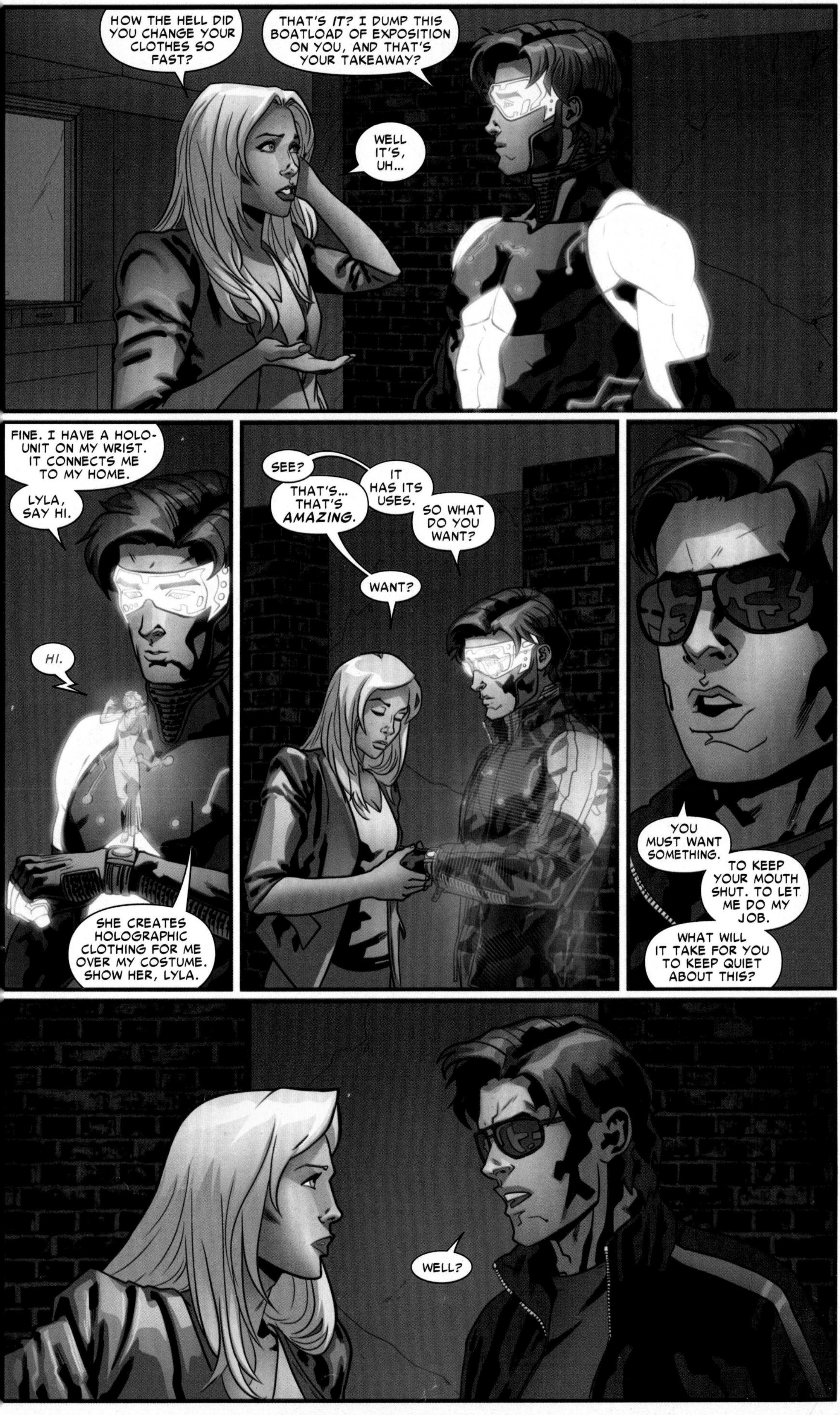
HOW THE HELL DID YOU CHANGE YOUR CLOTHES SO FAST?
THAT'S *IT*? I DUMP THIS BOATLOAD OF EXPOSITION ON YOU, AND THAT'S YOUR TAKEAWAY?
WELL IT'S, UH...
FINE. I HAVE A HOLO-UNIT ON MY WRIST. IT CONNECTS ME TO MY HOME.
LYLA, SAY HI.
HI.
SHE CREATES HOLOGRAPHIC CLOTHING FOR ME OVER MY COSTUME. SHOW HER, LYLA.
SEE?
THAT'S... THAT'S *AMAZING*.
IT HAS ITS USES.
SO WHAT DO YOU WANT?
WANT?
YOU MUST WANT SOMETHING.
TO KEEP YOUR MOUTH SHUT. TO LET ME DO MY JOB.
WHAT WILL IT TAKE FOR YOU TO KEEP QUIET ABOUT THIS?
WELL?

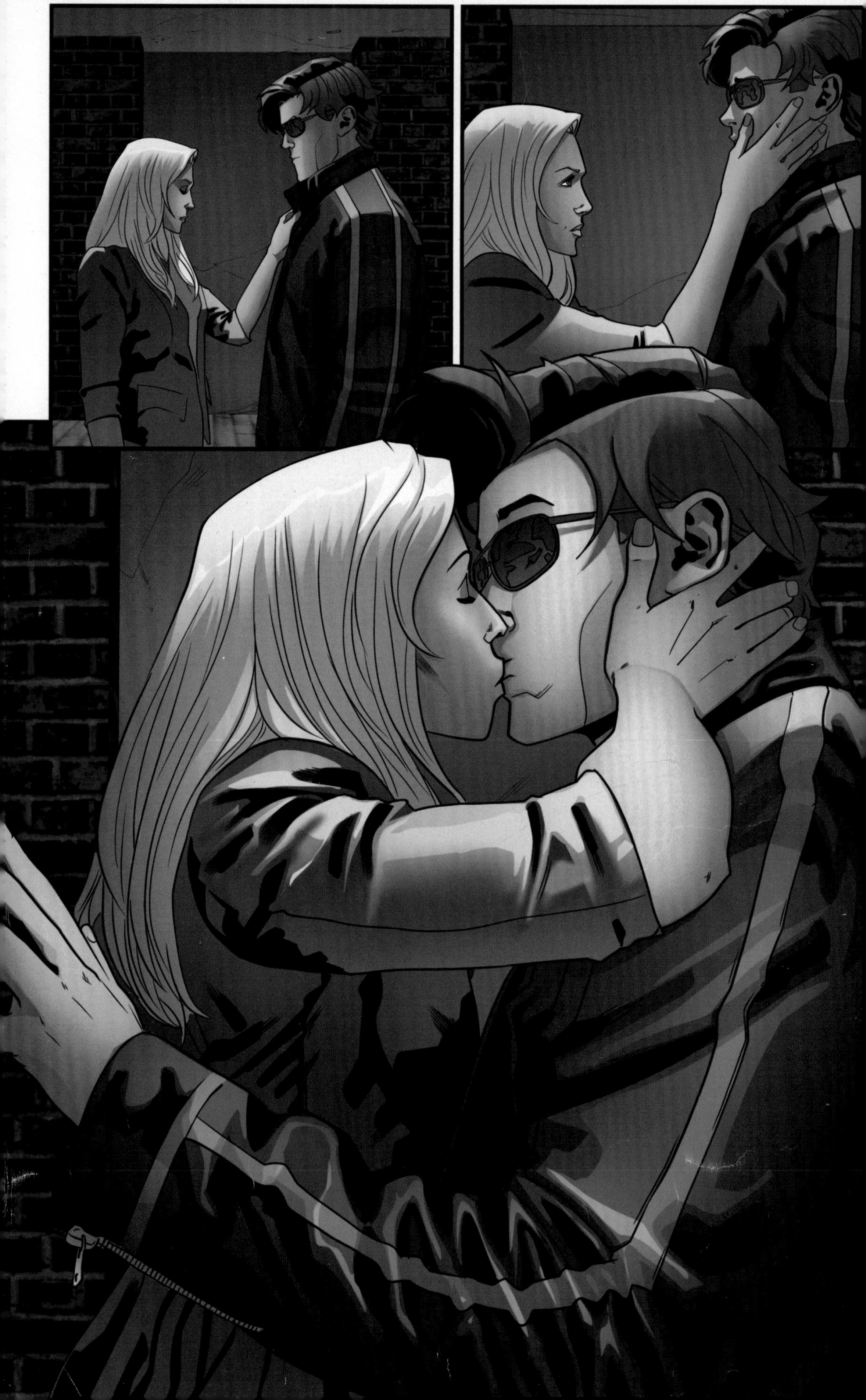

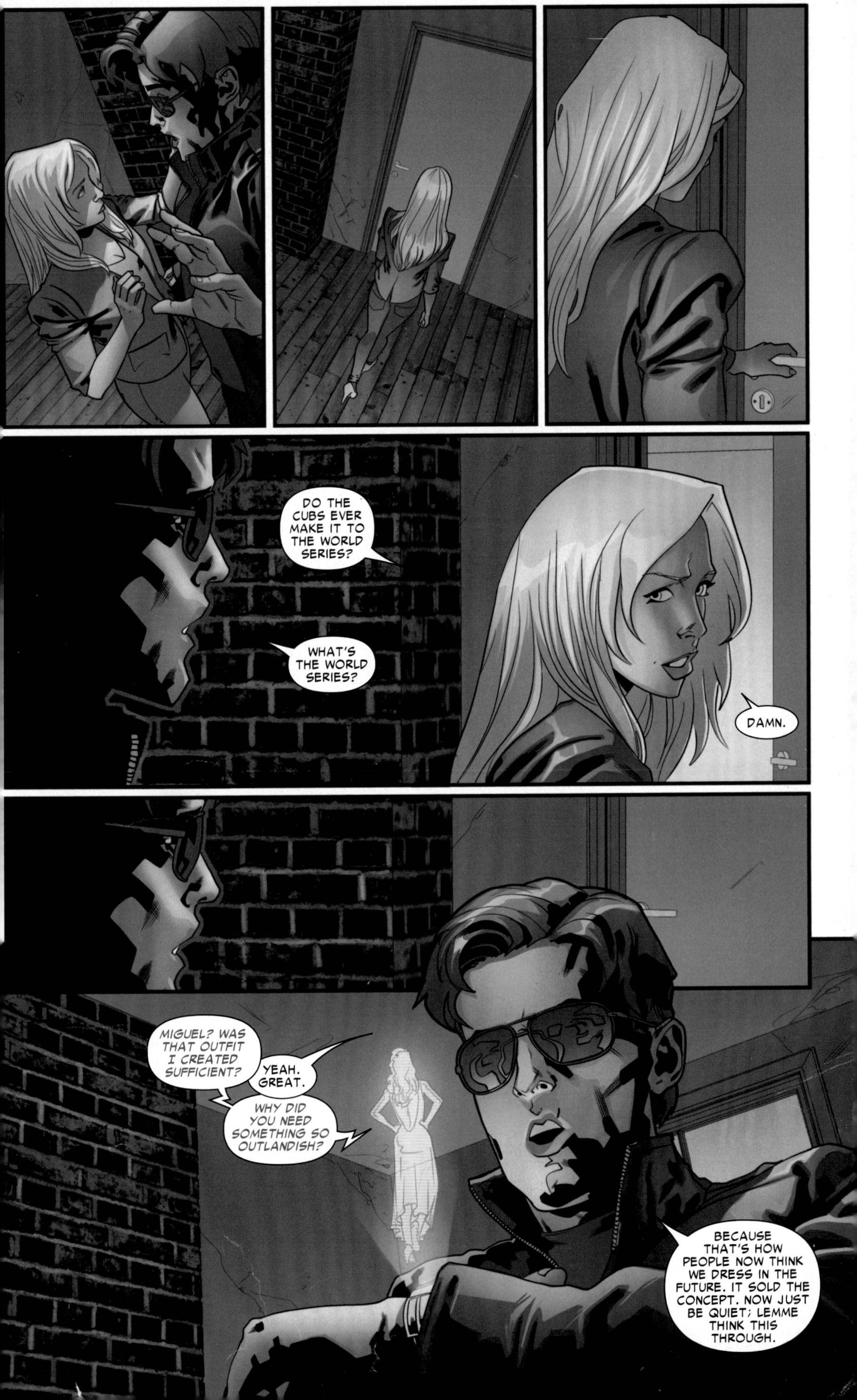
DO THE CUBS EVER MAKE IT TO THE WORLD SERIES?
WHAT'S THE WORLD SERIES?
DAMN.
MIGUEL? WAS THAT OUTFIT I CREATED SUFFICIENT?
YEAH. GREAT.
WHY DID YOU NEED SOMETHING SO OUTLANDISH?
BECAUSE THAT'S HOW PEOPLE NOW THINK WE DRESS IN THE FUTURE. IT SOLD THE CONCEPT. NOW JUST BE QUIET; LEMME THINK THIS THROUGH.

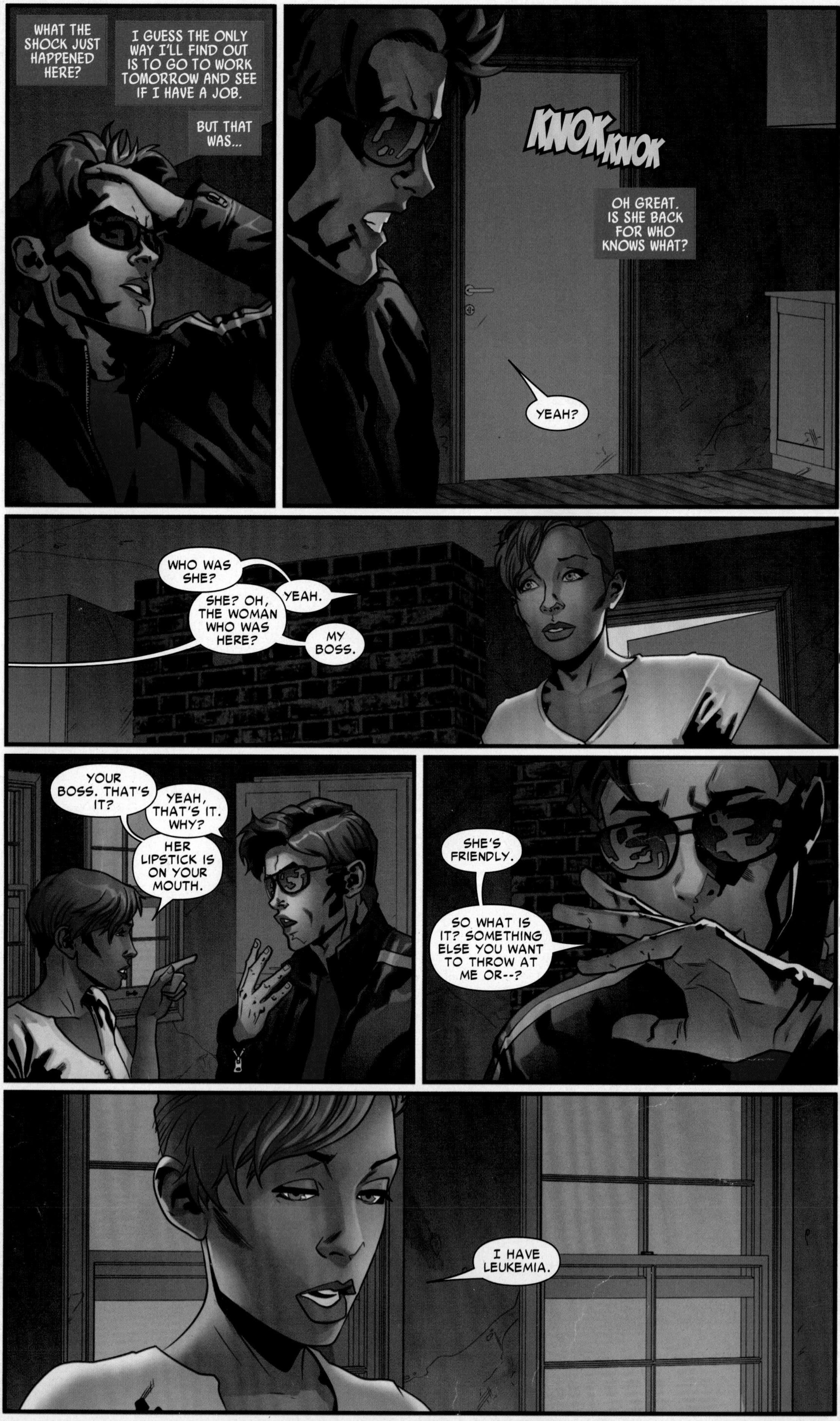

WHAT THE SHOCK JUST HAPPENED HERE?
I GUESS THE ONLY WAY I'LL FIND OUT IS TO GO TO WORK TOMORROW AND SEE IF I HAVE A JOB.
BUT THAT WAS...
KNOK KNOK
OH GREAT. IS SHE BACK FOR WHO KNOWS WHAT?
YEAH?
WHO WAS SHE?
YEAH.
SHE? OH, THE WOMAN WHO WAS HERE?
MY BOSS.
YOUR BOSS. THAT'S IT?
YEAH, THAT'S IT. WHY?
HER LIPSTICK IS ON YOUR MOUTH.
SHE'S FRIENDLY.
SO WHAT IS IT? SOMETHING ELSE YOU WANT TO THROW AT ME OR--?
I HAVE LEUKEMIA.

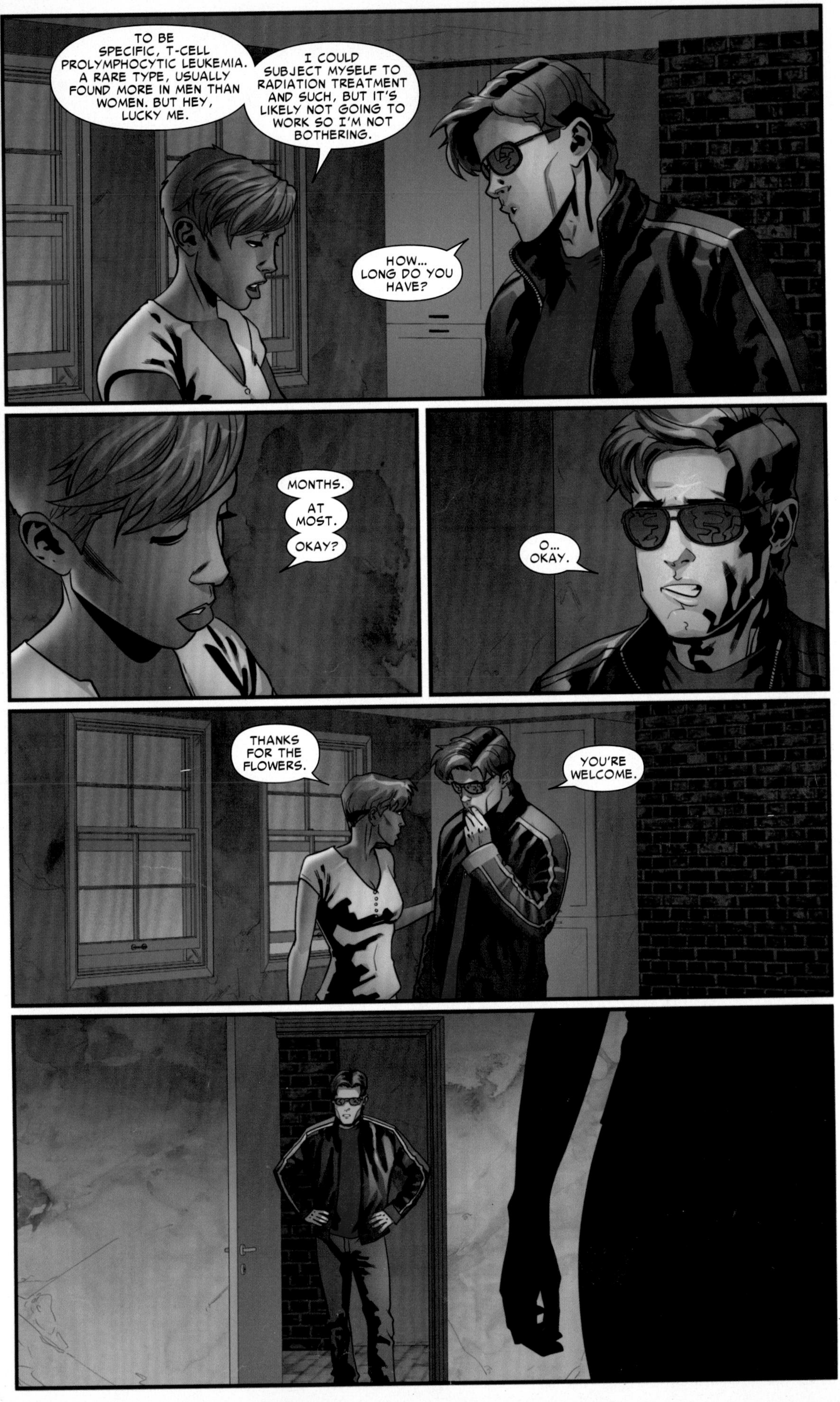
TO BE SPECIFIC, T-CELL PROLYMPHOCYTIC LEUKEMIA. A RARE TYPE, USUALLY FOUND MORE IN MEN THAN WOMEN. BUT HEY, LUCKY ME.
I COULD SUBJECT MYSELF TO RADIATION TREATMENT AND SUCH, BUT IT'S LIKELY NOT GOING TO WORK SO I'M NOT BOTHERING.
HOW... LONG DO YOU HAVE?
MONTHS.
AT MOST.
OKAY?
O... OKAY.
THANKS FOR THE FLOWERS.
YOU'RE WELCOME.

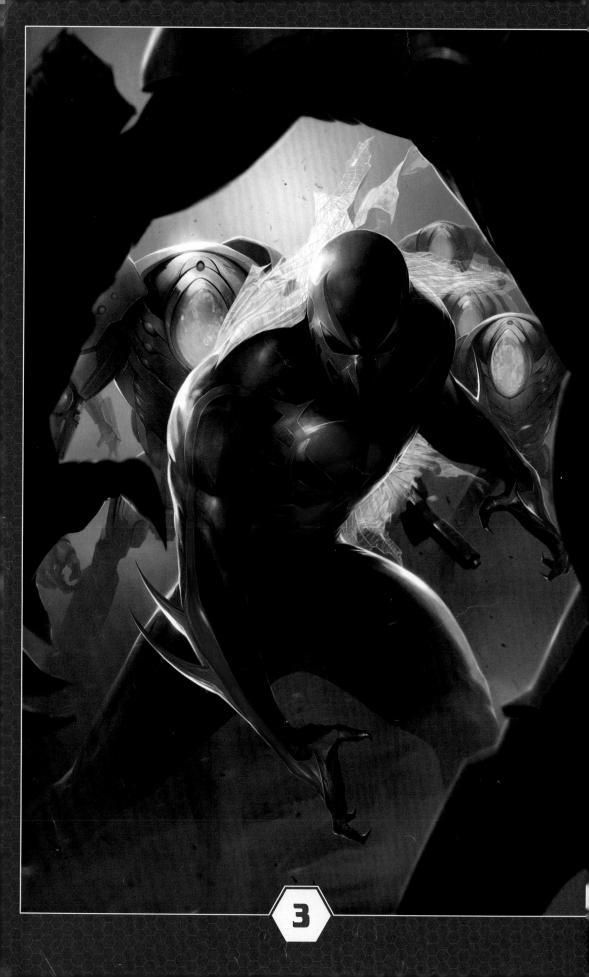

3

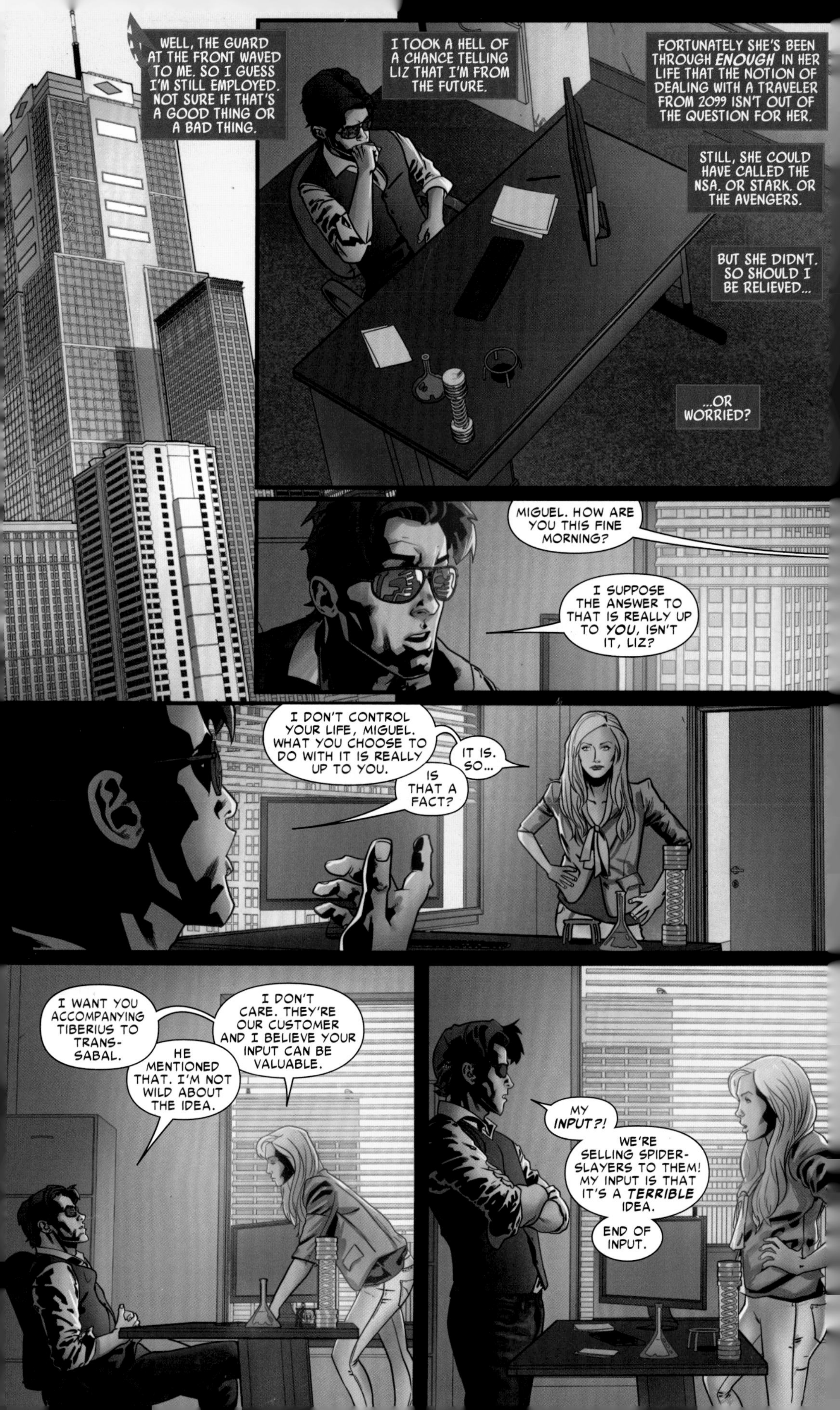
WELL, THE GUARD AT THE FRONT WAVED TO ME. SO I GUESS I'M STILL EMPLOYED. NOT SURE IF THAT'S A GOOD THING OR A BAD THING.
I TOOK A HELL OF A CHANCE TELLING LIZ THAT I'M FROM THE FUTURE.
FORTUNATELY SHE'S BEEN THROUGH ENOUGH IN HER LIFE THAT THE NOTION OF DEALING WITH A TRAVELER FROM 2099 ISN'T OUT OF THE QUESTION FOR HER.
STILL, SHE COULD HAVE CALLED THE NSA. OR STARK. OR THE AVENGERS.
BUT SHE DIDN'T. SO SHOULD I BE RELIEVED...
...OR WORRIED?
MIGUEL. HOW ARE YOU THIS FINE MORNING?
I SUPPOSE THE ANSWER TO THAT IS REALLY UP TO YOU, ISN'T IT, LIZ?
I DON'T CONTROL YOUR LIFE, MIGUEL. WHAT YOU CHOOSE TO DO WITH IT IS REALLY UP TO YOU.
IS THAT A FACT?
IT IS. SO...
I WANT YOU ACCOMPANYING TIBERIUS TO TRANS-SABAL.
HE MENTIONED THAT. I'M NOT WILD ABOUT THE IDEA.
I DON'T CARE. THEY'RE OUR CUSTOMER AND I BELIEVE YOUR INPUT CAN BE VALUABLE.
MY INPUT?!
WE'RE SELLING SPIDER-SLAYERS TO THEM! MY INPUT IS THAT IT'S A TERRIBLE IDEA.
END OF INPUT.

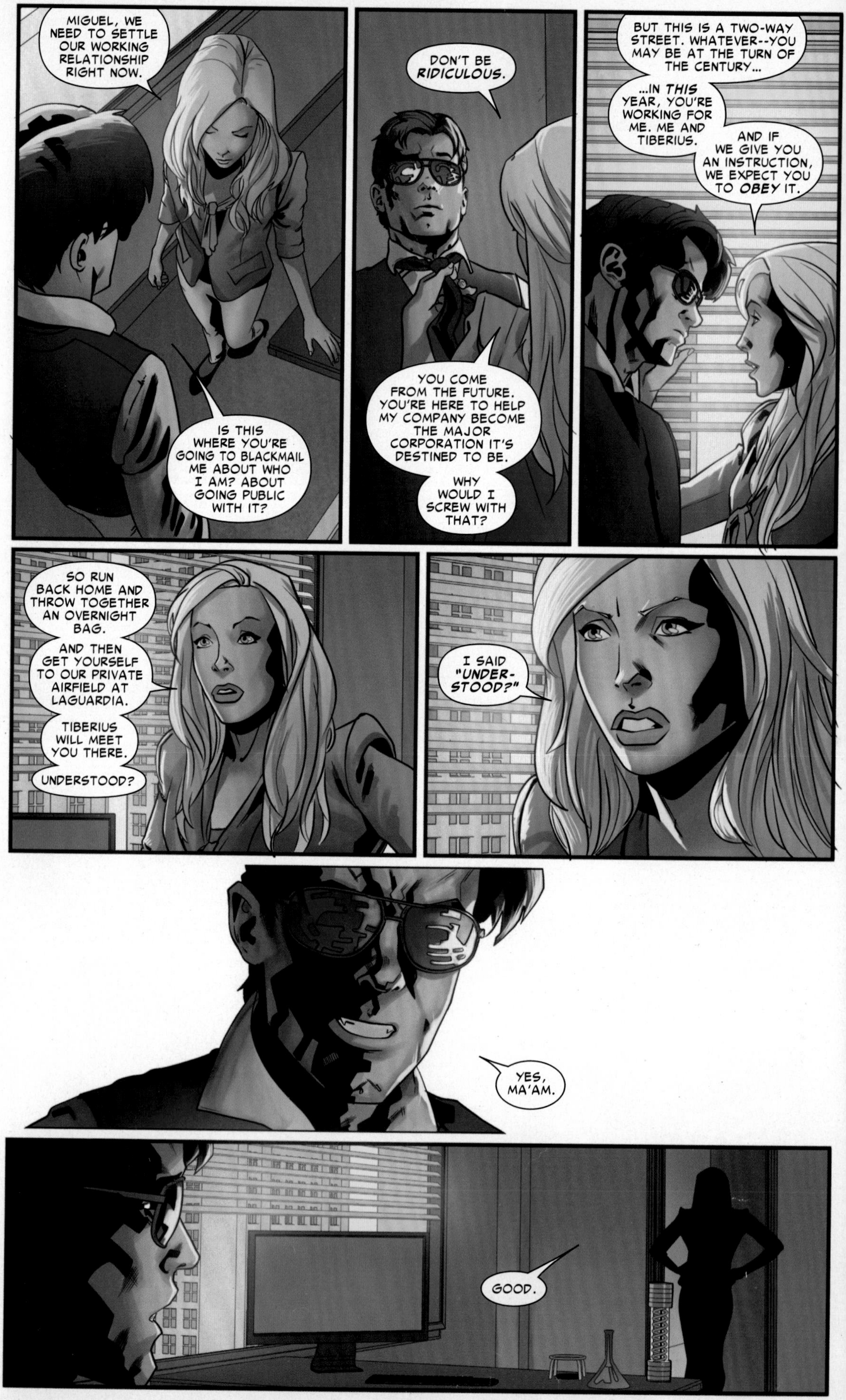
MIGUEL, WE NEED TO SETTLE OUR WORKING RELATIONSHIP RIGHT NOW.
IS THIS WHERE YOU'RE GOING TO BLACKMAIL ME ABOUT WHO I AM? ABOUT GOING PUBLIC WITH IT?
DON'T BE *RIDICULOUS*.
YOU COME FROM THE FUTURE. YOU'RE HERE TO HELP MY COMPANY BECOME THE MAJOR CORPORATION IT'S DESTINED TO BE.
WHY WOULD I SCREW WITH THAT?
BUT THIS IS A TWO-WAY STREET. WHATEVER--YOU MAY BE AT THE TURN OF THE CENTURY...
...IN *THIS* YEAR, YOU'RE WORKING FOR ME. ME AND TIBERIUS.
AND IF WE GIVE YOU AN INSTRUCTION, WE EXPECT YOU TO *OBEY* IT.
SO RUN BACK HOME AND THROW TOGETHER AN OVERNIGHT BAG.
AND THEN GET YOURSELF TO OUR PRIVATE AIRFIELD AT LAGUARDIA.
TIBERIUS WILL MEET YOU THERE.
UNDERSTOOD?
I SAID *"UNDER-STOOD?"*
YES, MA'AM.
GOOD.

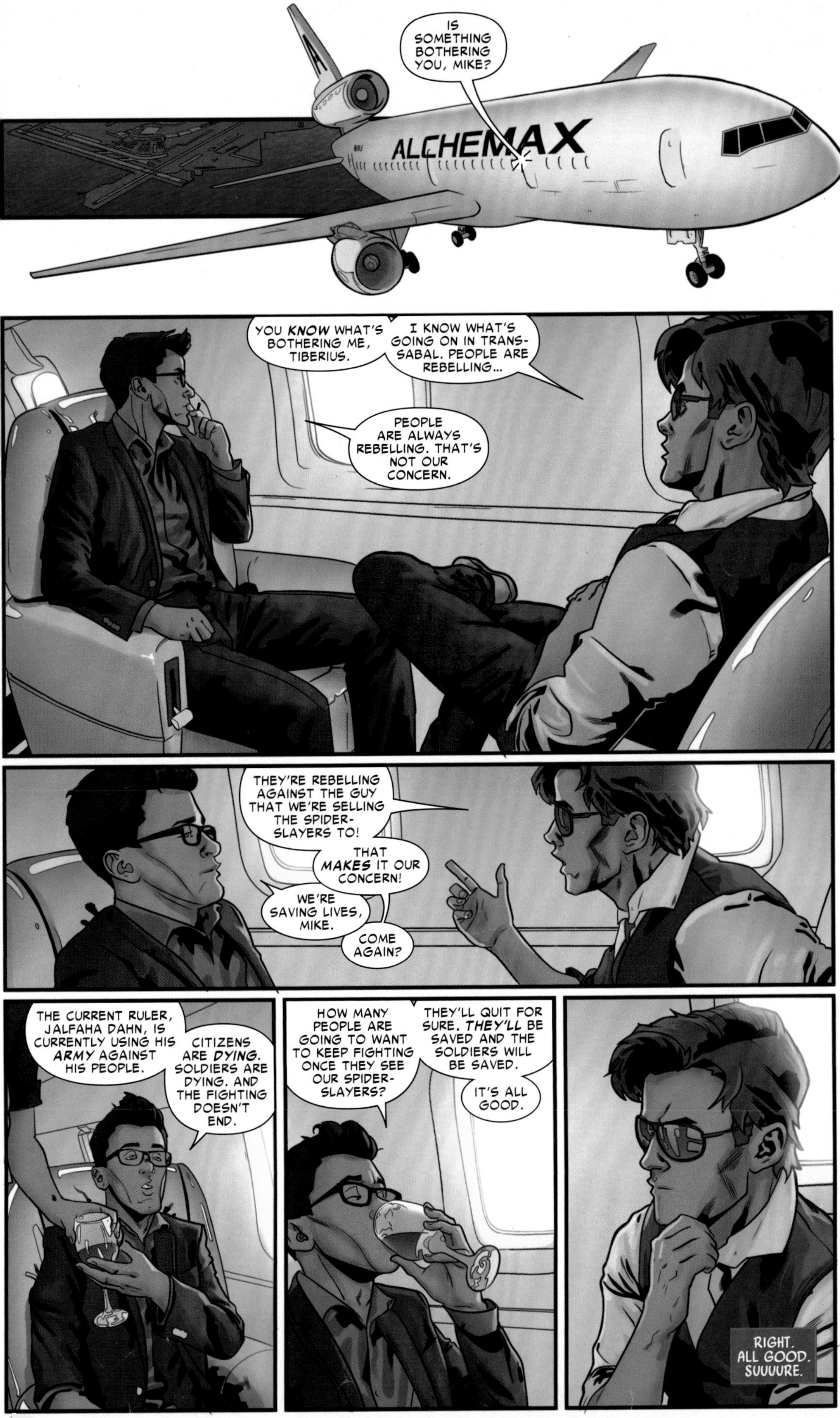

IS SOMETHING BOTHERING YOU, MIKE?
ALCHEMAX
YOU KNOW WHAT'S BOTHERING ME, TIBERIUS.
I KNOW WHAT'S GOING ON IN TRANS-SABAL. PEOPLE ARE REBELLING...
PEOPLE ARE ALWAYS REBELLING. THAT'S NOT OUR CONCERN.
THEY'RE REBELLING AGAINST THE GUY THAT WE'RE SELLING THE SPIDER-SLAYERS TO!
THAT MAKES IT OUR CONCERN!
WE'RE SAVING LIVES, MIKE.
COME AGAIN?
THE CURRENT RULER, JALFAHA DAHN, IS CURRENTLY USING HIS ARMY AGAINST HIS PEOPLE.
CITIZENS ARE DYING. SOLDIERS ARE DYING. AND THE FIGHTING DOESN'T END.
HOW MANY PEOPLE ARE GOING TO WANT TO KEEP FIGHTING ONCE THEY SEE OUR SPIDER-SLAYERS?
THEY'LL QUIT FOR SURE. THEY'LL BE SAVED AND THE SOLDIERS WILL BE SAVED.
IT'S ALL GOOD.
RIGHT. ALL GOOD. SUUUURE.

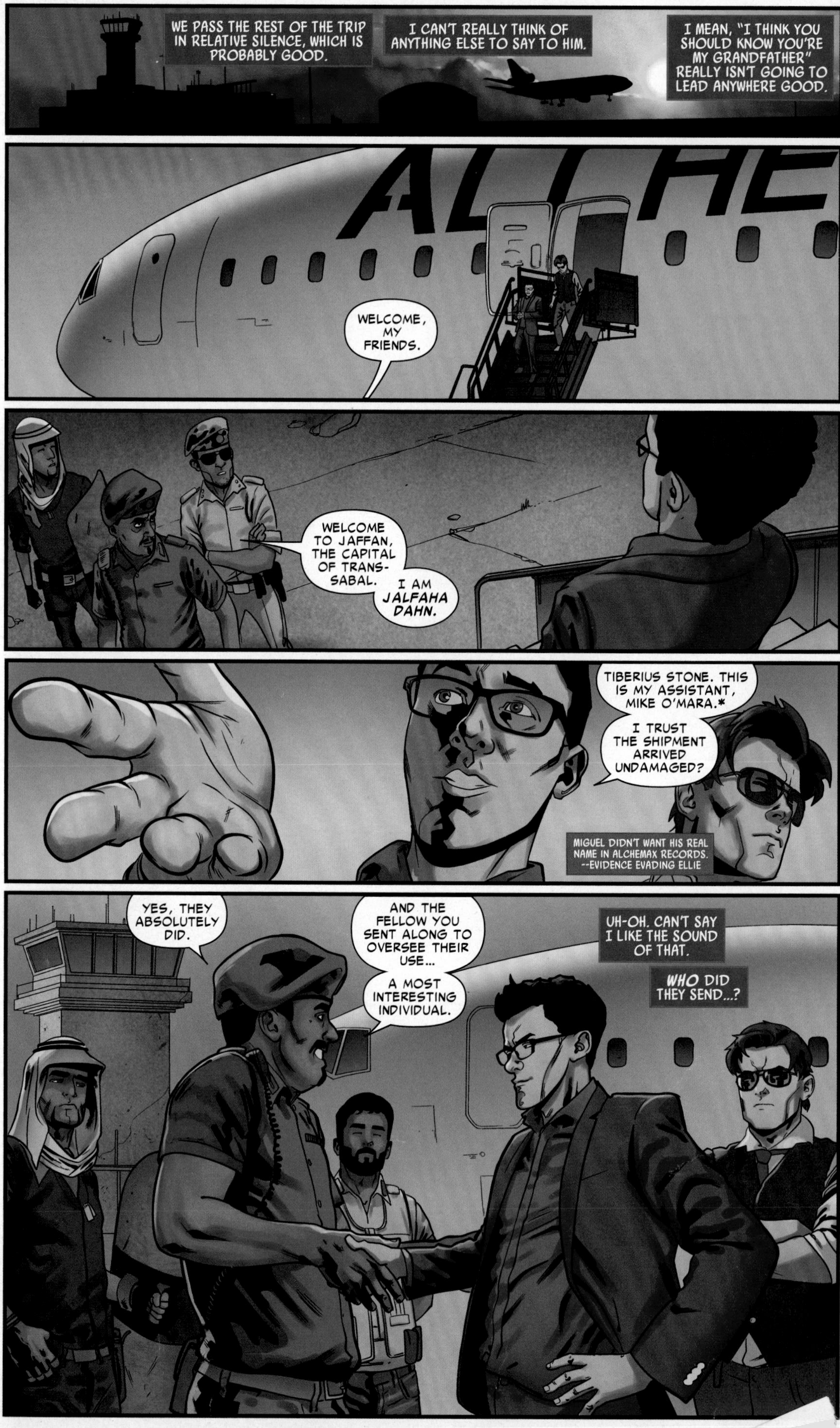
WE PASS THE REST OF THE TRIP IN RELATIVE SILENCE, WHICH IS PROBABLY GOOD.
I CAN'T REALLY THINK OF ANYTHING ELSE TO SAY TO HIM.
I MEAN, "I THINK YOU SHOULD KNOW YOU'RE MY GRANDFATHER" REALLY ISN'T GOING TO LEAD ANYWHERE GOOD.
ALCHE
WELCOME, MY FRIENDS.
WELCOME TO JAFFAN, THE CAPITAL OF TRANS-SABAL.
I AM *JALFAHA DAHN.*
TIBERIUS STONE. THIS IS MY ASSISTANT, MIKE O'MARA.*
I TRUST THE SHIPMENT ARRIVED UNDAMAGED?
MIGUEL DIDN'T WANT HIS REAL NAME IN ALCHEMAX RECORDS. --EVIDENCE EVADING ELLIE
YES, THEY ABSOLUTELY DID.
AND THE FELLOW YOU SENT ALONG TO OVERSEE THEIR USE...
A MOST INTERESTING INDIVIDUAL.
UH-OH. CAN'T SAY I LIKE THE SOUND OF THAT.
WHO DID THEY SEND...?

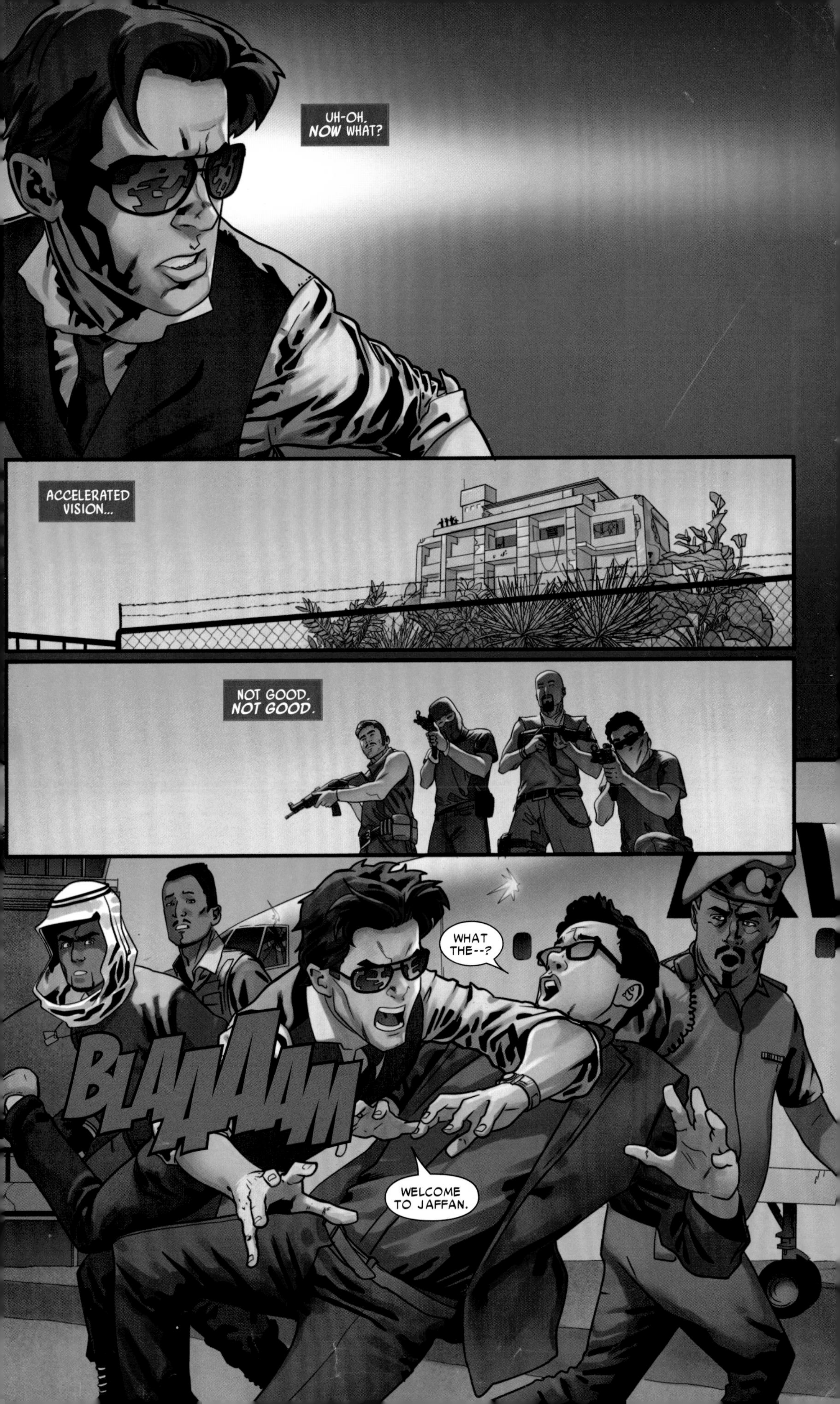
UH-OH. NOW WHAT?
ACCELERATED VISION...
NOT GOOD. NOT GOOD.
WHAT THE--?
BLAAAAM
WELCOME TO JAFFAN.

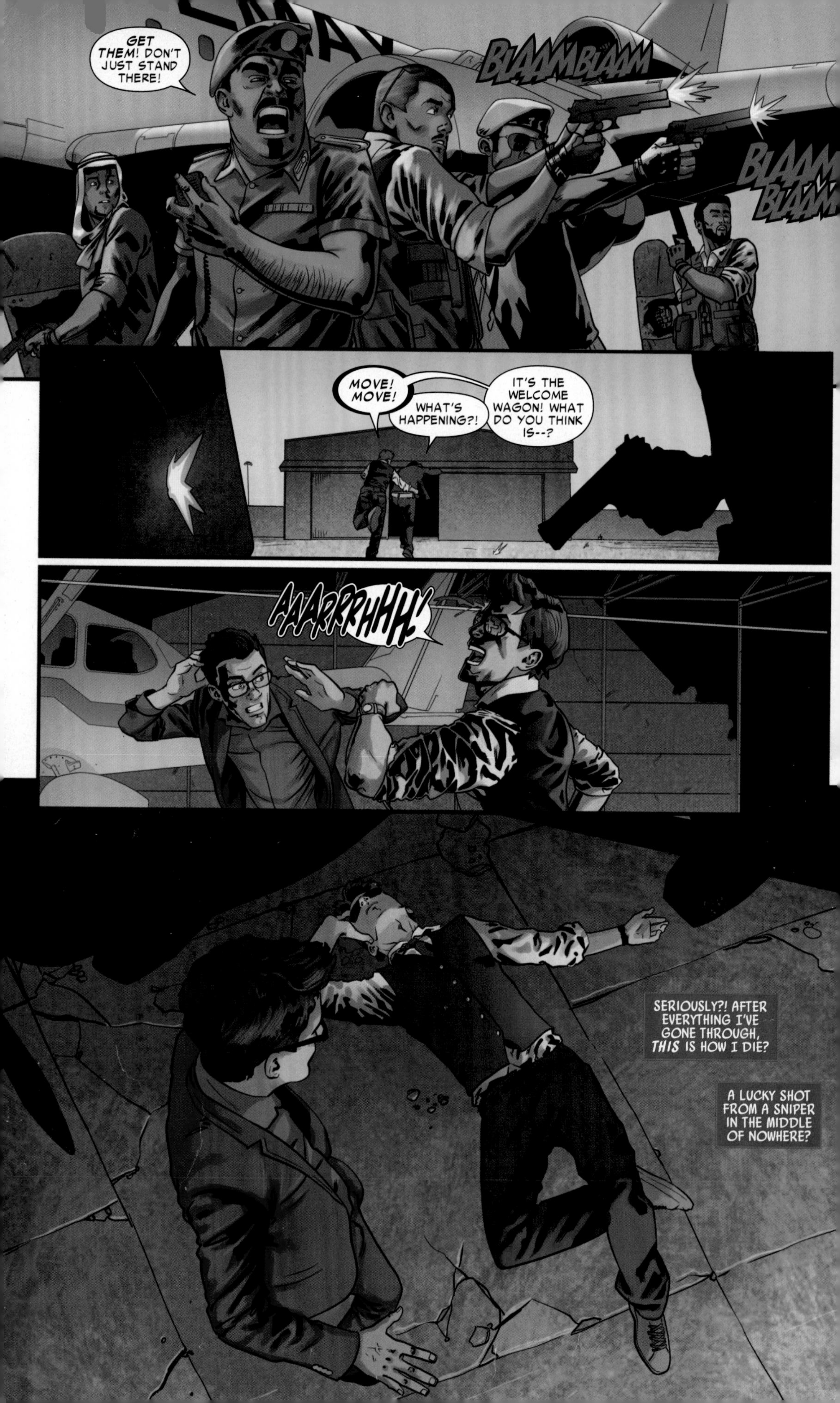

GET THEM! DON'T JUST STAND THERE!
BLAAM BLAAM
BLAAM BLAAM
MOVE! MOVE!
WHAT'S HAPPENING?!
IT'S THE WELCOME WAGON! WHAT DO YOU THINK IS--?
AAARRRHHH!
SERIOUSLY?! AFTER EVERYTHING I'VE GONE THROUGH, THIS IS HOW I DIE?
A LUCKY SHOT FROM A SNIPER IN THE MIDDLE OF NOWHERE?

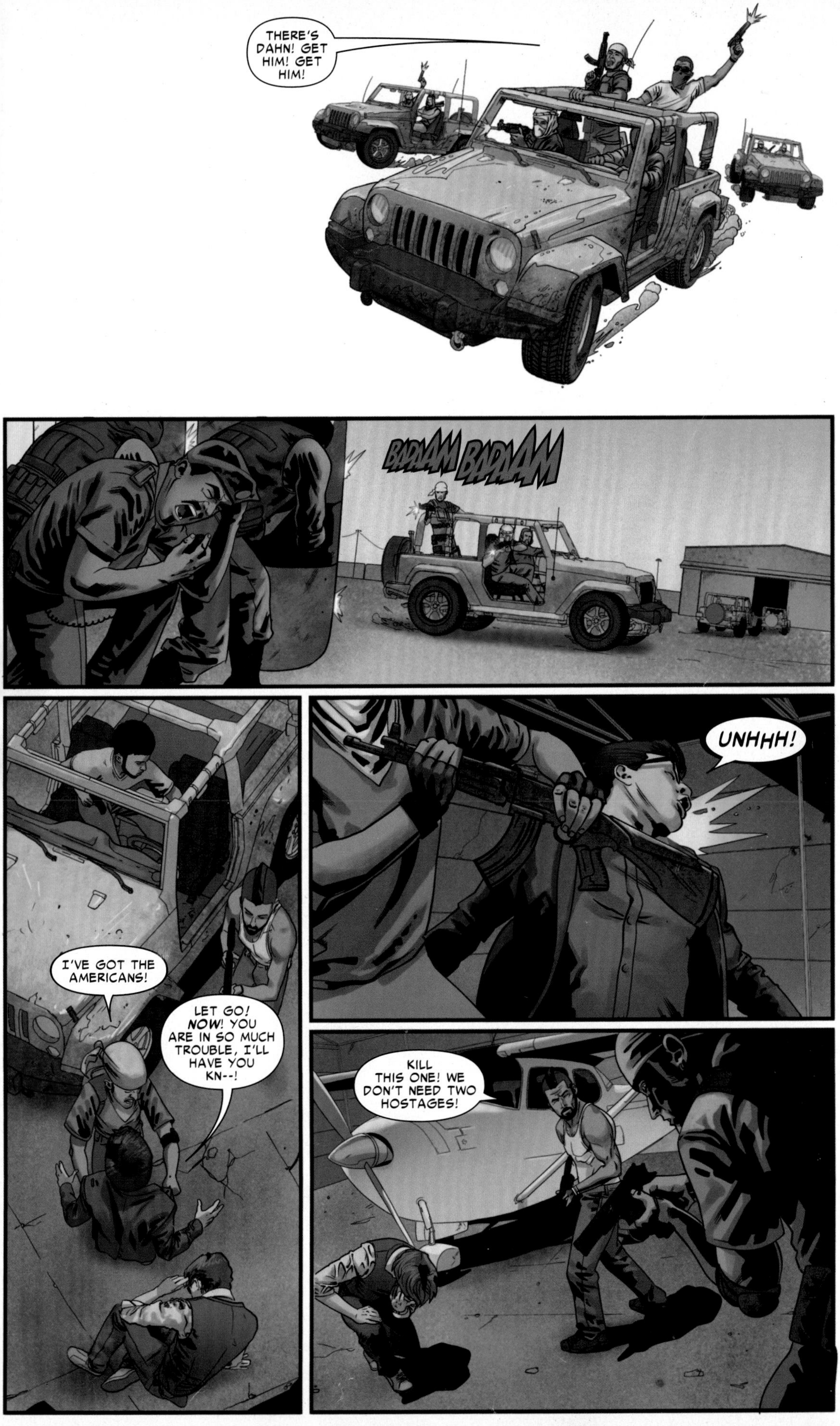
THERE'S DAHN! GET HIM! GET HIM!
BADAAM BADAAM
UNHHH!
I'VE GOT THE AMERICANS!
LET GO! NOW! YOU ARE IN SO MUCH TROUBLE, I'LL HAVE YOU KN--!
KILL THIS ONE! WE DON'T NEED TWO HOSTAGES!

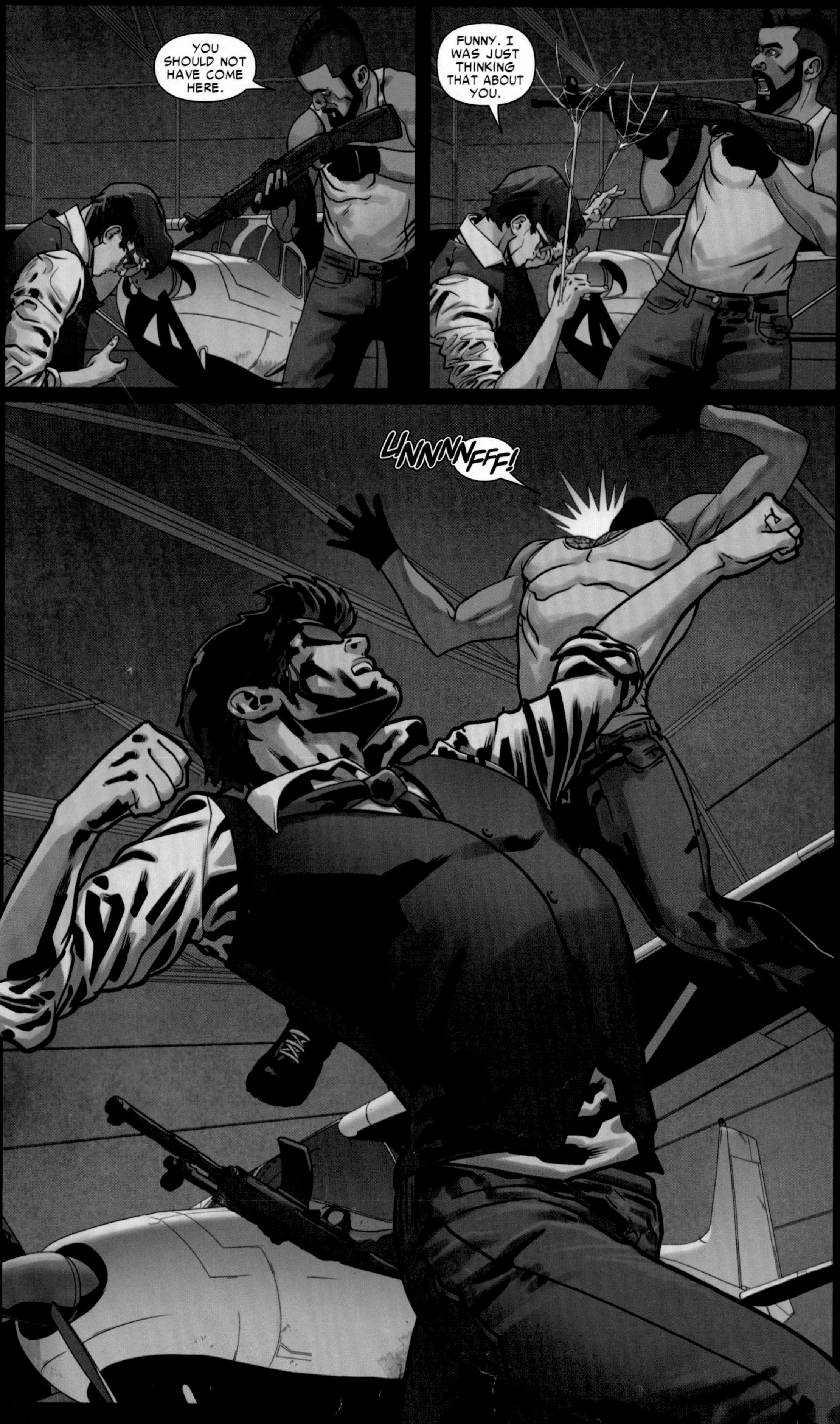
YOU SHOULD NOT HAVE COME HERE.
FUNNY. I WAS JUST THINKING THAT ABOUT YOU.
UNNNNFFF!

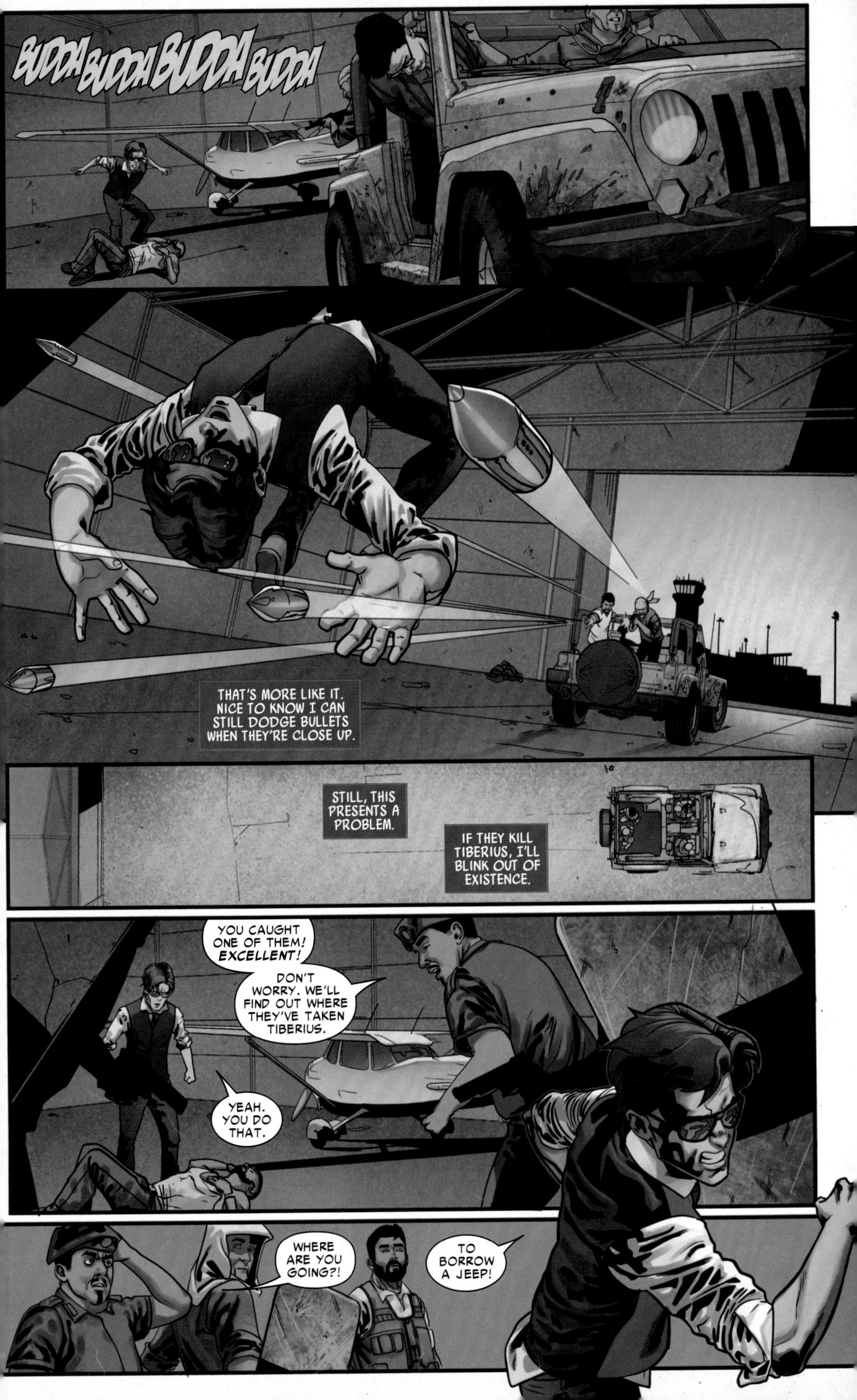
BUDDA BUDDA BUDDA BUDDA
THAT'S MORE LIKE IT. NICE TO KNOW I CAN STILL DODGE BULLETS WHEN THEY'RE CLOSE UP.
STILL, THIS PRESENTS A PROBLEM.
IF THEY KILL TIBERIUS, I'LL BLINK OUT OF EXISTENCE.
YOU CAUGHT ONE OF THEM! EXCELLENT!
DON'T WORRY. WE'LL FIND OUT WHERE THEY'VE TAKEN TIBERIUS.
YEAH. YOU DO THAT.
WHERE ARE YOU GOING?!
TO BORROW A JEEP!

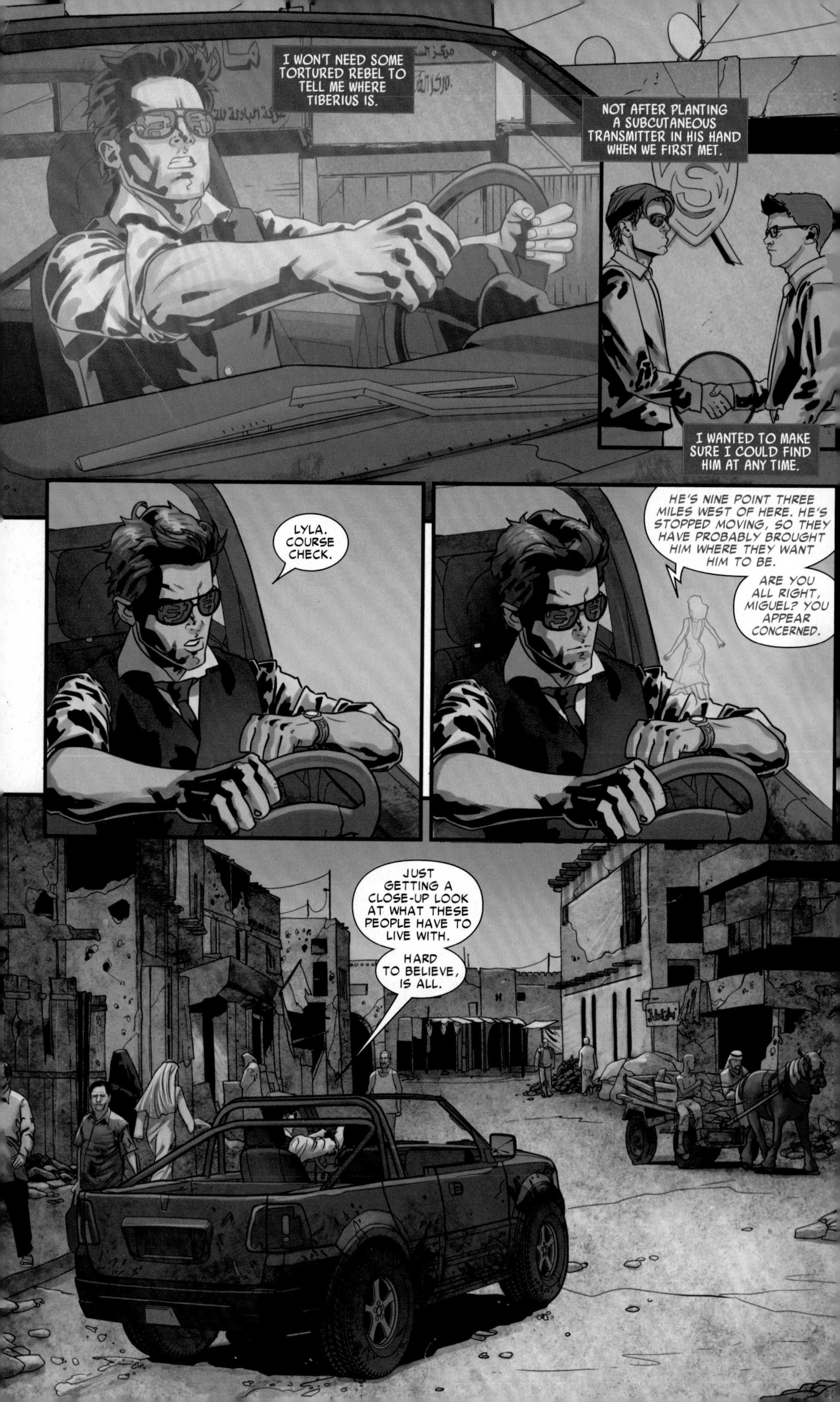

I WON'T NEED SOME TORTURED REBEL TO TELL ME WHERE TIBERIUS IS.
NOT AFTER PLANTING A SUBCUTANEOUS TRANSMITTER IN HIS HAND WHEN WE FIRST MET.
I WANTED TO MAKE SURE I COULD FIND HIM AT ANY TIME.
LYLA. COURSE CHECK.
HE'S NINE POINT THREE MILES WEST OF HERE. HE'S STOPPED MOVING, SO THEY HAVE PROBABLY BROUGHT HIM WHERE THEY WANT HIM TO BE.
ARE YOU ALL RIGHT, MIGUEL? YOU APPEAR CONCERNED.
JUST GETTING A CLOSE-UP LOOK AT WHAT THESE PEOPLE HAVE TO LIVE WITH.
HARD TO BELIEVE, IS ALL.

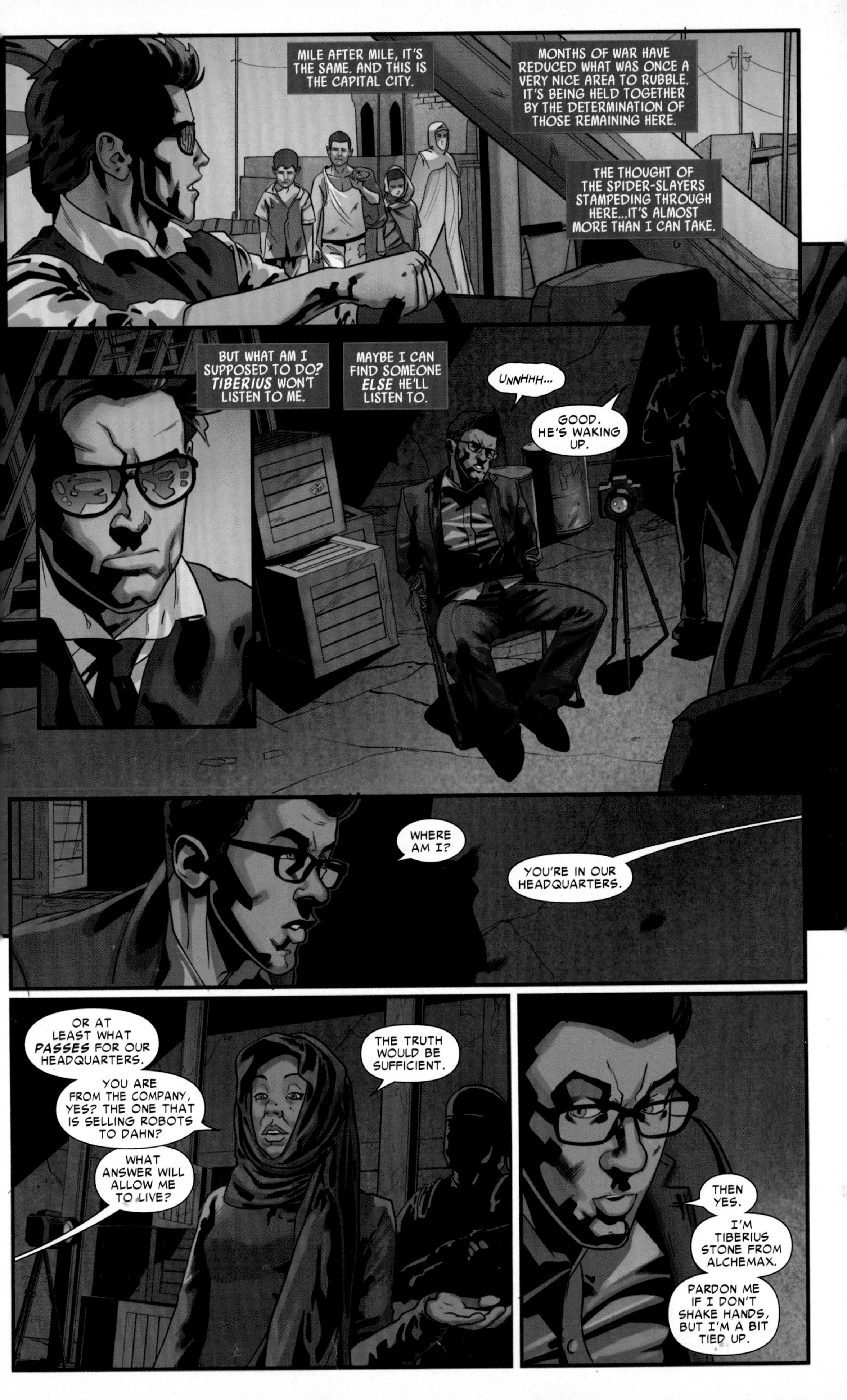
MILE AFTER MILE, IT'S THE SAME. AND THIS IS THE CAPITAL CITY.
MONTHS OF WAR HAVE REDUCED WHAT WAS ONCE A VERY NICE AREA TO RUBBLE. IT'S BEING HELD TOGETHER BY THE DETERMINATION OF THOSE REMAINING HERE.
THE THOUGHT OF THE SPIDER-SLAYERS STAMPEDING THROUGH HERE...IT'S ALMOST MORE THAN I CAN TAKE.
BUT WHAT AM I SUPPOSED TO DO? TIBERIUS WON'T LISTEN TO ME.
MAYBE I CAN FIND SOMEONE ELSE HE'LL LISTEN TO.
UNNHHH...
GOOD. HE'S WAKING UP.
WHERE AM I?
YOU'RE IN OUR HEADQUARTERS.
OR AT LEAST WHAT PASSES FOR OUR HEADQUARTERS.
YOU ARE FROM THE COMPANY, YES? THE ONE THAT IS SELLING ROBOTS TO DAHN?
WHAT ANSWER WILL ALLOW ME TO LIVE?
THE TRUTH WOULD BE SUFFICIENT.
THEN YES.
I'M TIBERIUS STONE FROM ALCHEMAX.
PARDON ME IF I DON'T SHAKE HANDS, BUT I'M A BIT TIED UP.

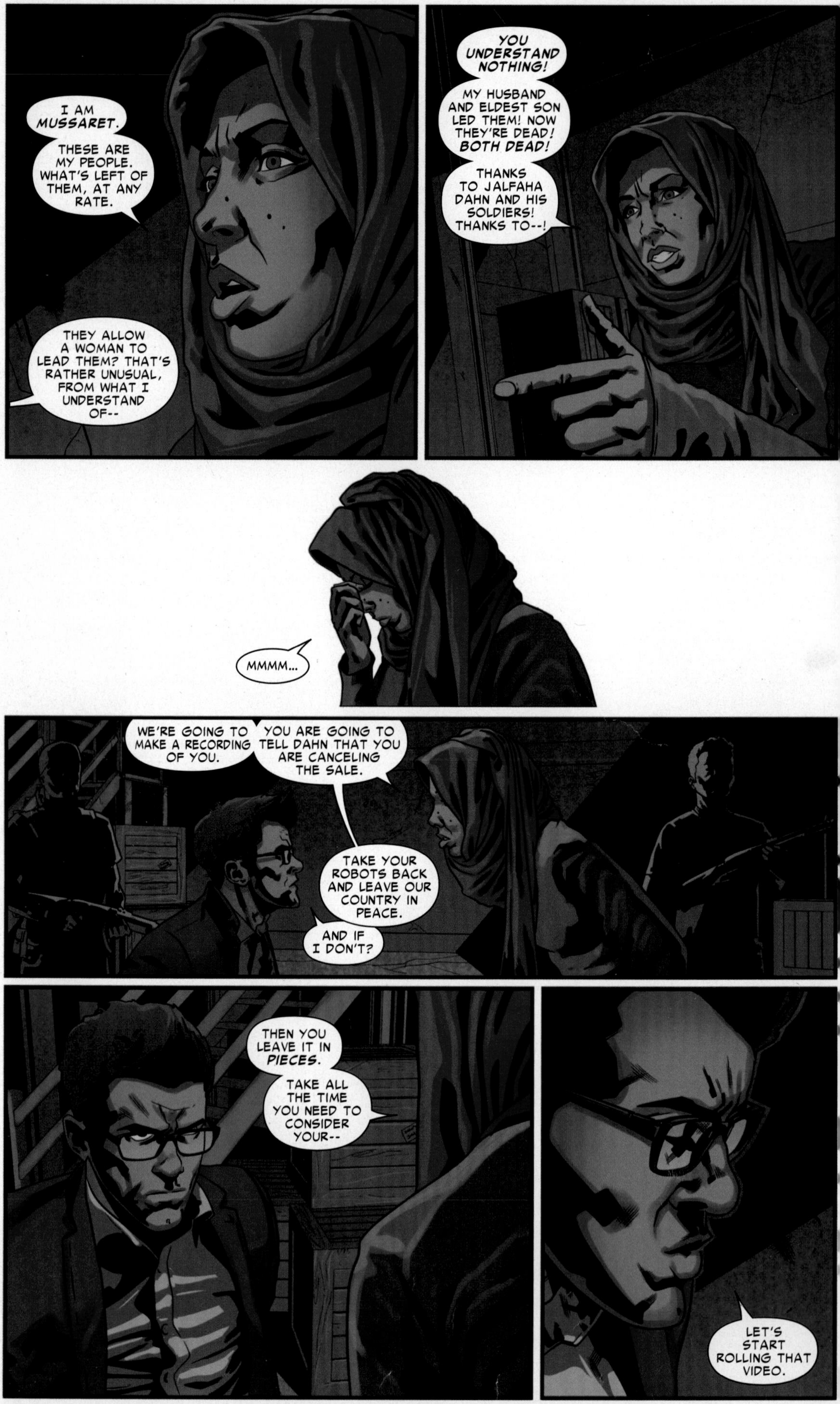
I AM MUSSARET.
THESE ARE MY PEOPLE. WHAT'S LEFT OF THEM, AT ANY RATE.
THEY ALLOW A WOMAN TO LEAD THEM? THAT'S RATHER UNUSUAL, FROM WHAT I UNDERSTAND OF--
YOU UNDERSTAND NOTHING!
MY HUSBAND AND ELDEST SON LED THEM! NOW THEY'RE DEAD! BOTH DEAD!
THANKS TO JALFAHA DAHN AND HIS SOLDIERS! THANKS TO--!
MMMM...
WE'RE GOING TO MAKE A RECORDING OF YOU.
YOU ARE GOING TO TELL DAHN THAT YOU ARE CANCELING THE SALE.
TAKE YOUR ROBOTS BACK AND LEAVE OUR COUNTRY IN PEACE.
AND IF I DON'T?
THEN YOU LEAVE IT IN PIECES.
TAKE ALL THE TIME YOU NEED TO CONSIDER YOUR--
LET'S START ROLLING THAT VIDEO.

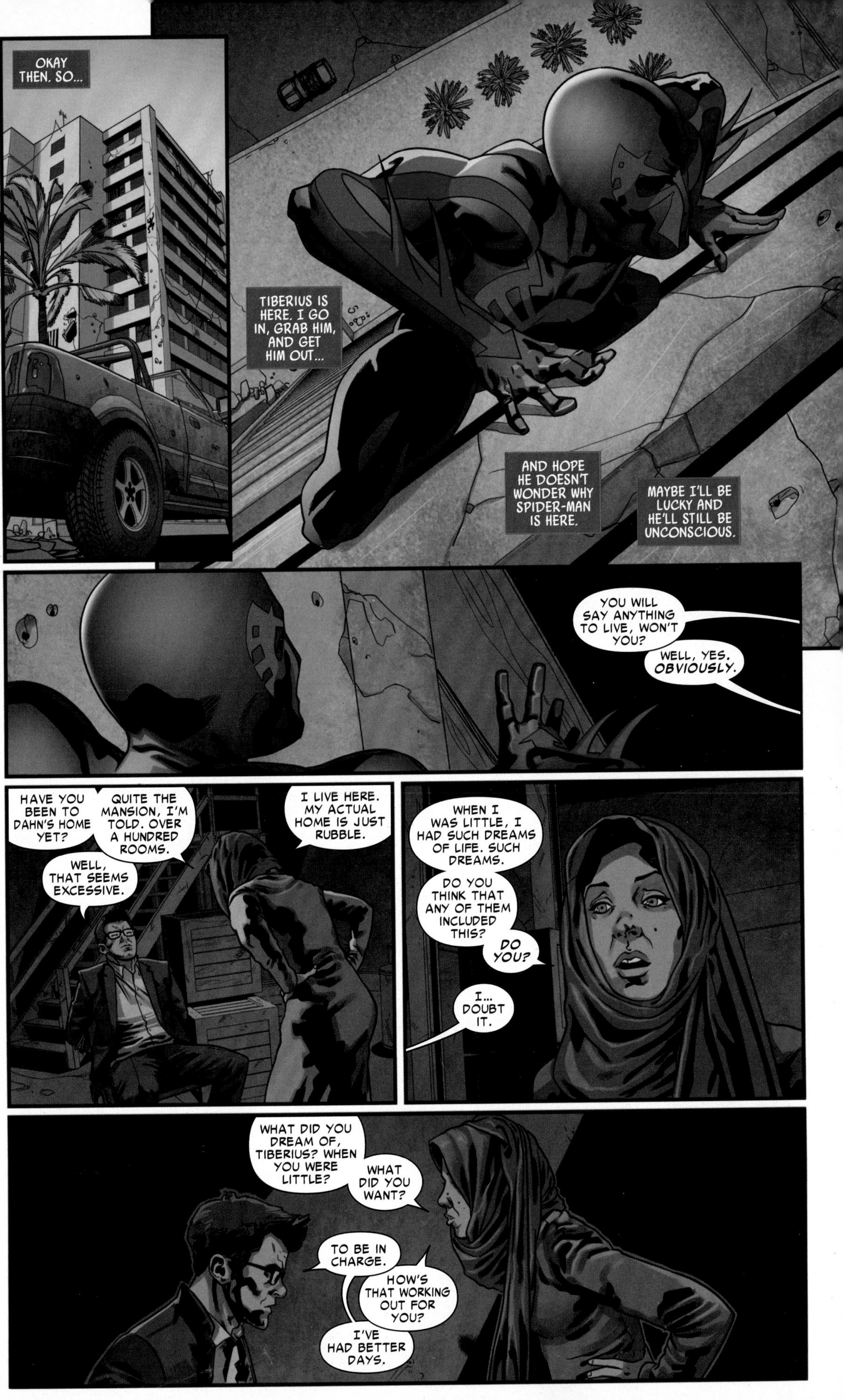
OKAY THEN. SO...
TIBERIUS IS HERE. I GO IN, GRAB HIM, AND GET HIM OUT...
AND HOPE HE DOESN'T WONDER WHY SPIDER-MAN IS HERE.
MAYBE I'LL BE LUCKY AND HE'LL STILL BE UNCONSCIOUS.
YOU WILL SAY ANYTHING TO LIVE, WON'T YOU?
WELL, YES. OBVIOUSLY.
HAVE YOU BEEN TO DAHN'S HOME YET?
QUITE THE MANSION, I'M TOLD. OVER A HUNDRED ROOMS.
WELL, THAT SEEMS EXCESSIVE.
I LIVE HERE. MY ACTUAL HOME IS JUST RUBBLE.
WHEN I WAS LITTLE, I HAD SUCH DREAMS OF LIFE. SUCH DREAMS.
DO YOU THINK THAT ANY OF THEM INCLUDED THIS?
DO YOU?
I... DOUBT IT.
WHAT DID YOU DREAM OF, TIBERIUS? WHEN YOU WERE LITTLE?
WHAT DID YOU WANT?
TO BE IN CHARGE.
HOW'S THAT WORKING OUT FOR YOU?
I'VE HAD BETTER DAYS.

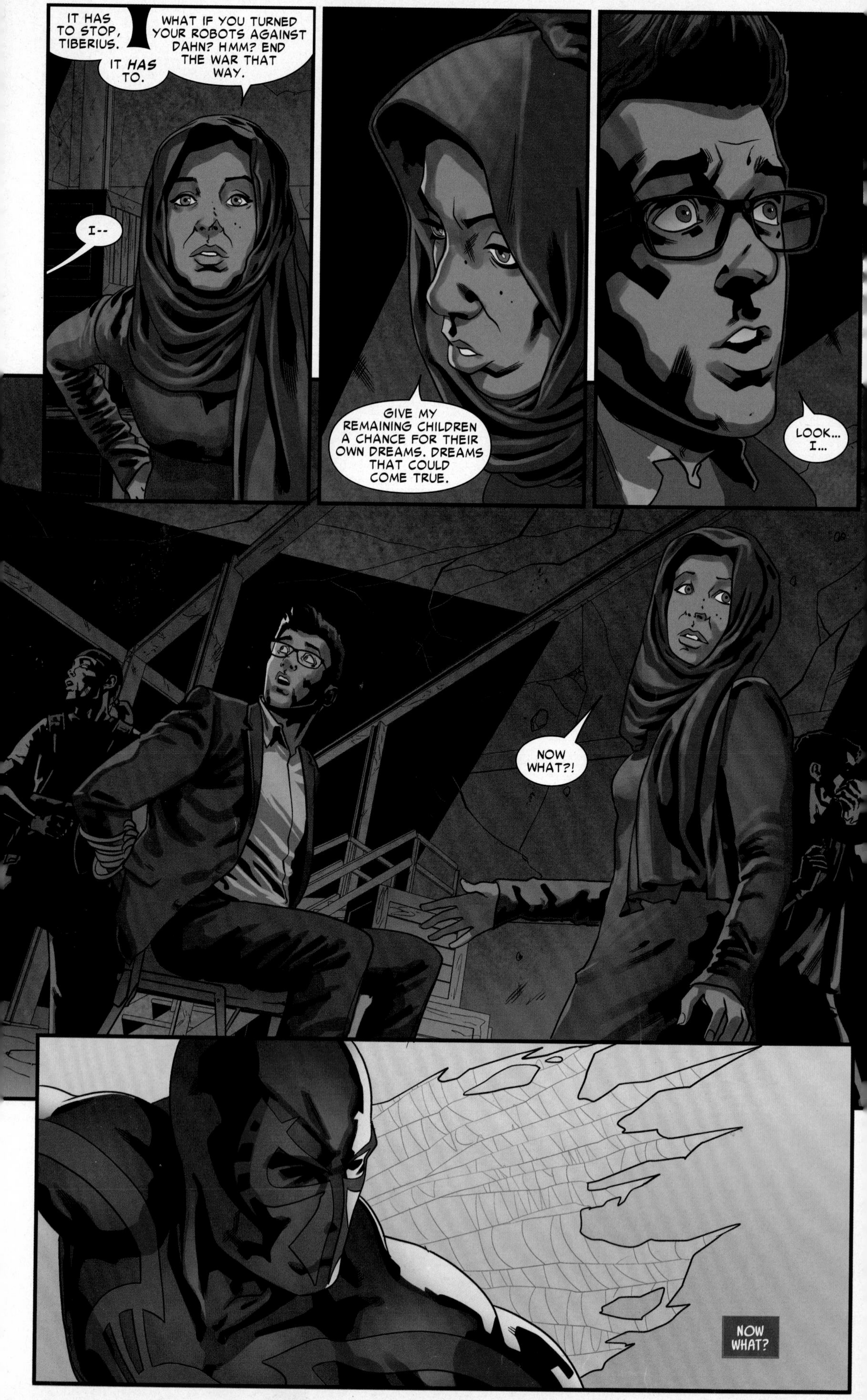
IT HAS TO STOP, TIBERIUS.
IT *HAS* TO.
WHAT IF YOU TURNED YOUR ROBOTS AGAINST DAHN? HMM? END THE WAR THAT WAY.
I--
GIVE MY REMAINING CHILDREN A CHANCE FOR THEIR OWN DREAMS. DREAMS THAT COULD COME TRUE.
LOOK... I...
NOW WHAT?!
NOW WHAT?

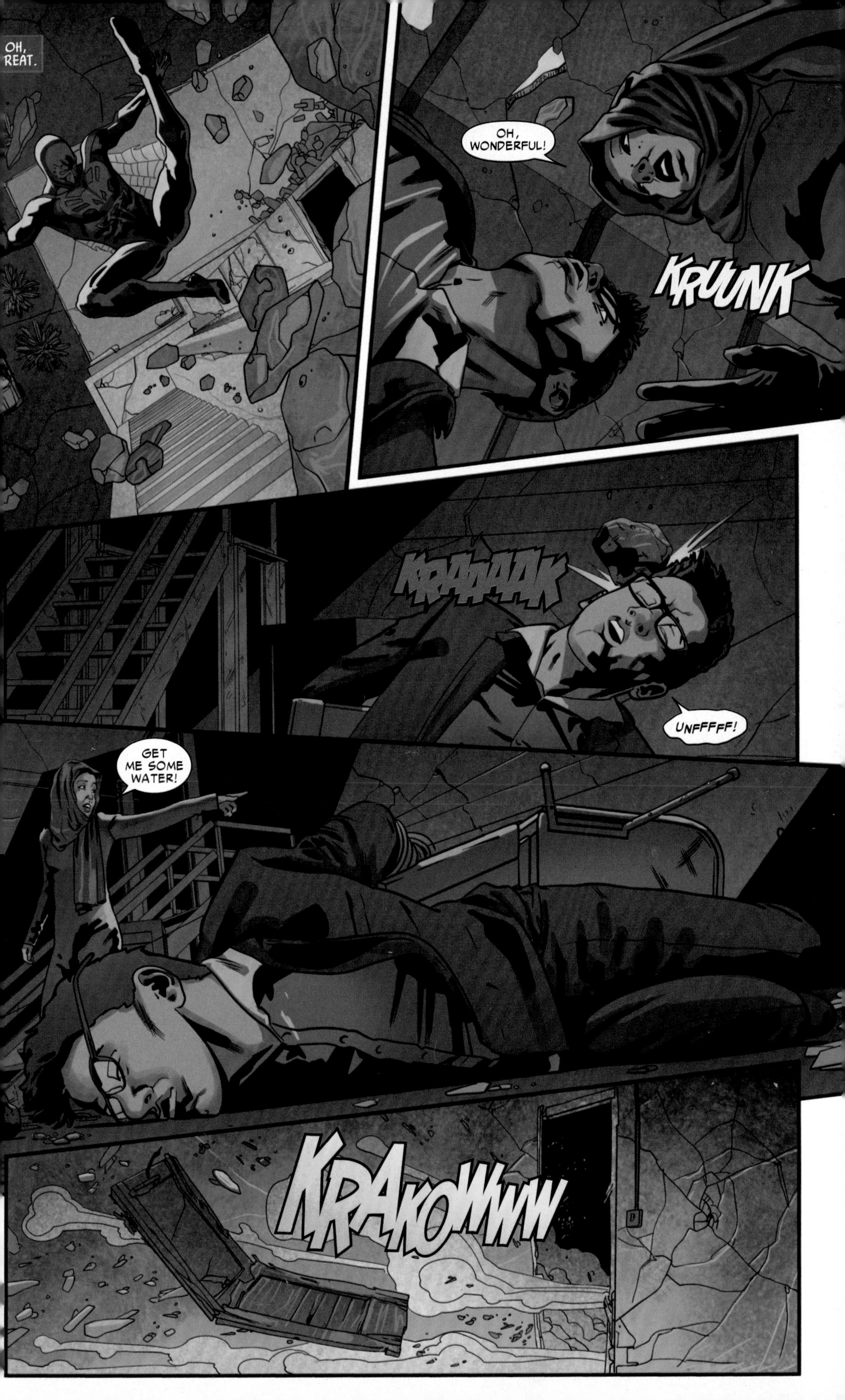
OH,
REAT.
OH, WONDERFUL!
KRUUNK
KRAAAAK
UNFFFFF!
GET ME SOME WATER!
KRAKOWWW

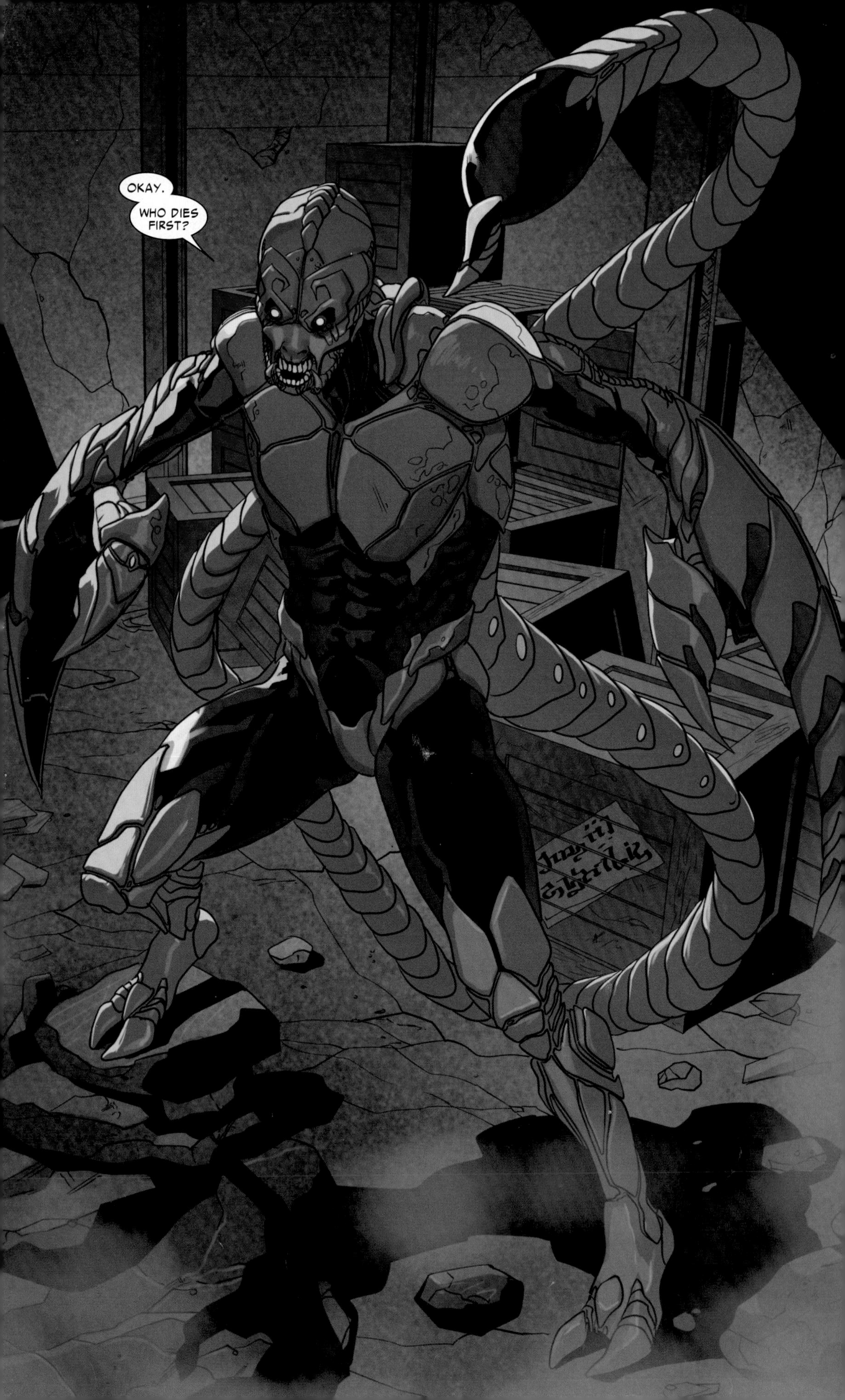
OKAY.
WHO DIES FIRST?

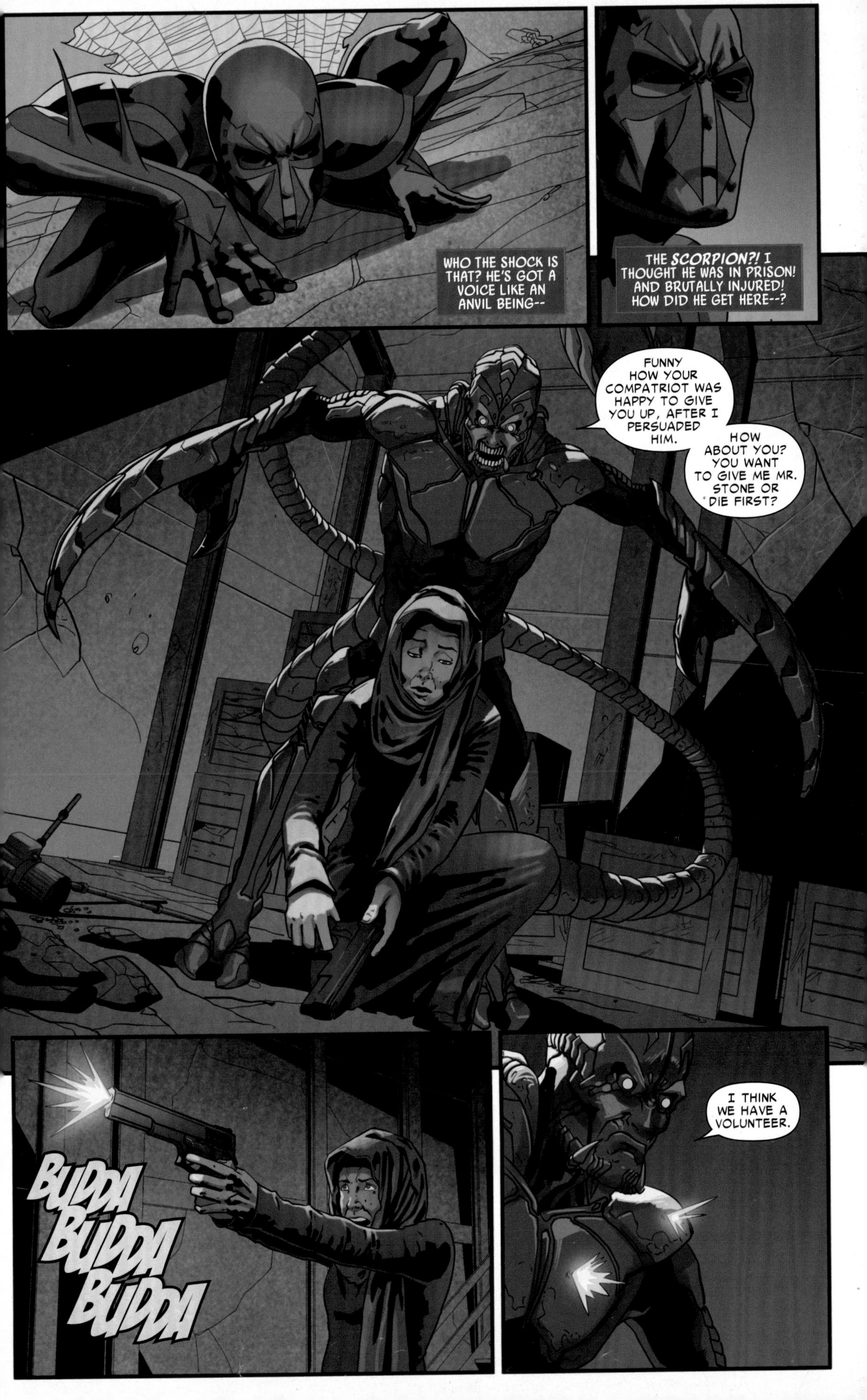
WHO THE SHOCK IS THAT? HE'S GOT A VOICE LIKE AN ANVIL BEING--
THE *SCORPION?!* I THOUGHT HE WAS IN PRISON! AND BRUTALLY INJURED! HOW DID HE GET HERE--?
FUNNY HOW YOUR COMPATRIOT WAS HAPPY TO GIVE YOU UP, AFTER I PERSUADED HIM.
HOW ABOUT YOU? YOU WANT TO GIVE ME MR. STONE OR DIE FIRST?
BUDDA BUDDA BUDDA
I THINK WE HAVE A VOLUNTEER.

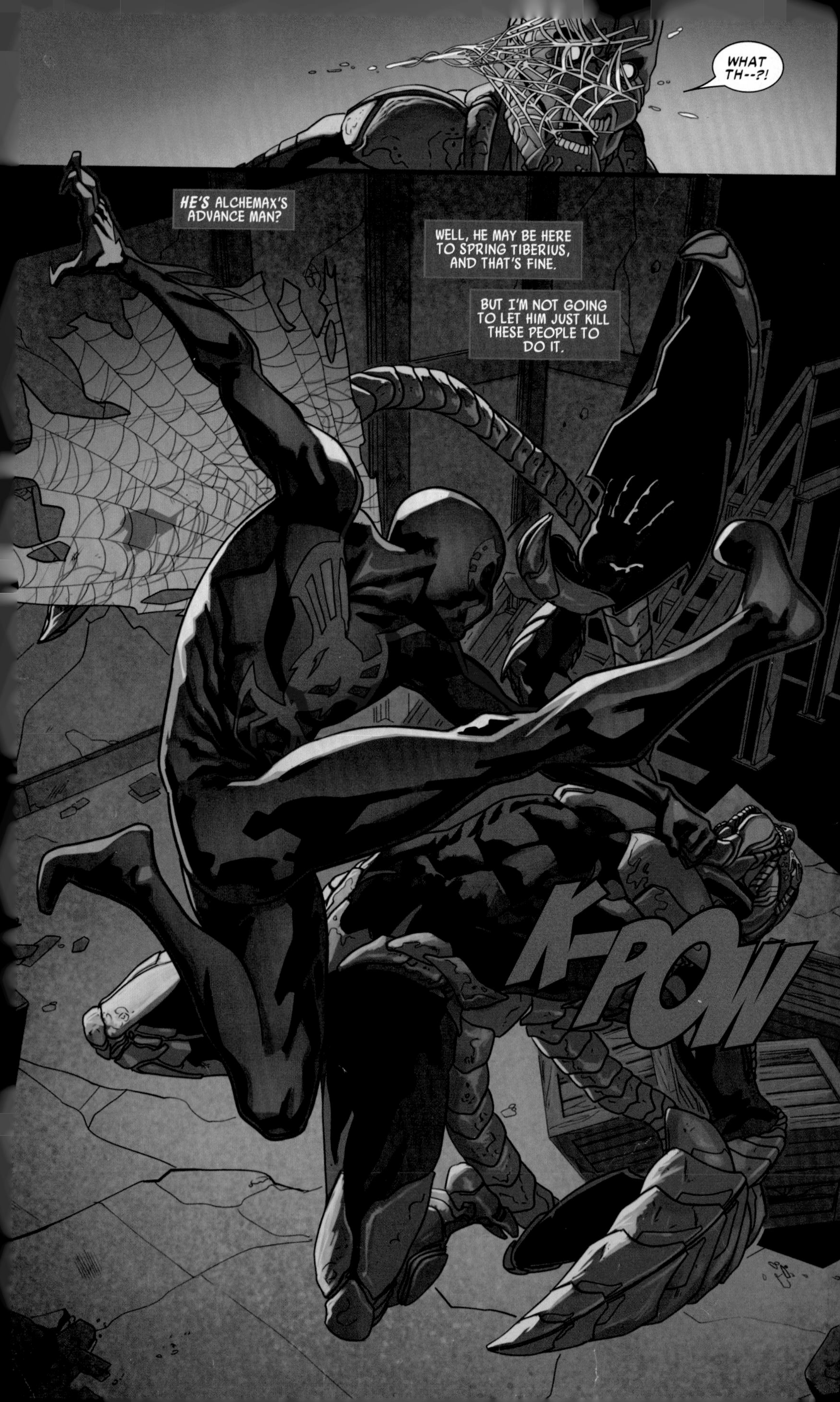
WHAT TH--?!
HE'S ALCHEMAX'S ADVANCE MAN?
WELL, HE MAY BE HERE TO SPRING TIBERIUS, AND THAT'S FINE.
BUT I'M NOT GOING TO LET HIM JUST KILL THESE PEOPLE TO DO IT.
K-POW

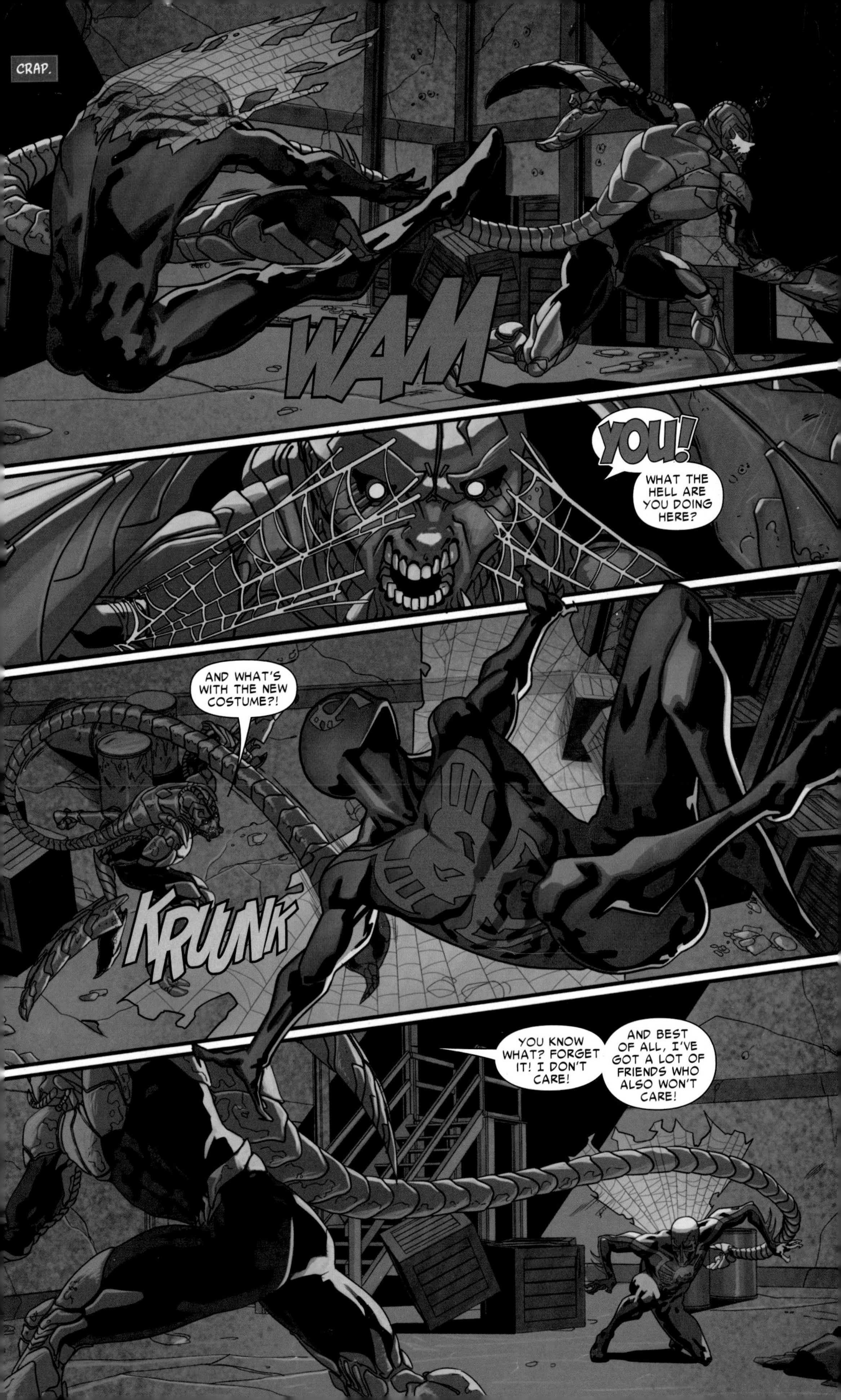

CRAP.
WAM
YOU!
WHAT THE HELL ARE YOU DOING HERE?
AND WHAT'S WITH THE NEW COSTUME?!
KRUNK
YOU KNOW WHAT? FORGET IT! I DON'T CARE!
AND BEST OF ALL, I'VE GOT A LOT OF FRIENDS WHO ALSO WON'T CARE!

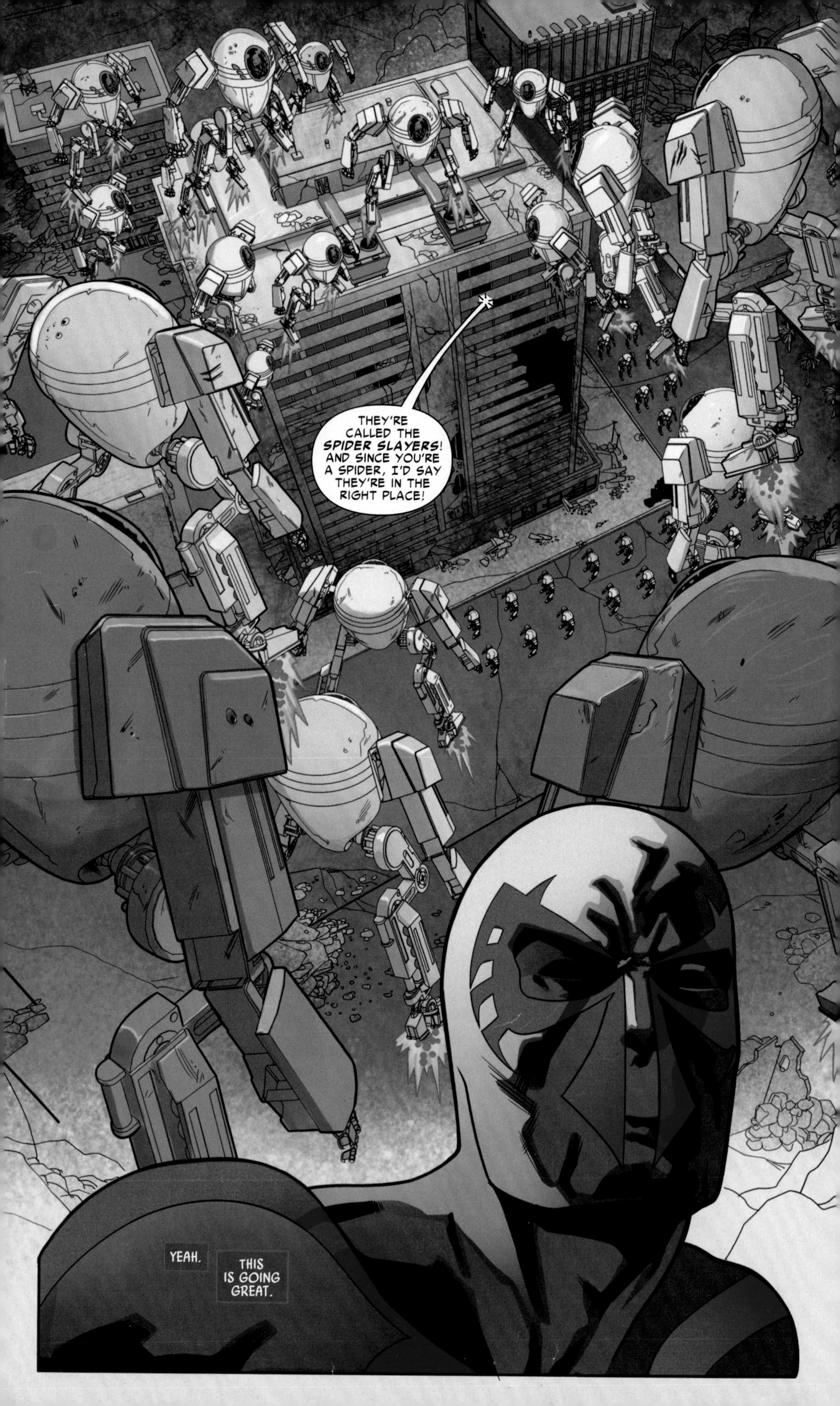
THEY'RE CALLED THE SPIDER SLAYERS! AND SINCE YOU'RE A SPIDER, I'D SAY THEY'RE IN THE RIGHT PLACE!
YEAH.
THIS IS GOING GREAT.

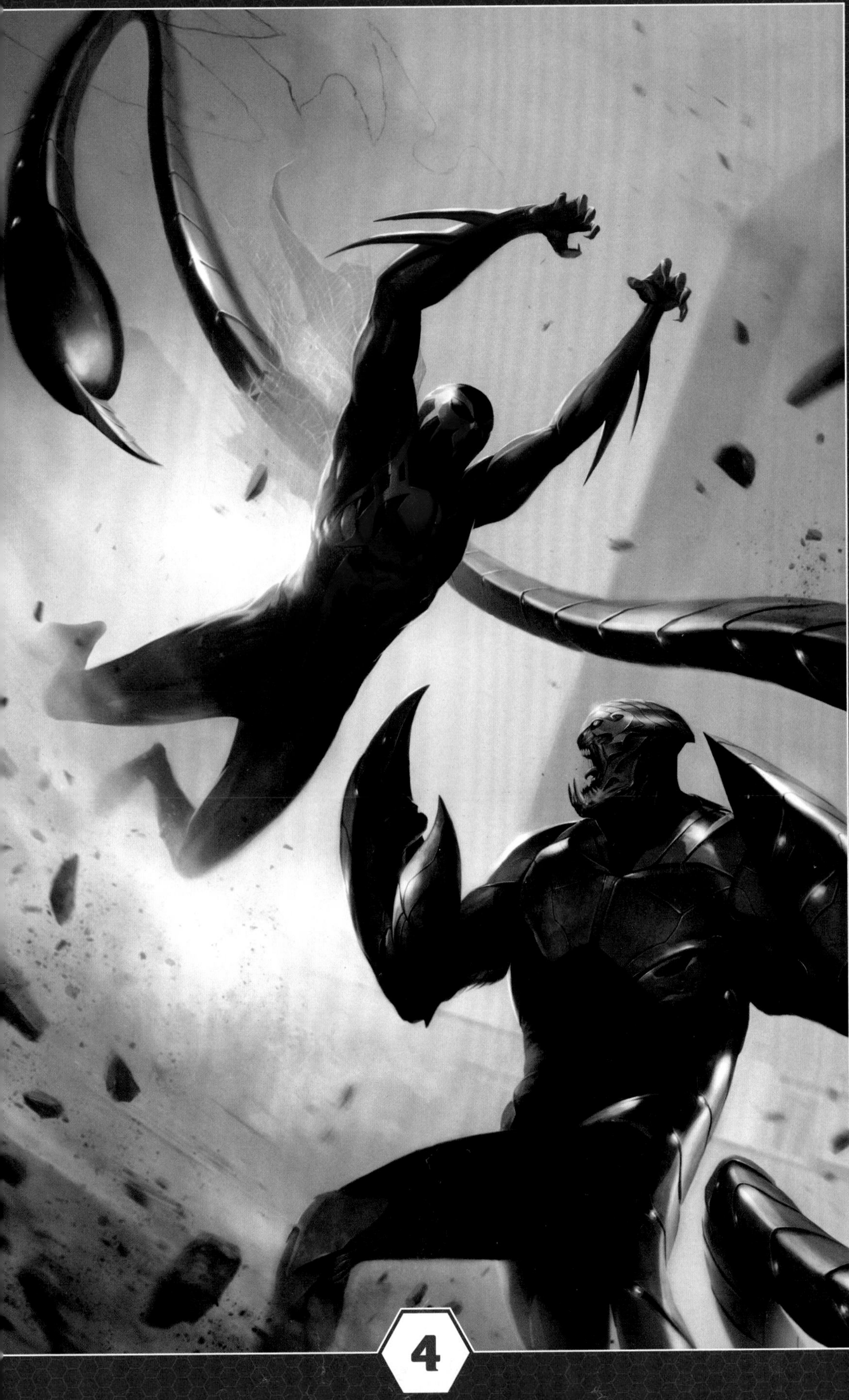

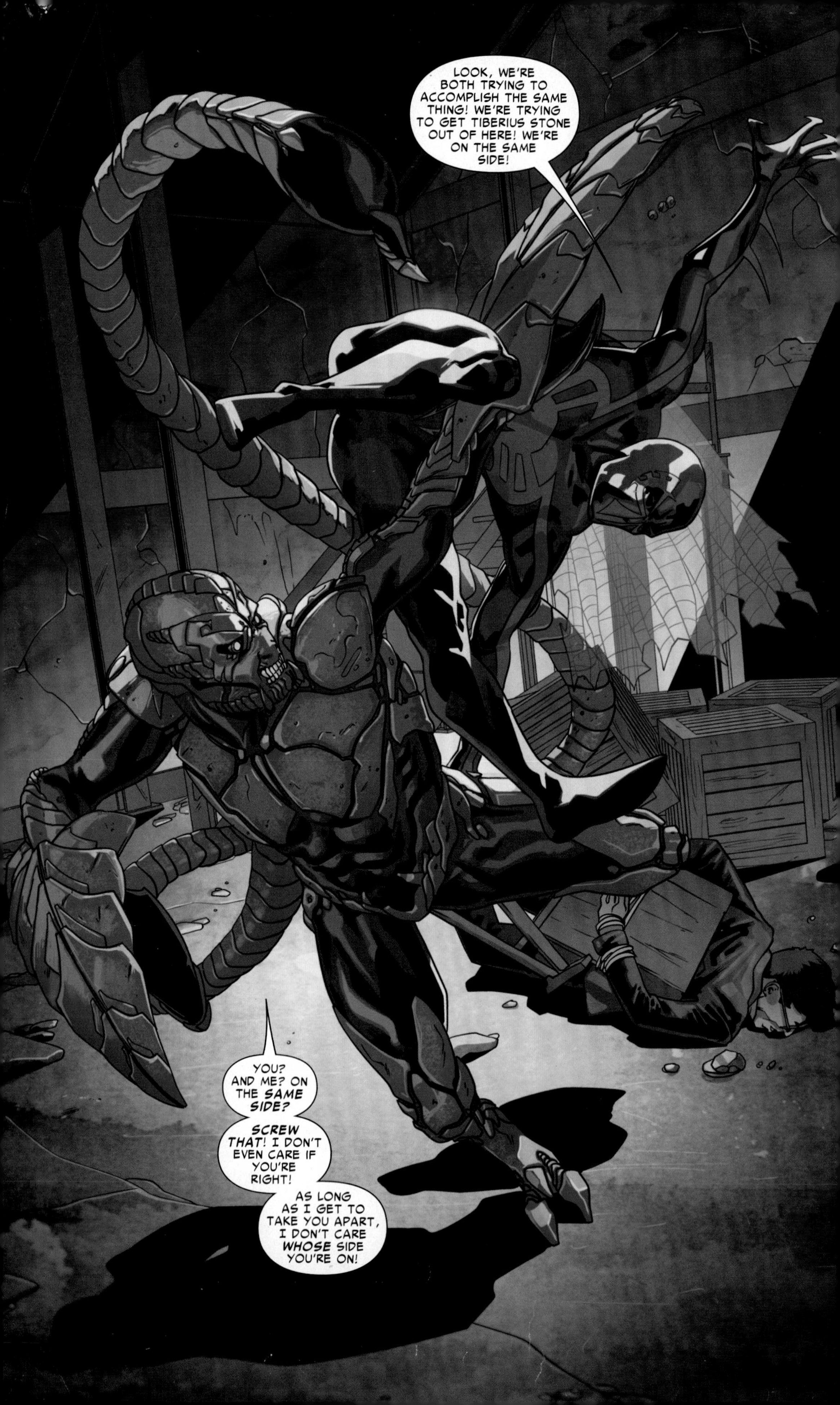

LOOK, WE'RE BOTH TRYING TO ACCOMPLISH THE SAME THING! WE'RE TRYING TO GET TIBERIUS STONE OUT OF HERE! WE'RE ON THE SAME SIDE!
YOU? AND ME? ON THE *SAME SIDE?*
SCREW THAT! I DON'T EVEN CARE IF YOU'RE RIGHT!
AS LONG AS I GET TO TAKE YOU APART, I DON'T CARE *WHOSE* SIDE YOU'RE ON!

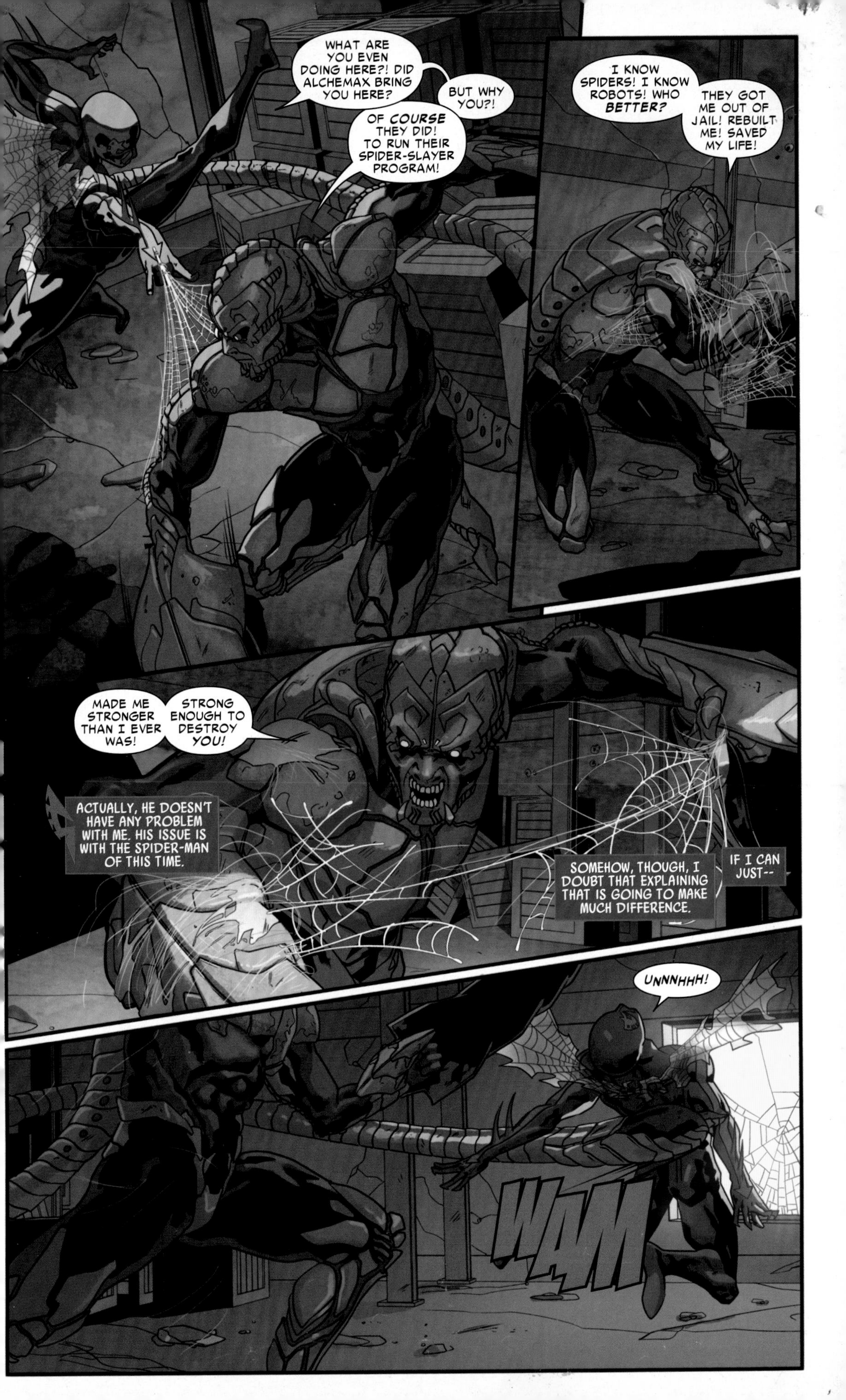
WHAT ARE YOU EVEN DOING HERE?! DID ALCHEMAX BRING YOU HERE?
BUT WHY YOU?!
OF COURSE THEY DID! TO RUN THEIR SPIDER-SLAYER PROGRAM!
I KNOW SPIDERS! I KNOW ROBOTS! WHO BETTER?
THEY GOT ME OUT OF JAIL! REBUILT ME! SAVED MY LIFE!
MADE ME STRONGER THAN I EVER WAS!
STRONG ENOUGH TO DESTROY YOU!
ACTUALLY, HE DOESN'T HAVE ANY PROBLEM WITH ME. HIS ISSUE IS WITH THE SPIDER-MAN OF THIS TIME.
SOMEHOW, THOUGH, I DOUBT THAT EXPLAINING THAT IS GOING TO MAKE MUCH DIFFERENCE.
IF I CAN JUST--
UNNNHHH!
WAM

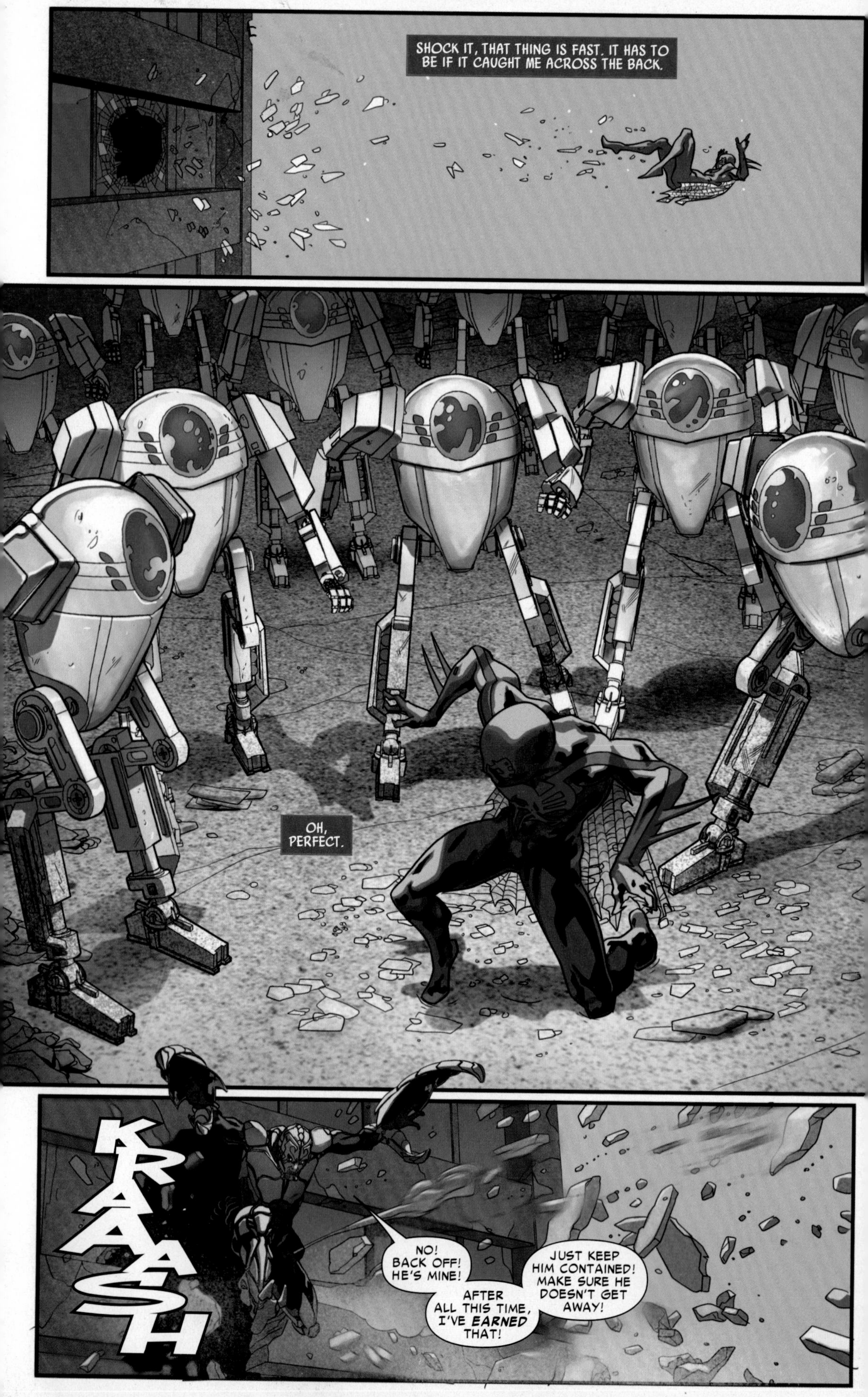
SHOCK IT, THAT THING IS FAST. IT HAS TO BE IF IT CAUGHT ME ACROSS THE BACK.
OH, PERFECT.
KRAAASH
NO! BACK OFF! HE'S MINE!
AFTER ALL THIS TIME, I'VE EARNED THAT!
JUST KEEP HIM CONTAINED! MAKE SURE HE DOESN'T GET AWAY!

HA. I'D LIKE TO SEE THEM TRY--

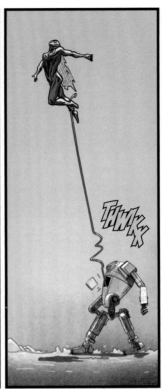

THWK-K

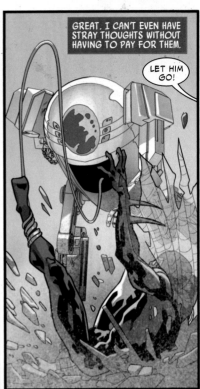

GREAT. I CAN'T EVEN HAVE STRAY THOUGHTS WITHOUT HAVING TO PAY FOR THEM.

LET HIM GO!

I'VE GOT HIM!

WAAAAM

HISTORY ALWAYS DEPICTED THE SCORPION AS A MINOR ANNOYANCE FOR SPIDER-MAN AT BEST.

MY GUESS IS THAT NO HISTORIANS EVER FOUND THEMSELVES IN PITCHED BATTLE WITH HIM.

HE'S QUICK AND HE'S VICIOUS. AND IF I SLOW DOWN FOR EVEN A SECOND, HE'LL TAKE ME APART.

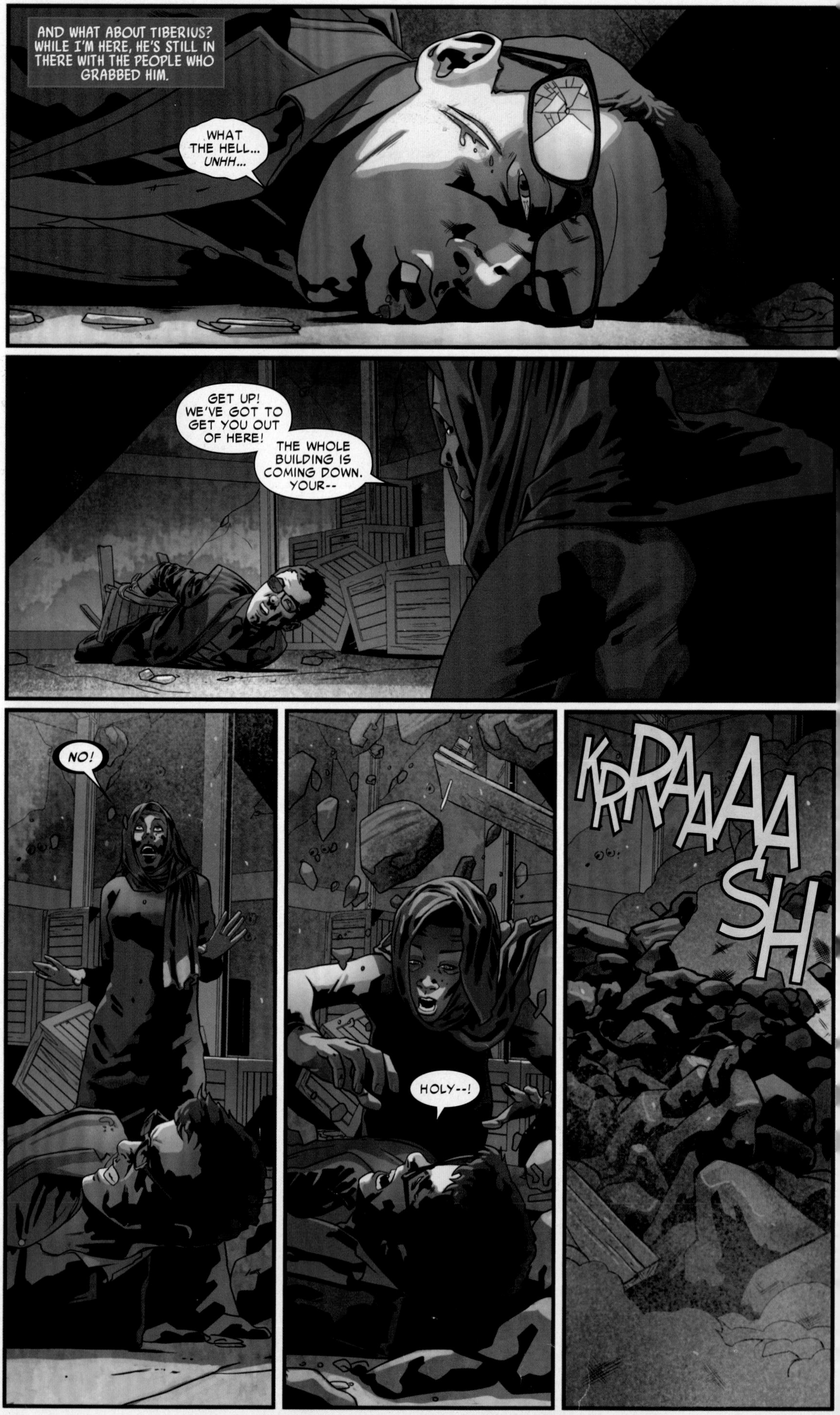
AND WHAT ABOUT TIBERIUS? WHILE I'M HERE, HE'S STILL IN THERE WITH THE PEOPLE WHO GRABBED HIM.
WHAT THE HELL... UNHH...
GET UP! WE'VE GOT TO GET YOU OUT OF HERE!
THE WHOLE BUILDING IS COMING DOWN. YOUR--
NO!
HOLY--!
KRRAAAAASH

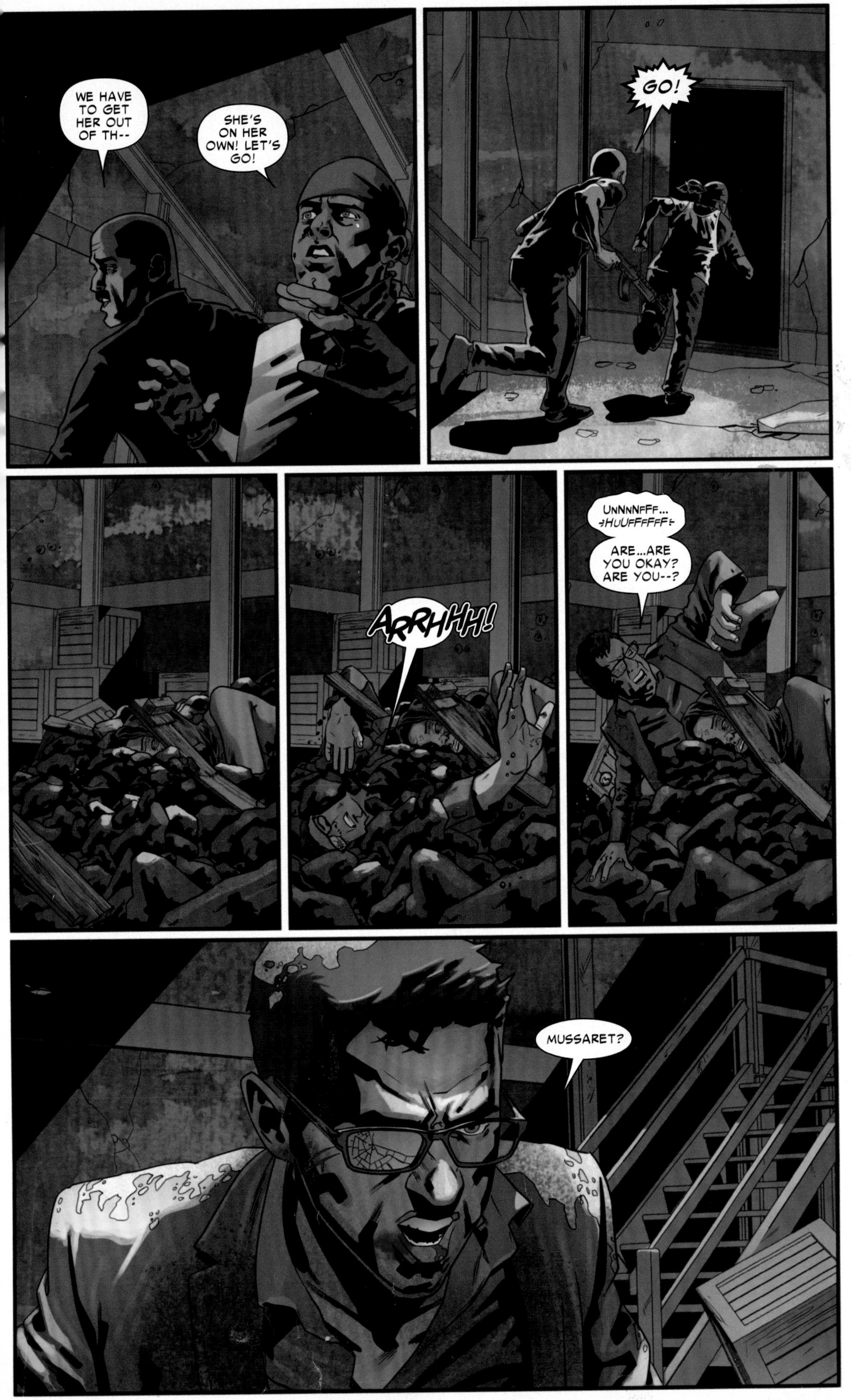
WE HAVE TO GET HER OUT OF TH--
SHE'S ON HER OWN! LET'S GO!
GO!
ARRHHH!
UNNNNFFF... HUUFFFFFF
ARE...ARE YOU OKAY? ARE YOU--?
MUSSARET?

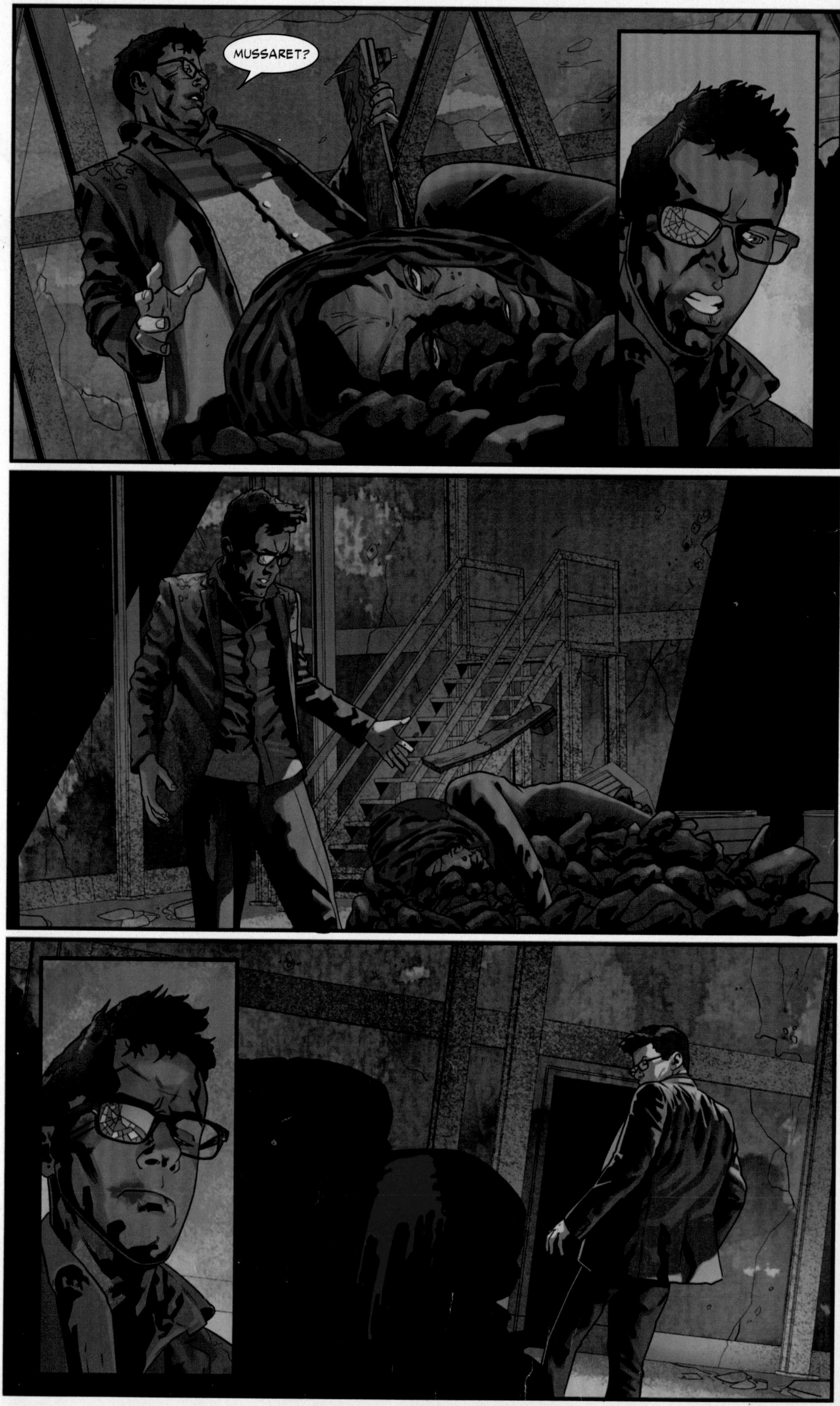
MUSSARET?

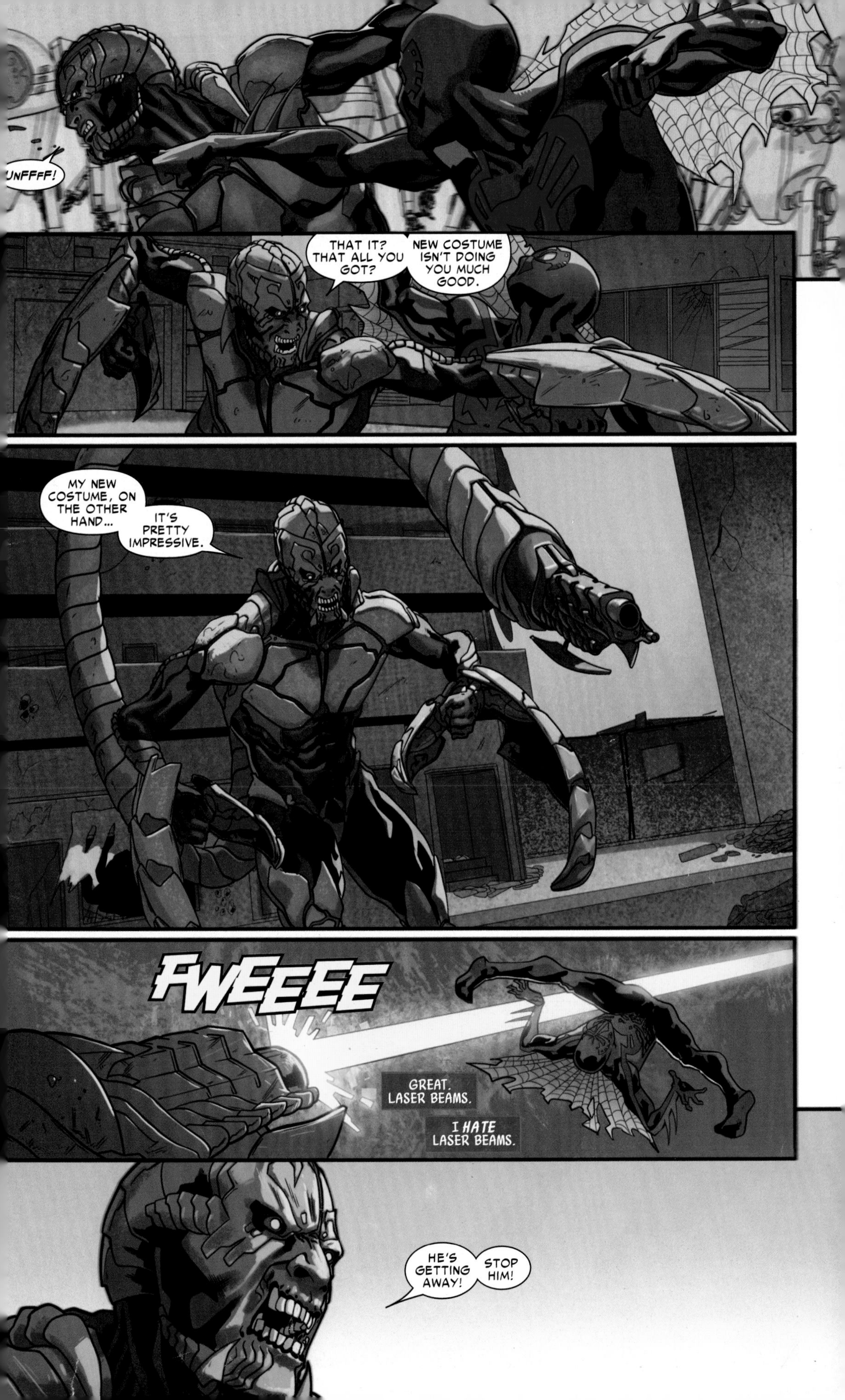
UNFFFF!
THAT IT? THAT ALL YOU GOT?
NEW COSTUME ISN'T DOING YOU MUCH GOOD.
MY NEW COSTUME, ON THE OTHER HAND...
IT'S PRETTY IMPRESSIVE.
FWEEEE
GREAT. LASER BEAMS.
I *HATE* LASER BEAMS.
HE'S GETTING AWAY!
STOP HIM!

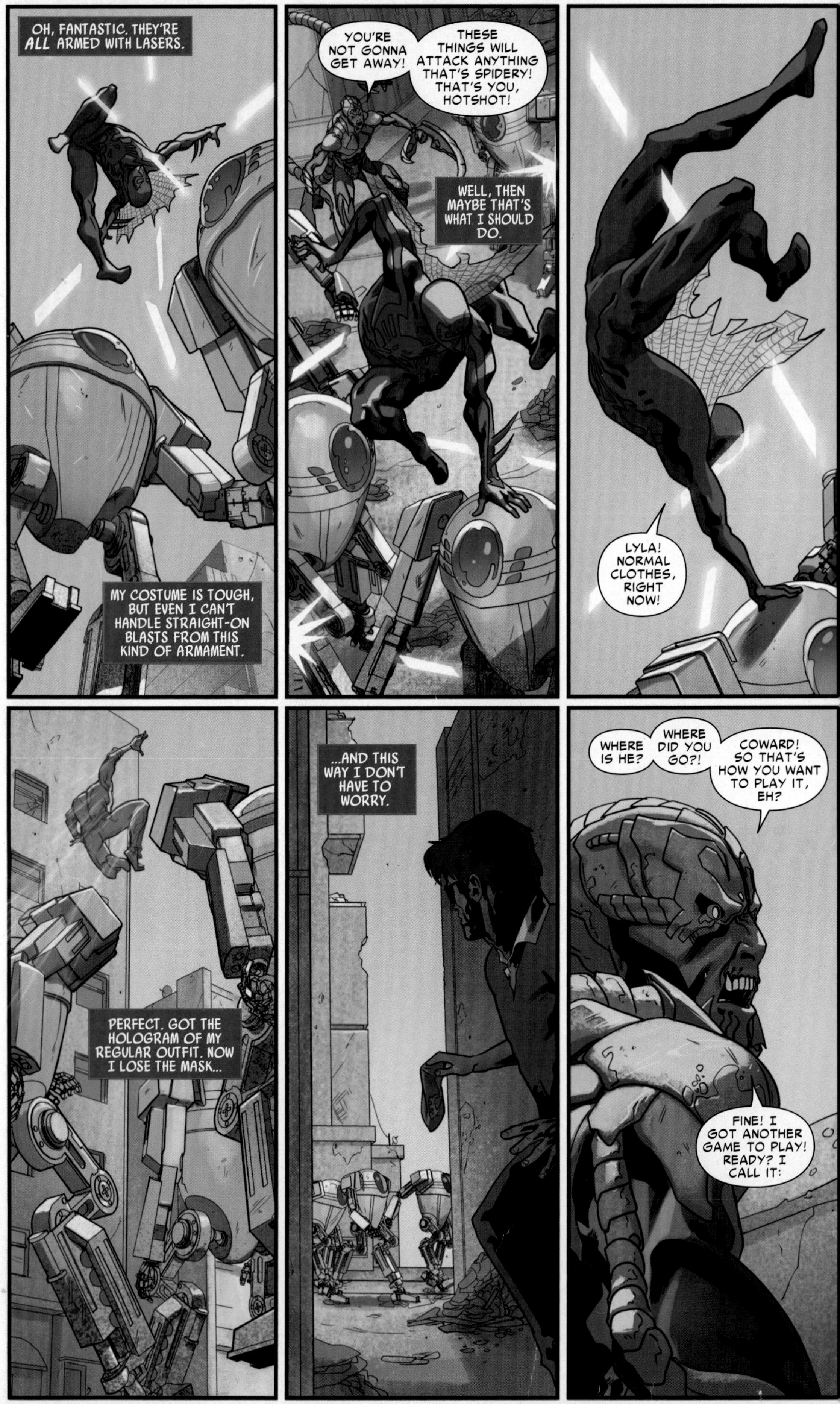

OH, FANTASTIC. THEY'RE ALL ARMED WITH LASERS.
MY COSTUME IS TOUGH, BUT EVEN I CAN'T HANDLE STRAIGHT-ON BLASTS FROM THIS KIND OF ARMAMENT.
YOU'RE NOT GONNA GET AWAY!
THESE THINGS WILL ATTACK ANYTHING THAT'S SPIDERY! THAT'S YOU, HOTSHOT!
WELL, THEN MAYBE THAT'S WHAT I SHOULD DO.
LYLA! NORMAL CLOTHES, RIGHT NOW!
PERFECT. GOT THE HOLOGRAM OF MY REGULAR OUTFIT. NOW I LOSE THE MASK...
...AND THIS WAY I DON'T HAVE TO WORRY.
WHERE IS HE?
WHERE DID YOU GO?!
COWARD! SO THAT'S HOW YOU WANT TO PLAY IT, EH?
FINE! I GOT ANOTHER GAME TO PLAY! READY? I CALL IT:

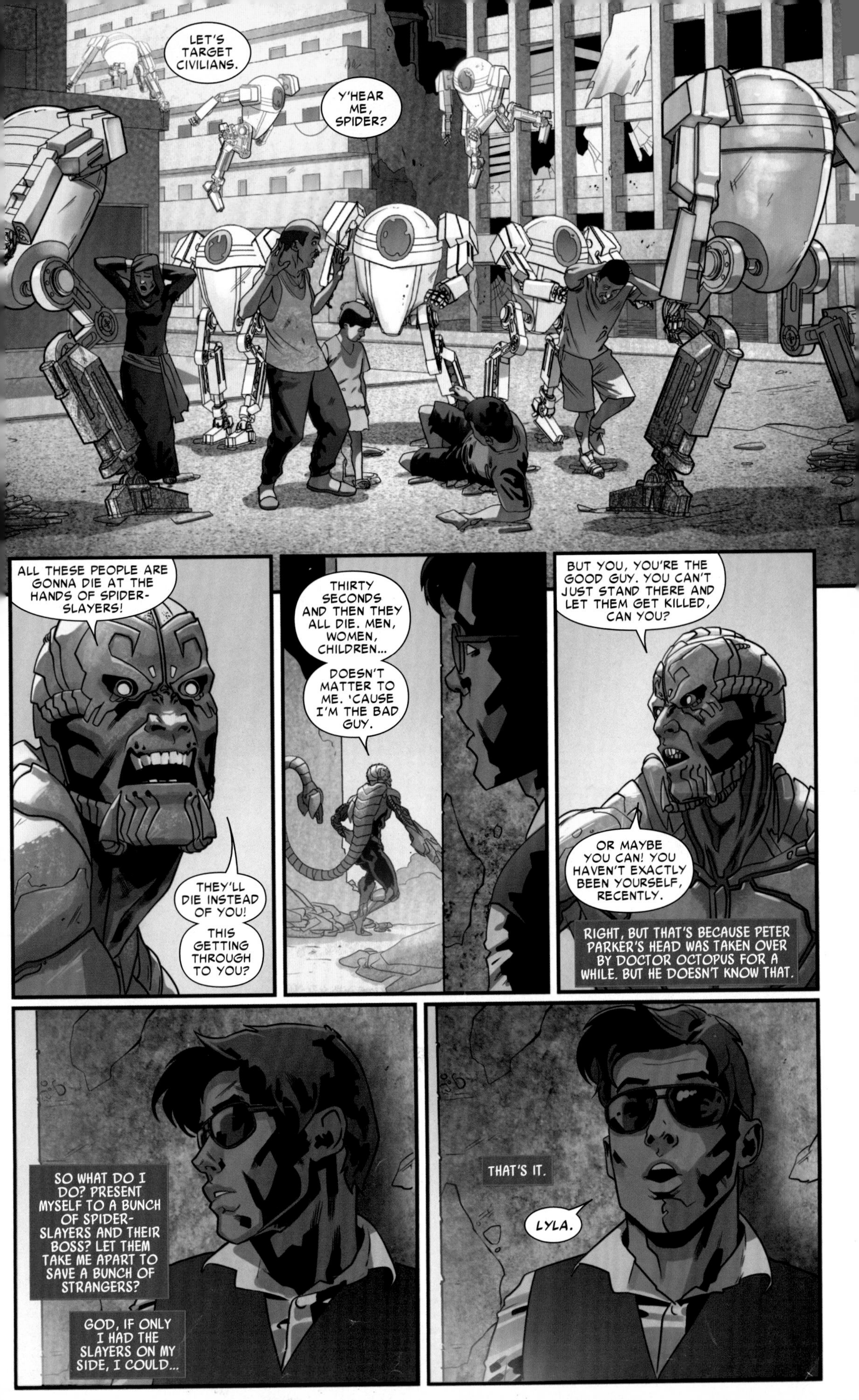

LET'S TARGET CIVILIANS.
Y'HEAR ME, SPIDER?
ALL THESE PEOPLE ARE GONNA DIE AT THE HANDS OF SPIDER-SLAYERS!
THEY'LL DIE INSTEAD OF YOU!
THIS GETTING THROUGH TO YOU?
THIRTY SECONDS AND THEN THEY ALL DIE. MEN, WOMEN, CHILDREN...
DOESN'T MATTER TO ME. 'CAUSE I'M THE BAD GUY.
BUT YOU, YOU'RE THE GOOD GUY. YOU CAN'T JUST STAND THERE AND LET THEM GET KILLED, CAN YOU?
OR MAYBE YOU CAN! YOU HAVEN'T EXACTLY BEEN YOURSELF, RECENTLY.
RIGHT, BUT THAT'S BECAUSE PETER PARKER'S HEAD WAS TAKEN OVER BY DOCTOR OCTOPUS FOR A WHILE. BUT HE DOESN'T KNOW THAT.
SO WHAT DO I DO? PRESENT MYSELF TO A BUNCH OF SPIDER-SLAYERS AND THEIR BOSS? LET THEM TAKE ME APART TO SAVE A BUNCH OF STRANGERS?
GOD, IF ONLY I HAD THE SLAYERS ON MY SIDE, I COULD...
THAT'S IT.
LYLA.

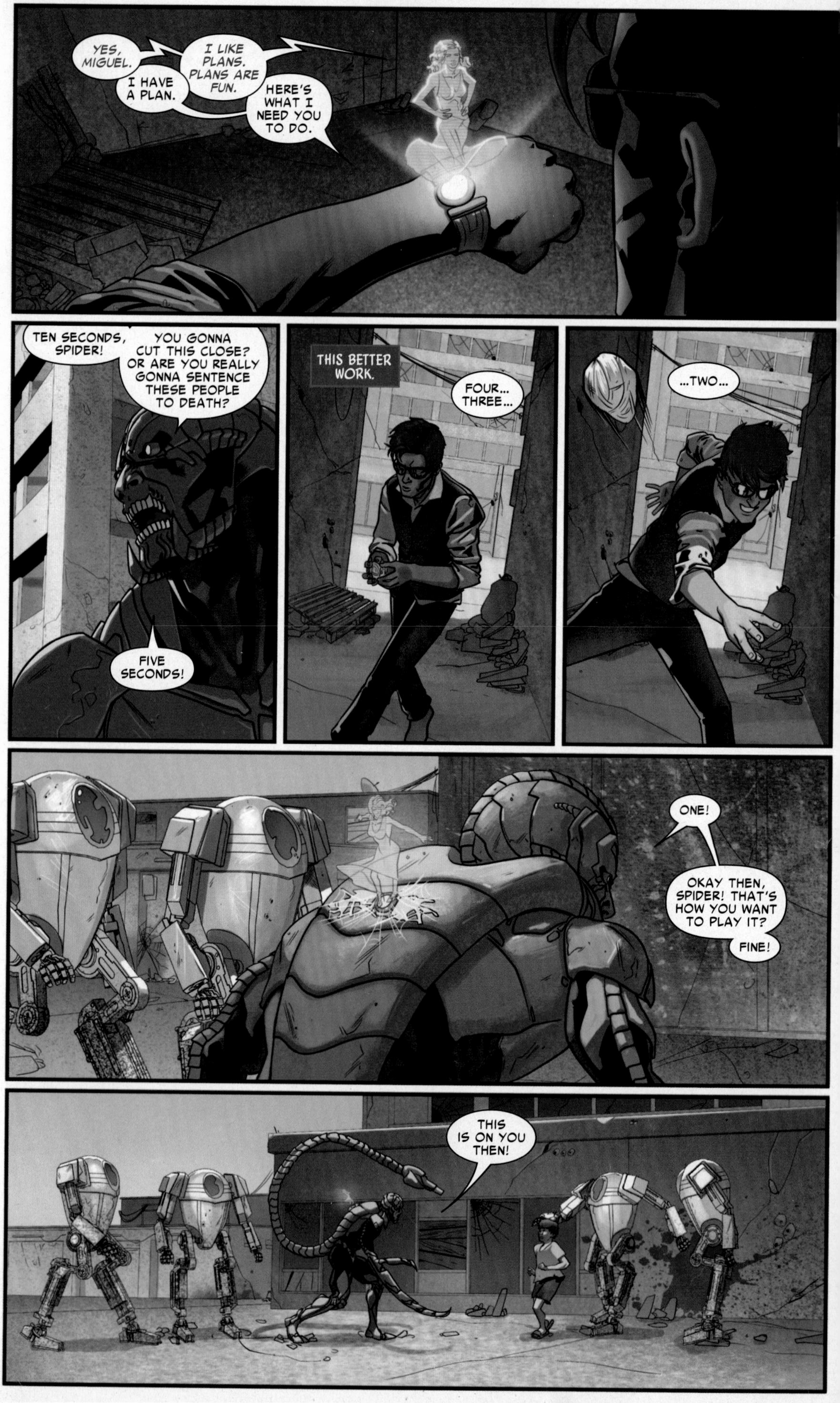
YES, MIGUEL.
I HAVE A PLAN.
I LIKE PLANS. PLANS ARE FUN.
HERE'S WHAT I NEED YOU TO DO.
TEN SECONDS, SPIDER!
YOU GONNA CUT THIS CLOSE? OR ARE YOU REALLY GONNA SENTENCE THESE PEOPLE TO DEATH?
FIVE SECONDS!
THIS BETTER WORK.
FOUR... THREE...
...TWO...
ONE!
OKAY THEN, SPIDER! THAT'S HOW YOU WANT TO PLAY IT?
FINE!
THIS IS ON YOU THEN!

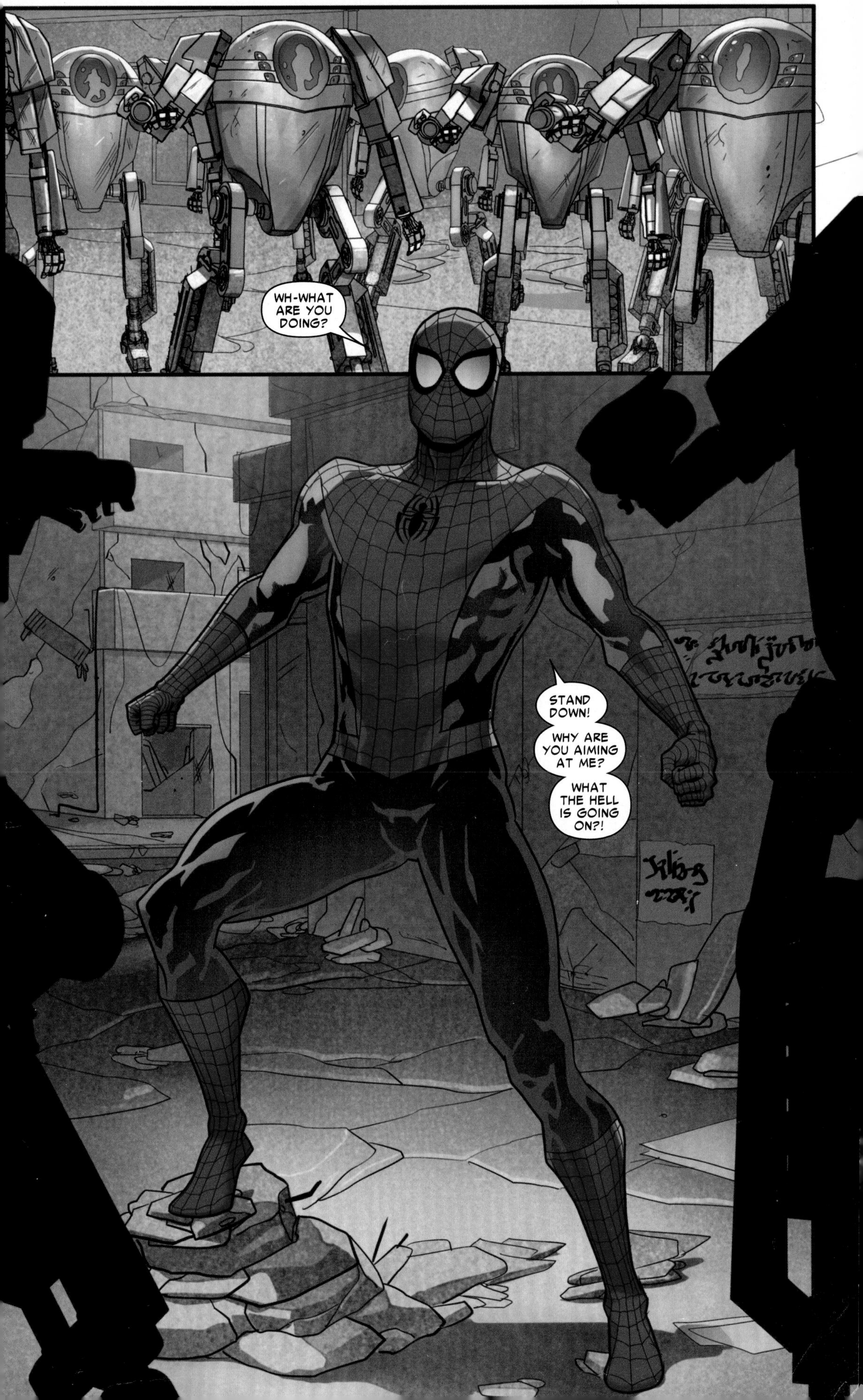
WH-WHAT ARE YOU DOING?
STAND DOWN!
WHY ARE YOU AIMING AT ME?
WHAT THE HELL IS GOING ON?!

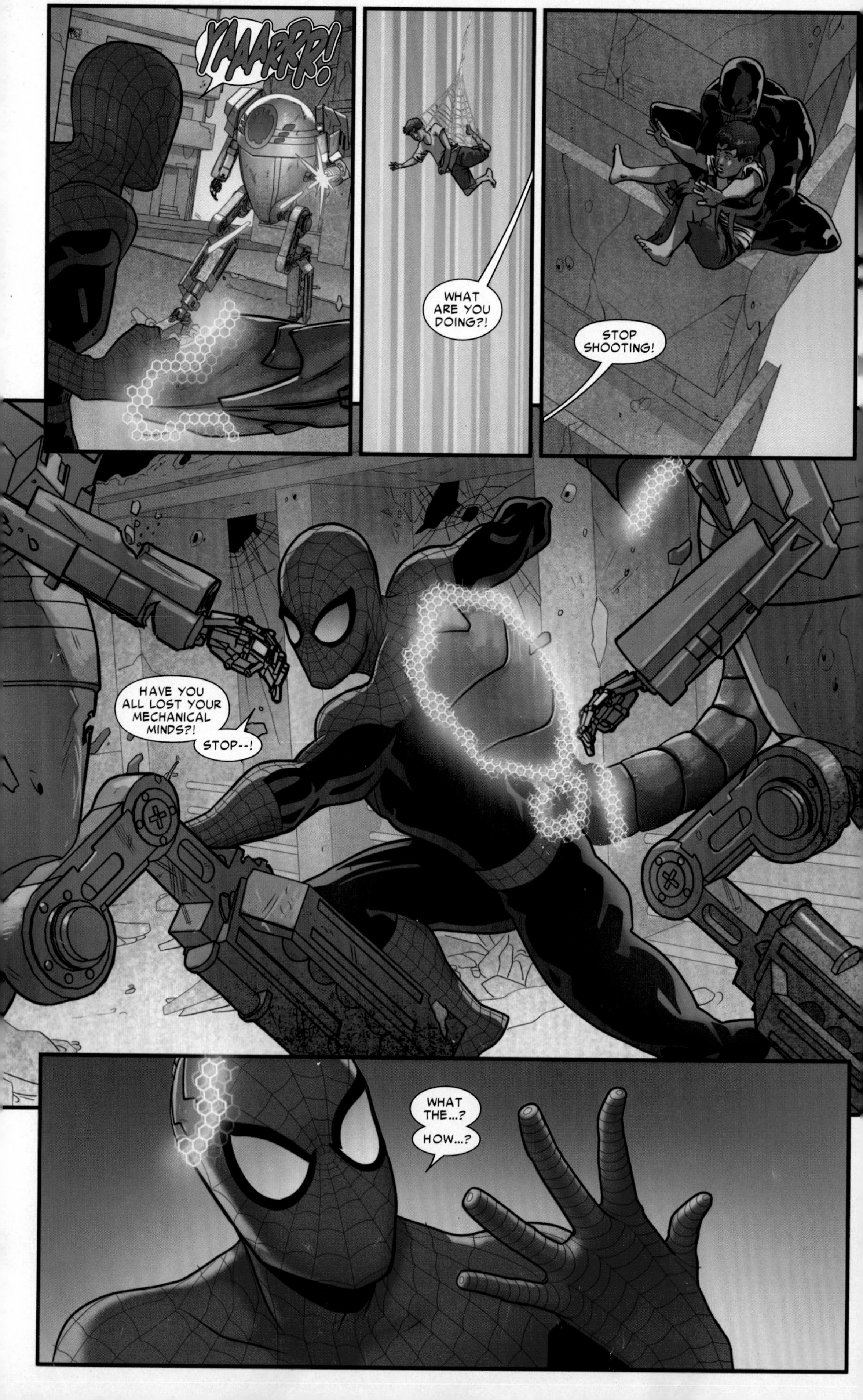
YAAARRR!
WHAT ARE YOU DOING?!
STOP SHOOTING!
HAVE YOU ALL LOST YOUR MECHANICAL MINDS?!
STOP--!
WHAT THE...?
HOW...?

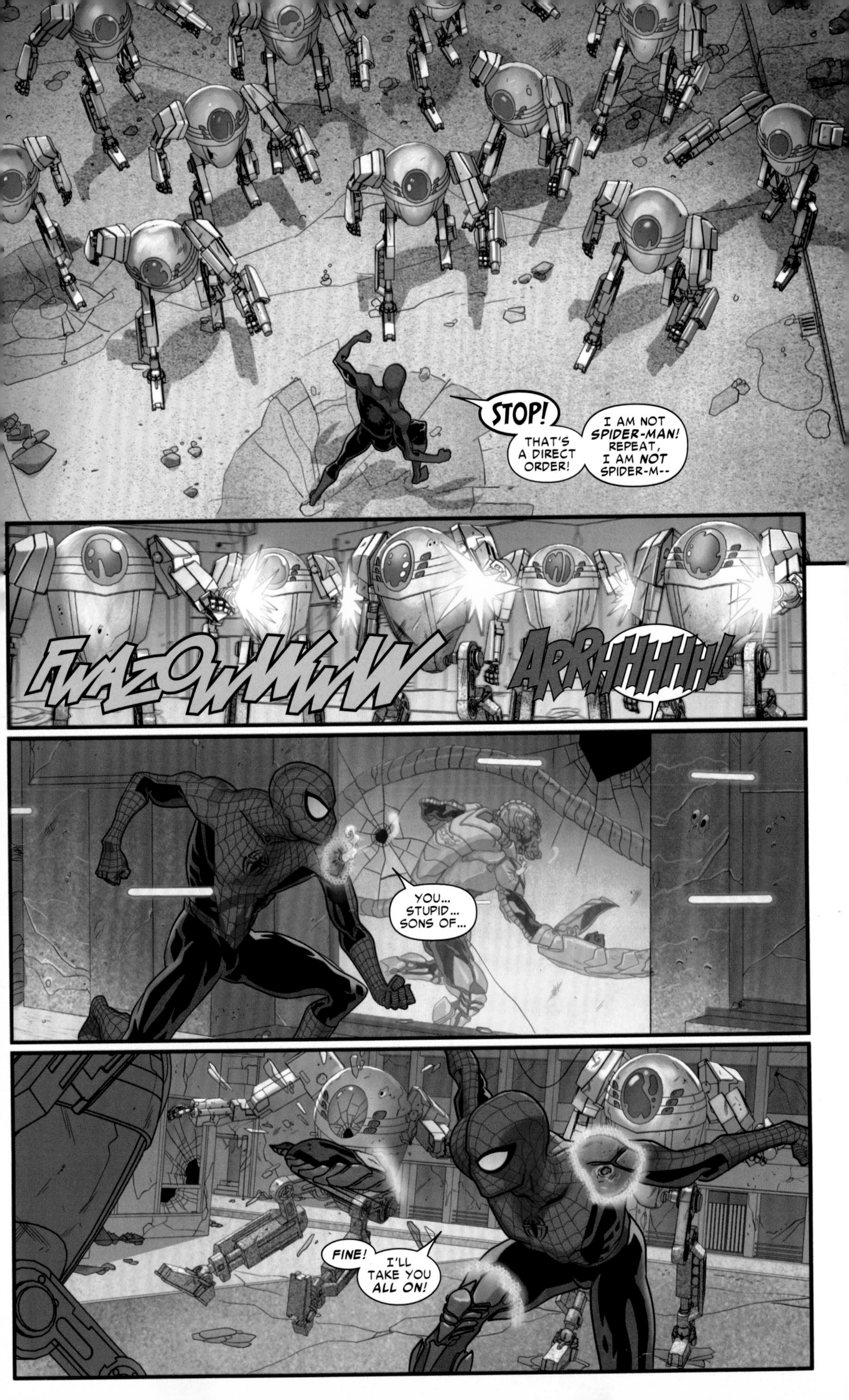
STOP!
THAT'S A DIRECT ORDER!
I AM NOT SPIDER-MAN! REPEAT, I AM NOT SPIDER-M--
FWAZOWMMWW
ARRHHHHH!
YOU... STUPID... SONS OF...
FINE!
I'LL TAKE YOU ALL ON!

VAMANOS! HERE! COME ON, LET'S GO!

HEY... IT'S ALL RIGHT.

RUN TO YOUR FOLKS. MOVE IT.

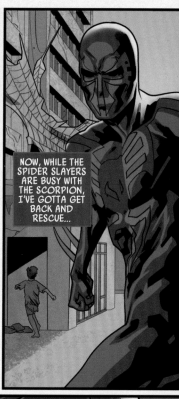

NOW, WHILE THE SPIDER SLAYERS ARE BUSY WITH THE SCORPION, I'VE GOTTA GET BACK AND RESCUE...

SHOCK ME.

THERE HE IS, HOW'D HE GET AWAY?

DID THEY LET HIM GO?

WHAT THE HELL?

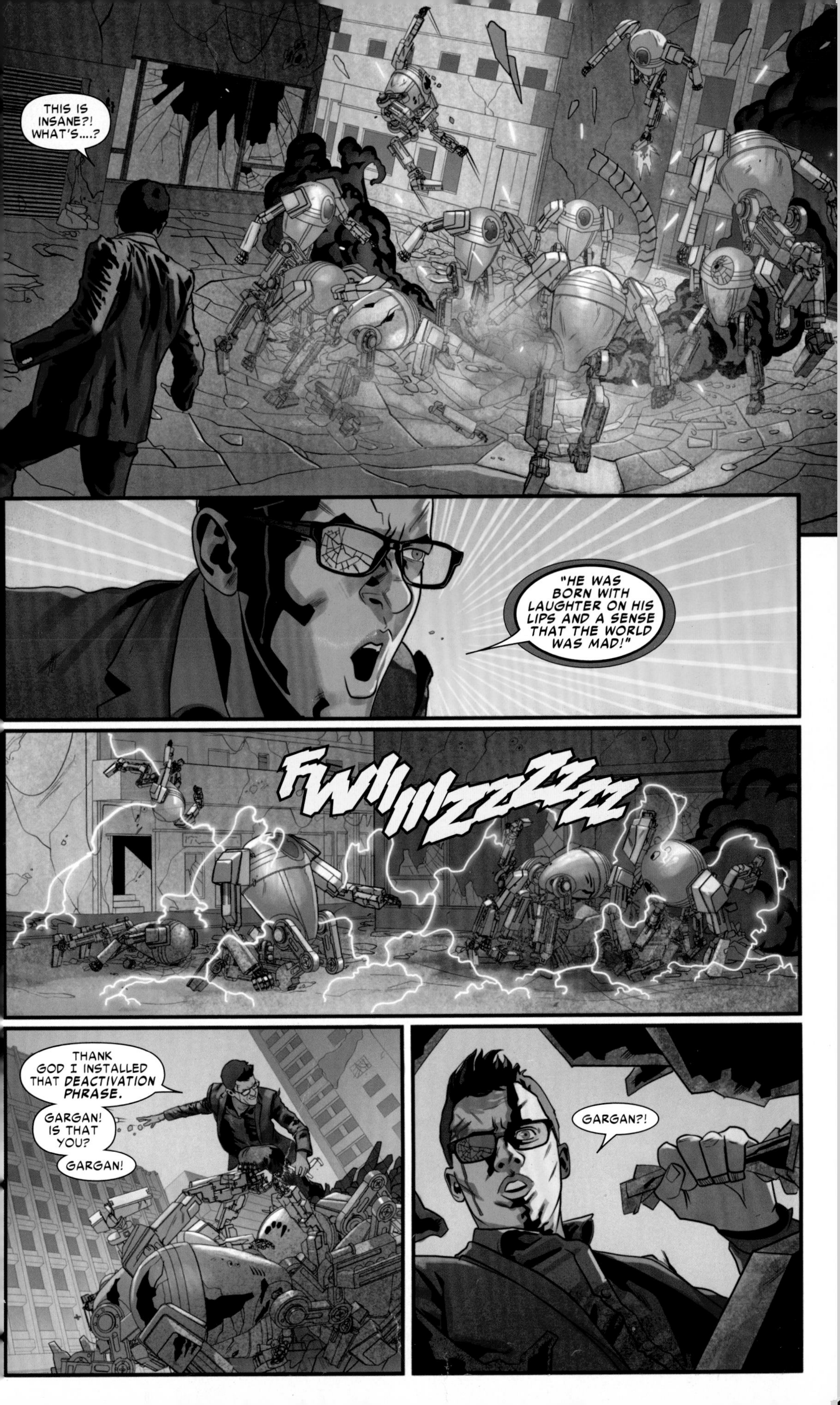
THIS IS INSANE?! WHAT'S....?
"HE WAS BORN WITH LAUGHTER ON HIS LIPS AND A SENSE THAT THE WORLD WAS MAD!"
FWIIIIIZZZZZZ
THANK GOD I INSTALLED THAT DEACTIVATION PHRASE.
GARGAN! IS THAT YOU?
GARGAN!
GARGAN?!

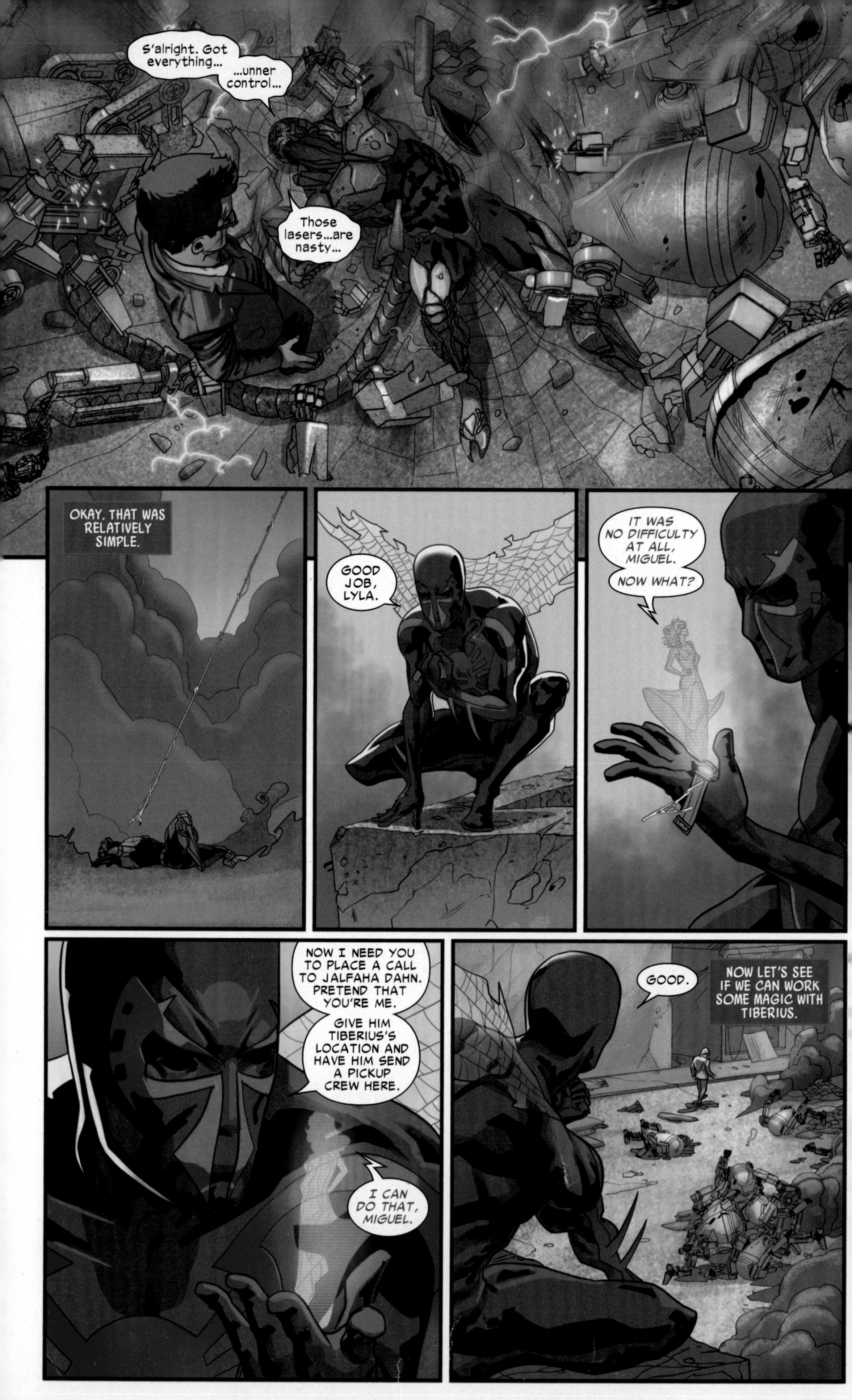

S'alright. Got everything...
...unner control...
Those lasers...are nasty...
OKAY. THAT WAS RELATIVELY SIMPLE.
GOOD JOB, LYLA.
IT WAS NO DIFFICULTY AT ALL, MIGUEL.
NOW WHAT?
NOW I NEED YOU TO PLACE A CALL TO JALFAHA DAHN. PRETEND THAT YOU'RE ME.
GIVE HIM TIBERIUS'S LOCATION AND HAVE HIM SEND A PICKUP CREW HERE.
I CAN DO THAT, MIGUEL.
GOOD.
NOW LET'S SEE IF WE CAN WORK SOME MAGIC WITH TIBERIUS.

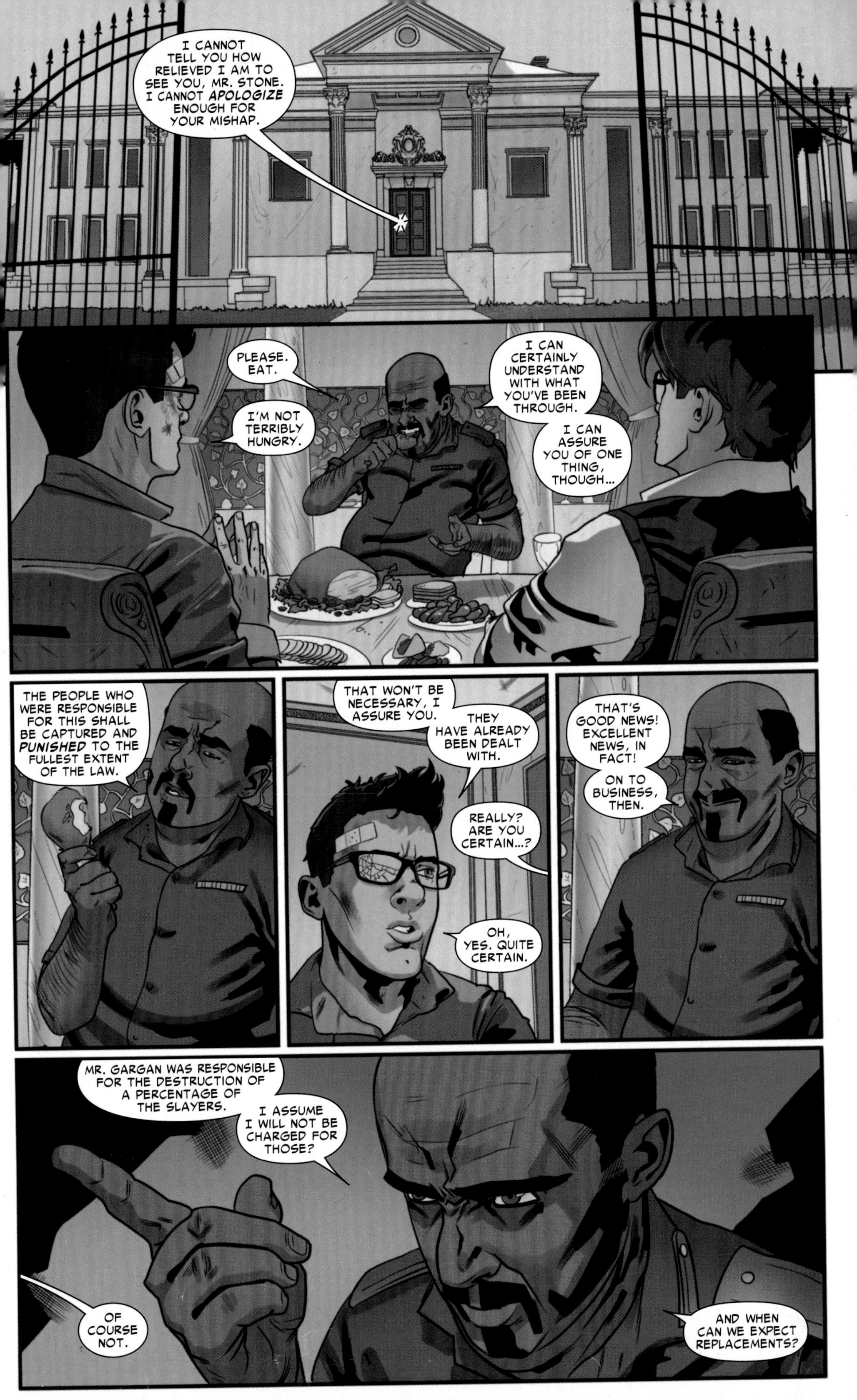
I CANNOT TELL YOU HOW RELIEVED I AM TO SEE YOU, MR. STONE. I CANNOT *APOLOGIZE* ENOUGH FOR YOUR MISHAP.
PLEASE. EAT.
I'M NOT TERRIBLY HUNGRY.
I CAN CERTAINLY UNDERSTAND WITH WHAT YOU'VE BEEN THROUGH.
I CAN ASSURE YOU OF ONE THING, THOUGH...
THE PEOPLE WHO WERE RESPONSIBLE FOR THIS SHALL BE CAPTURED AND *PUNISHED* TO THE FULLEST EXTENT OF THE LAW.
THAT WON'T BE NECESSARY, I ASSURE YOU.
THEY HAVE ALREADY BEEN DEALT WITH.
REALLY? ARE YOU CERTAIN...?
OH, YES. QUITE CERTAIN.
THAT'S GOOD NEWS! EXCELLENT NEWS, IN FACT!
ON TO BUSINESS, THEN.
MR. GARGAN WAS RESPONSIBLE FOR THE DESTRUCTION OF A PERCENTAGE OF THE SLAYERS.
I ASSUME I WILL NOT BE CHARGED FOR THOSE?
OF COURSE NOT.
AND WHEN CAN WE EXPECT REPLACEMENTS?

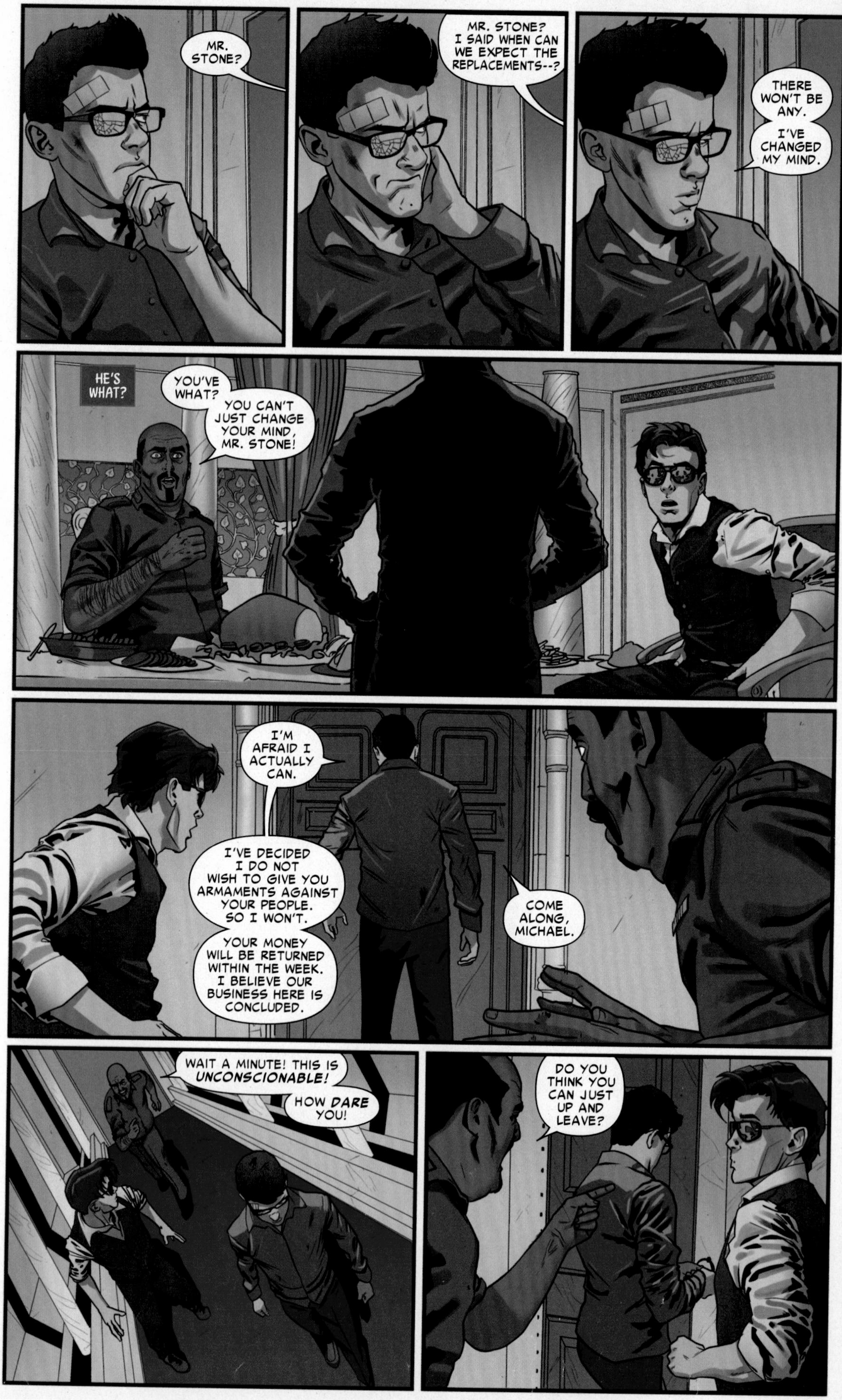
MR. STONE?
MR. STONE? I SAID WHEN CAN WE EXPECT THE REPLACEMENTS--?
THERE WON'T BE ANY.
I'VE CHANGED MY MIND.
HE'S WHAT?
YOU'VE WHAT?
YOU CAN'T JUST CHANGE YOUR MIND, MR. STONE!
I'M AFRAID I ACTUALLY CAN.
I'VE DECIDED I DO NOT WISH TO GIVE YOU ARMAMENTS AGAINST YOUR PEOPLE. SO I WON'T.
YOUR MONEY WILL BE RETURNED WITHIN THE WEEK. I BELIEVE OUR BUSINESS HERE IS CONCLUDED.
COME ALONG, MICHAEL.
WAIT A MINUTE! THIS IS UNCONSCIONABLE!
HOW DARE YOU!
DO YOU THINK YOU CAN JUST UP AND LEAVE?

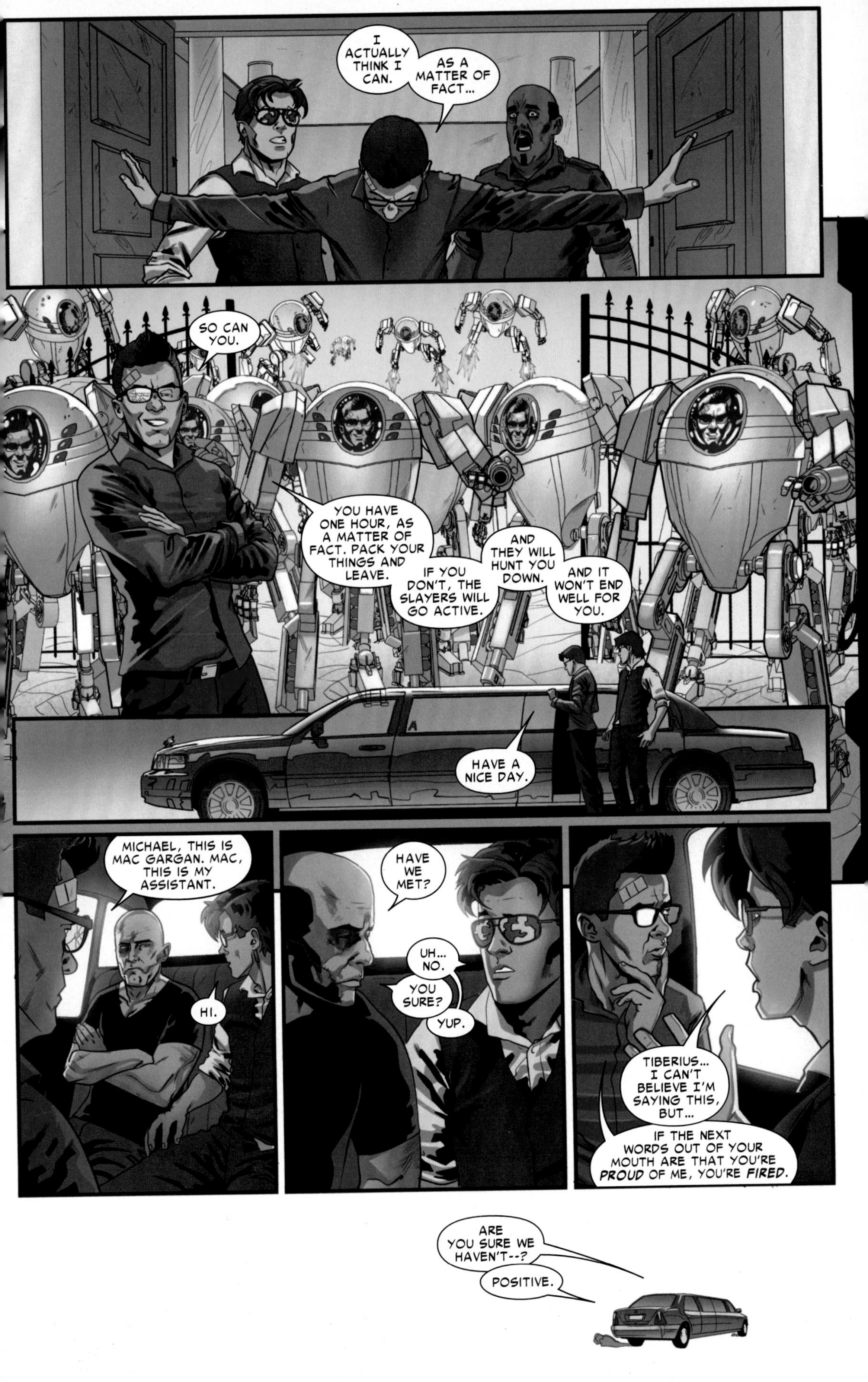
I ACTUALLY THINK I CAN.
AS A MATTER OF FACT...
SO CAN YOU.
YOU HAVE ONE HOUR, AS A MATTER OF FACT. PACK YOUR THINGS AND LEAVE.
IF YOU DON'T, THE SLAYERS WILL GO ACTIVE.
AND THEY WILL HUNT YOU DOWN.
AND IT WON'T END WELL FOR YOU.
HAVE A NICE DAY.
MICHAEL, THIS IS MAC GARGAN. MAC, THIS IS MY ASSISTANT.
HI.
HAVE WE MET?
UH... NO.
YOU SURE?
YUP.
TIBERIUS... I CAN'T BELIEVE I'M SAYING THIS, BUT...
IF THE NEXT WORDS OUT OF YOUR MOUTH ARE THAT YOU'RE *PROUD* OF ME, YOU'RE *FIRED*.
ARE YOU SURE WE HAVEN'T--?
POSITIVE.

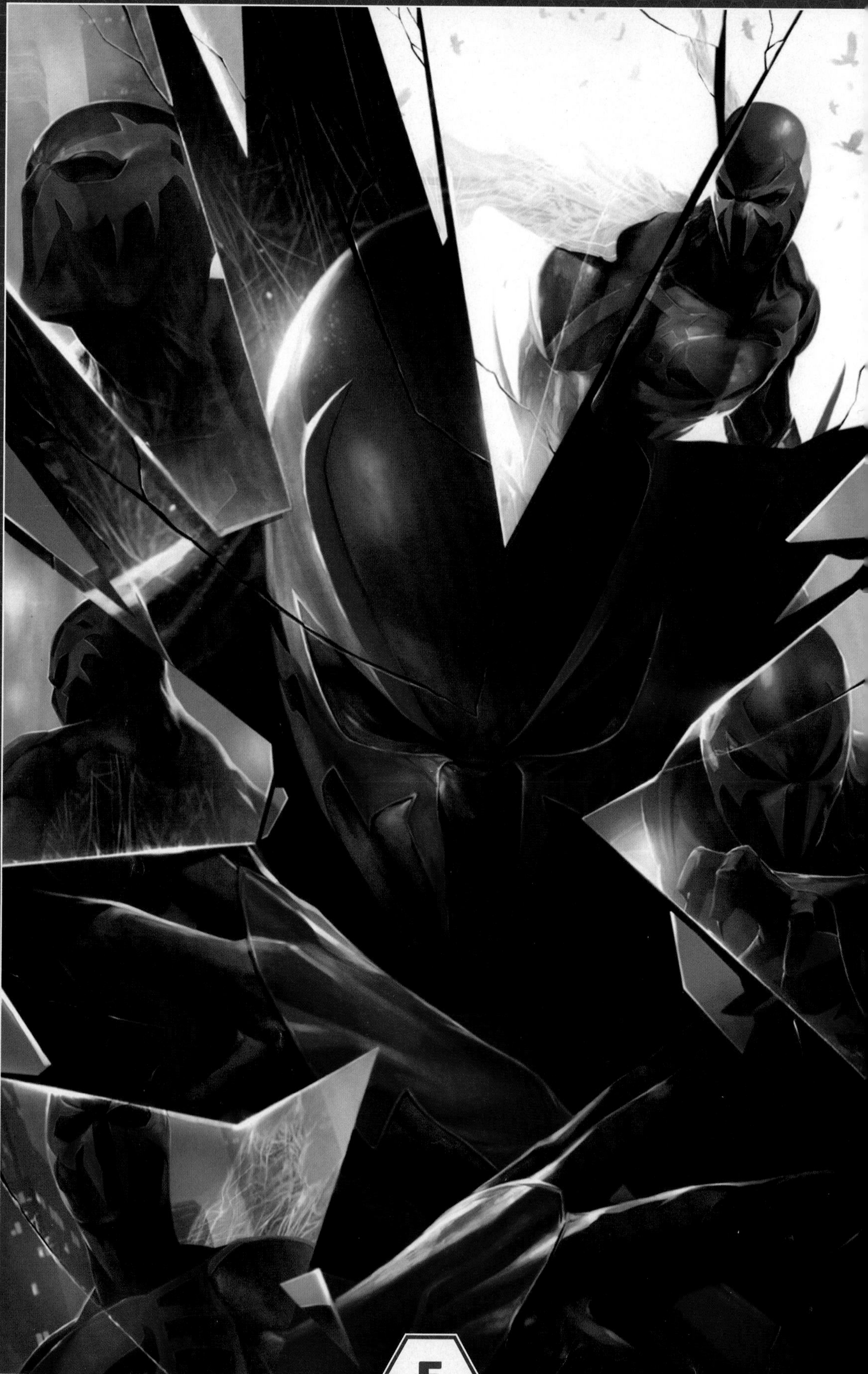

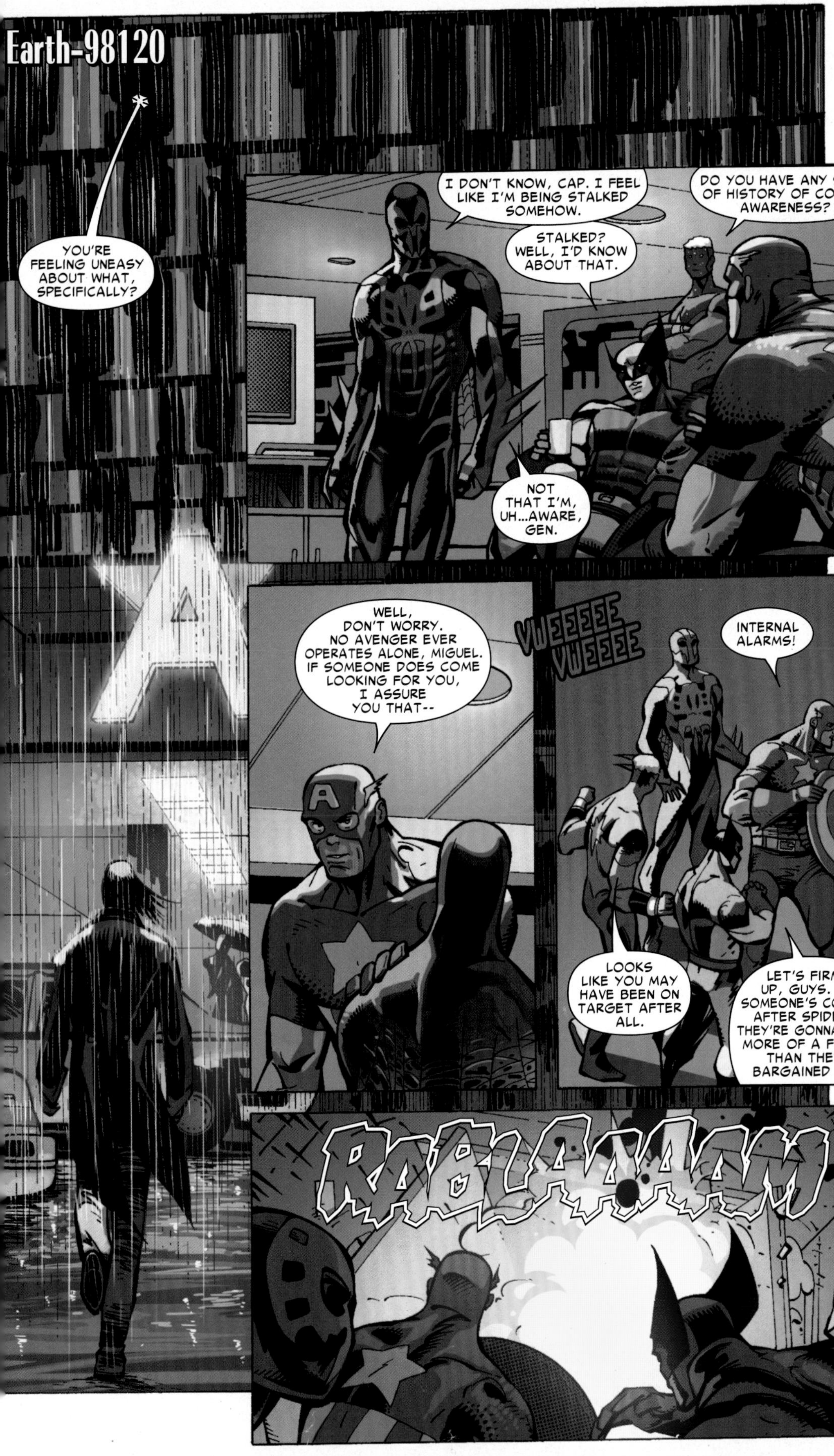
Earth-98120
YOU'RE FEELING UNEASY ABOUT WHAT, SPECIFICALLY?
I DON'T KNOW, CAP. I FEEL LIKE I'M BEING STALKED SOMEHOW.
STALKED? WELL, I'D KNOW ABOUT THAT.
DO YOU HAVE ANY SORT OF HISTORY OF COSMIC AWARENESS?
NOT THAT I'M, UH...AWARE, GEN.
WELL, DON'T WORRY. NO AVENGER EVER OPERATES ALONE, MIGUEL. IF SOMEONE DOES COME LOOKING FOR YOU, I ASSURE YOU THAT--
VWEEEEE VWEEEE
INTERNAL ALARMS!
LOOKS LIKE YOU MAY HAVE BEEN ON TARGET AFTER ALL.
LET'S FIRM UP, GUYS. IF SOMEONE'S COMIN' AFTER SPIDEY, THEY'RE GONNA FIND MORE OF A FIGHT THAN THEY BARGAINED F--
RABLAAAM

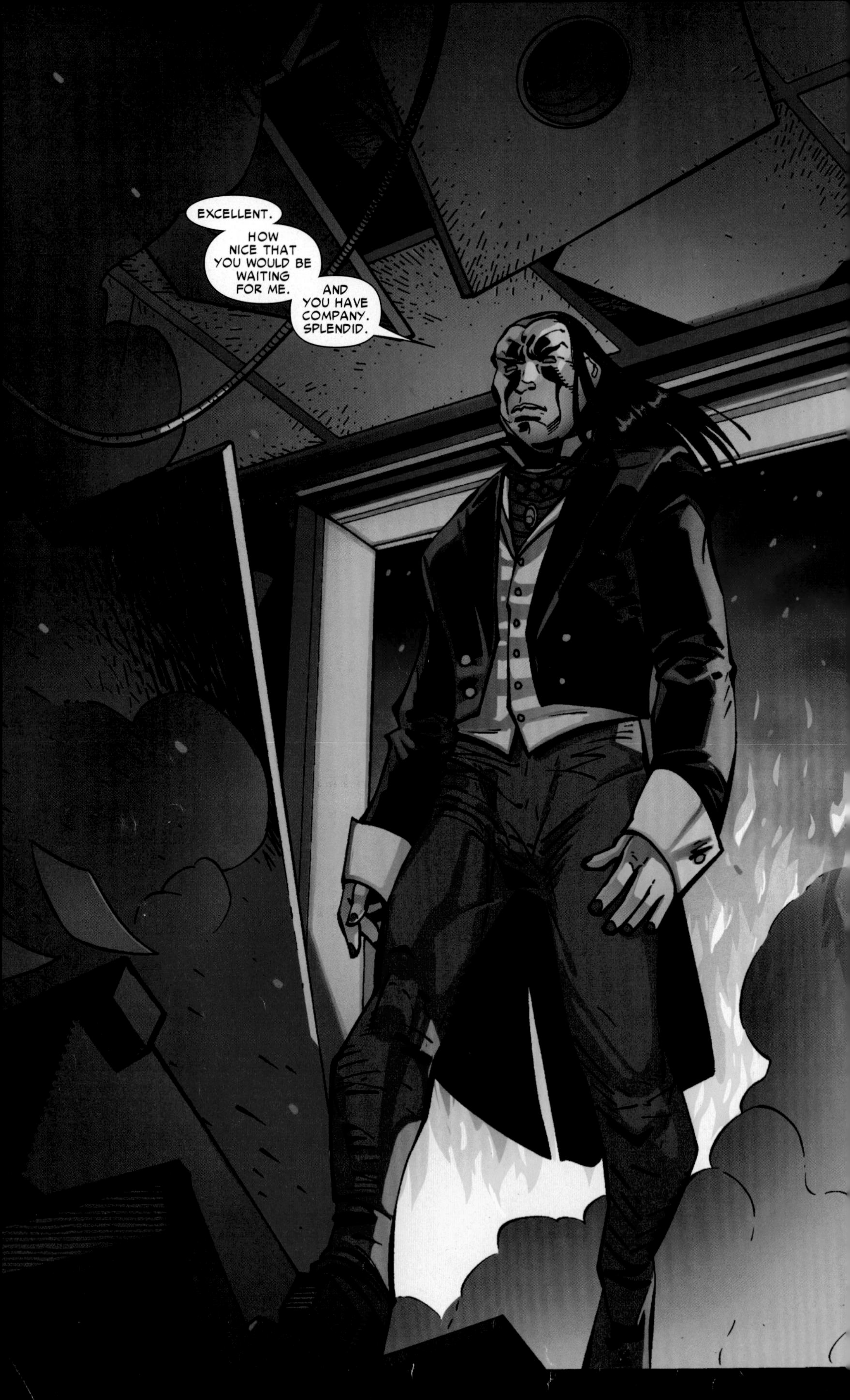
EXCELLENT.
HOW NICE THAT YOU WOULD BE WAITING FOR ME.
AND YOU HAVE COMPANY. SPLENDID.

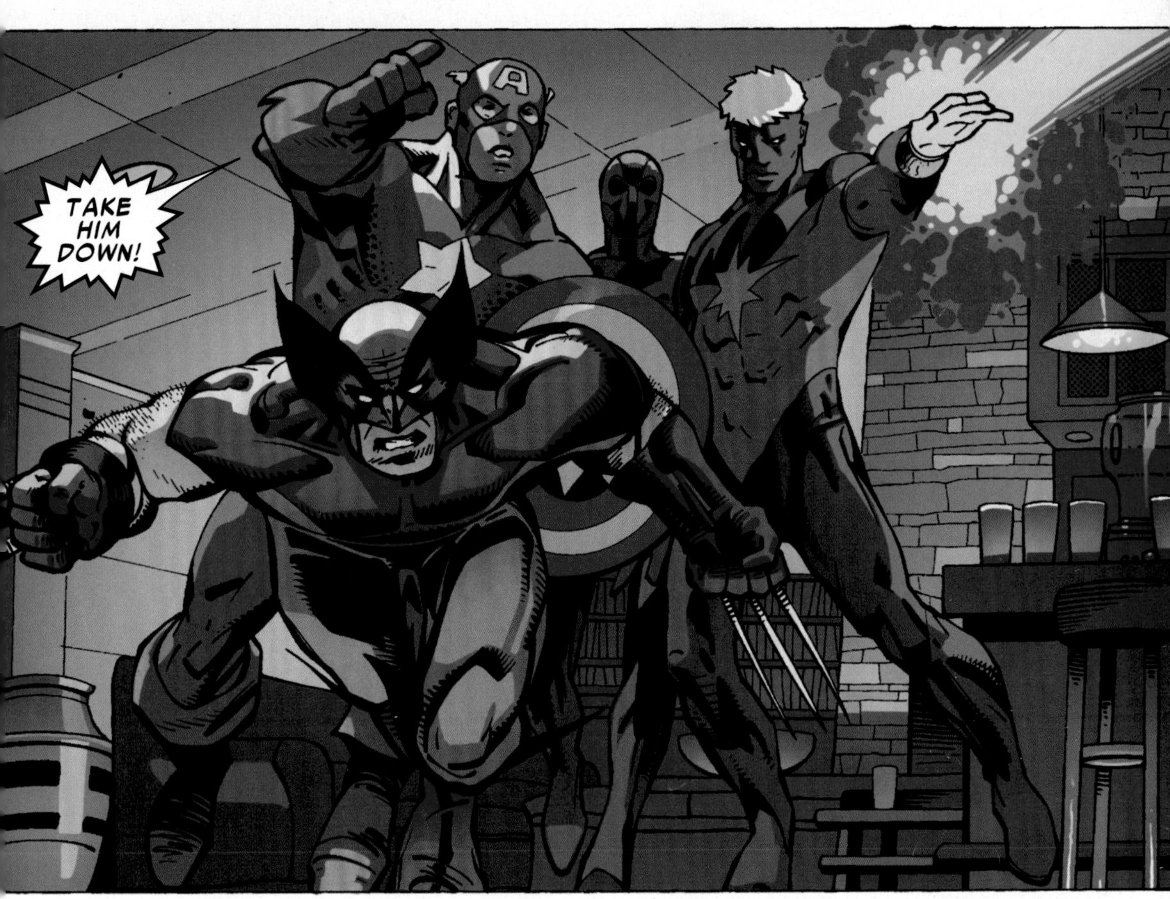
TAKE HIM DOWN!

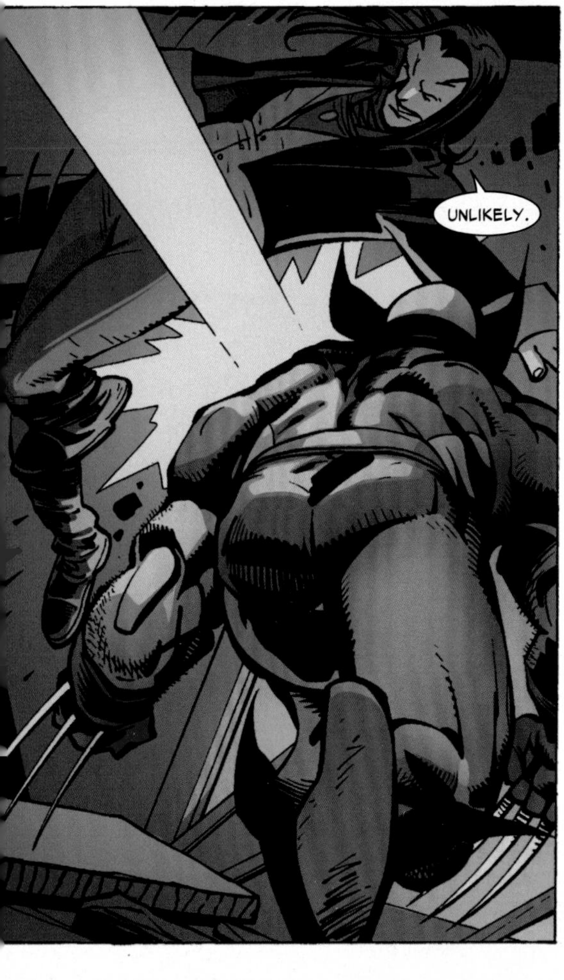
UNLIKELY.

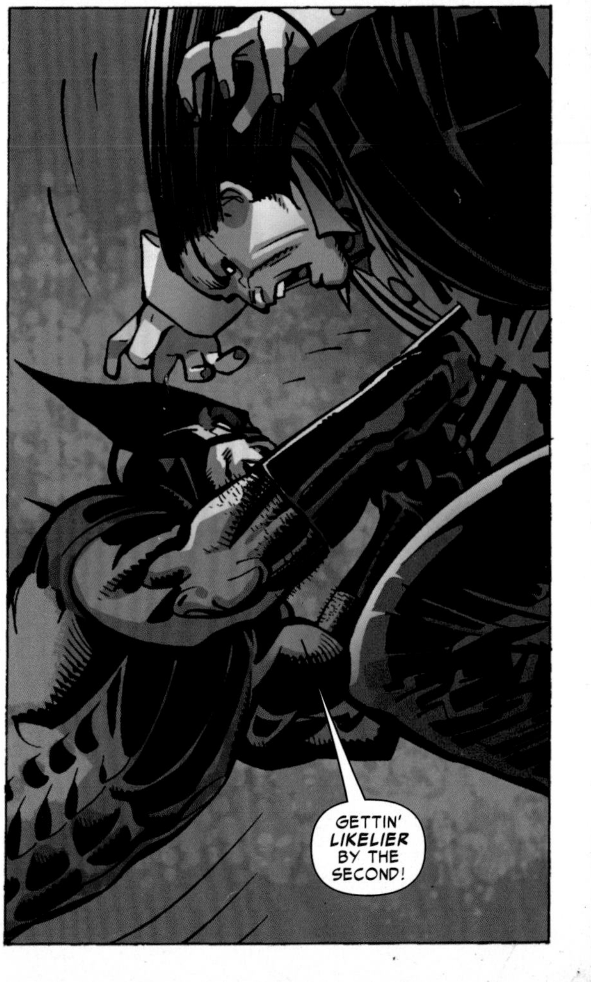
GETTIN' *LIKELIER* BY THE SECOND!

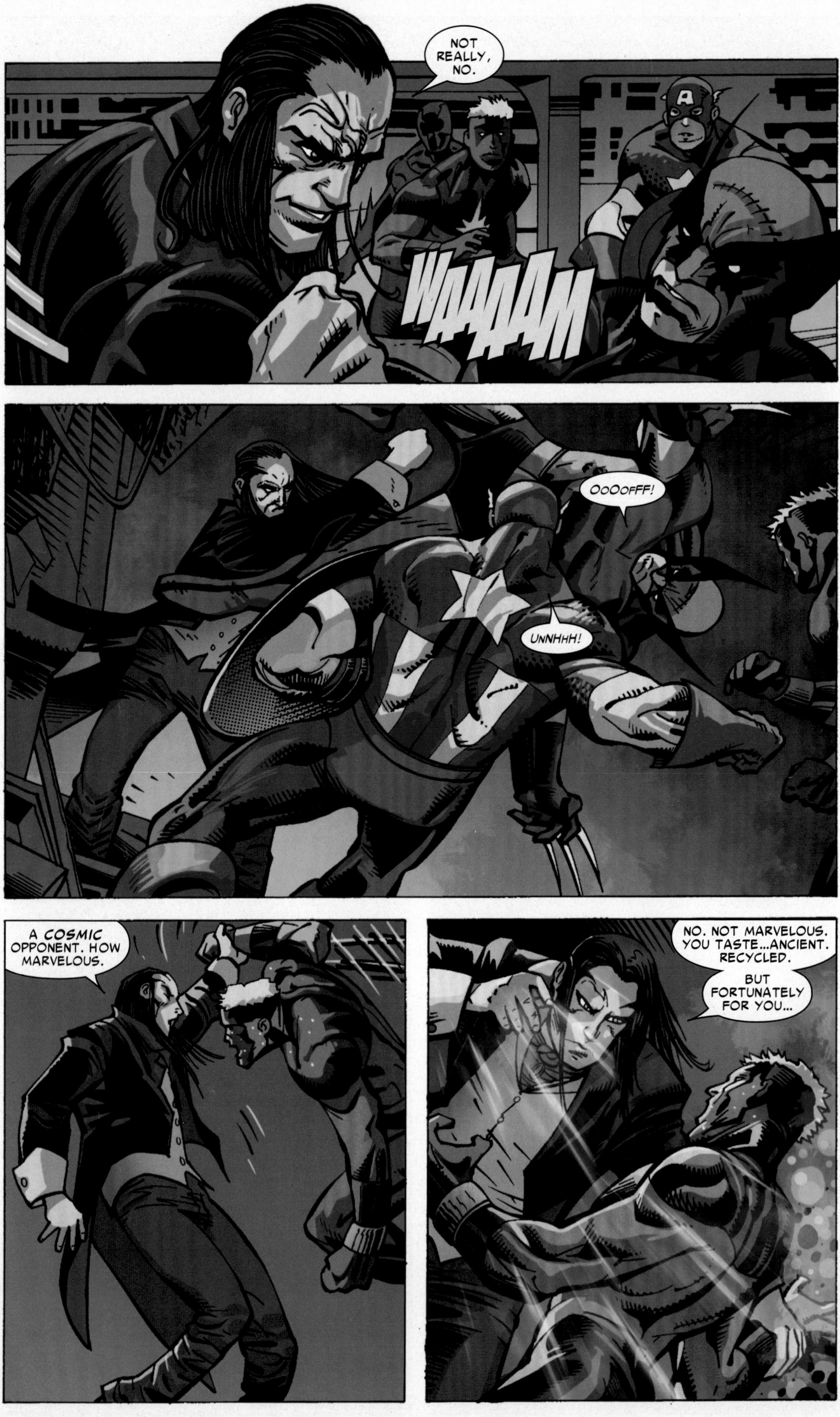
NOT REALLY, NO.
WAAAAM
OOOOFFF!
UNNHHH!
A COSMIC OPPONENT. HOW MARVELOUS.
NO. NOT MARVELOUS. YOU TASTE...ANCIENT. RECYCLED.
BUT FORTUNATELY FOR YOU...

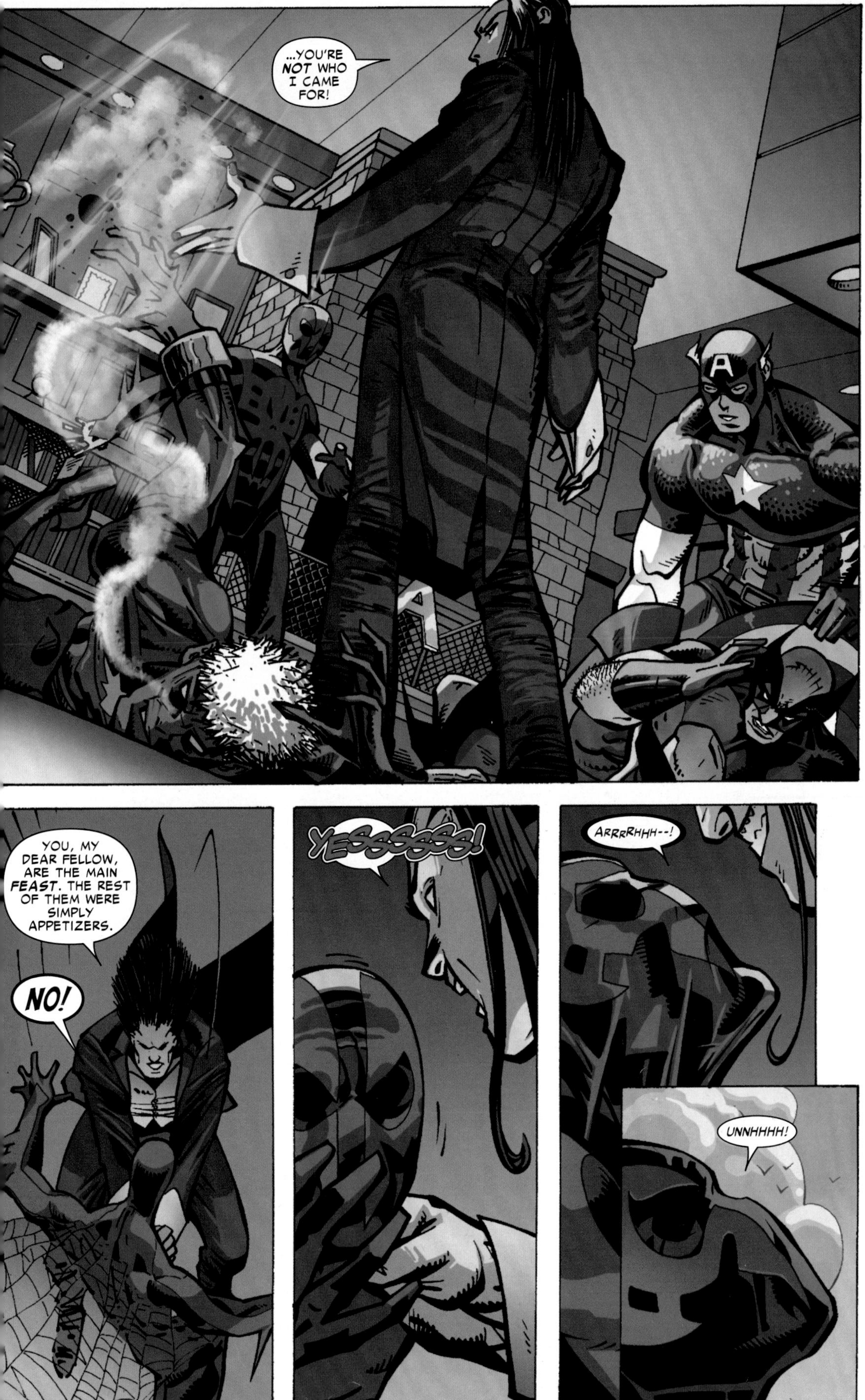
...YOU'RE NOT WHO I CAME FOR!
YOU, MY DEAR FELLOW, ARE THE MAIN FEAST. THE REST OF THEM WERE SIMPLY APPETIZERS.
NO!
YESSSSSS!
ARRRRHHH--!
UNNHHHH!

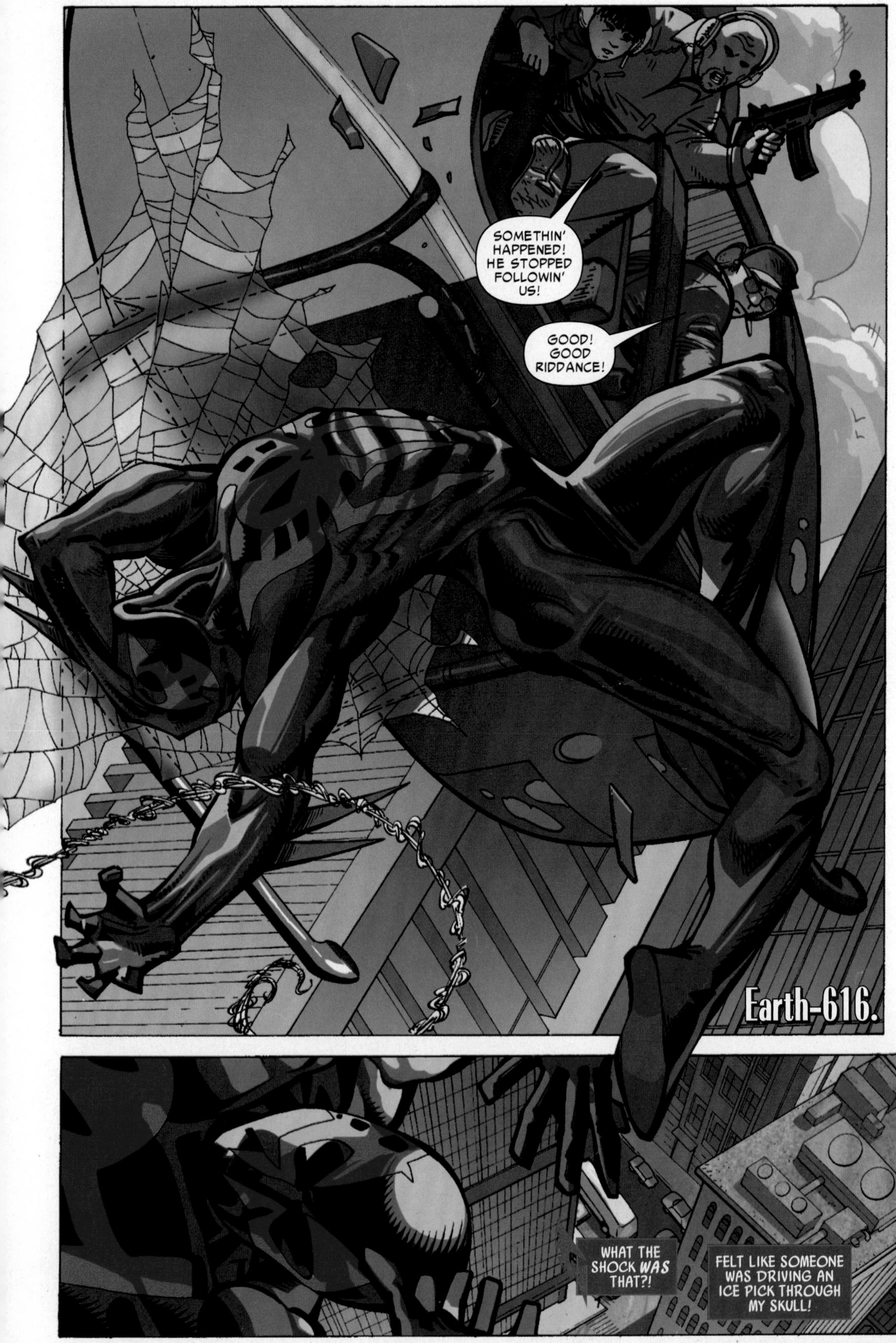
SOMETHIN' HAPPENED! HE STOPPED FOLLOWIN' US!
GOOD! GOOD RIDDANCE!
Earth-616.
WHAT THE SHOCK WAS THAT?!
FELT LIKE SOMEONE WAS DRIVING AN ICE PICK THROUGH MY SKULL!

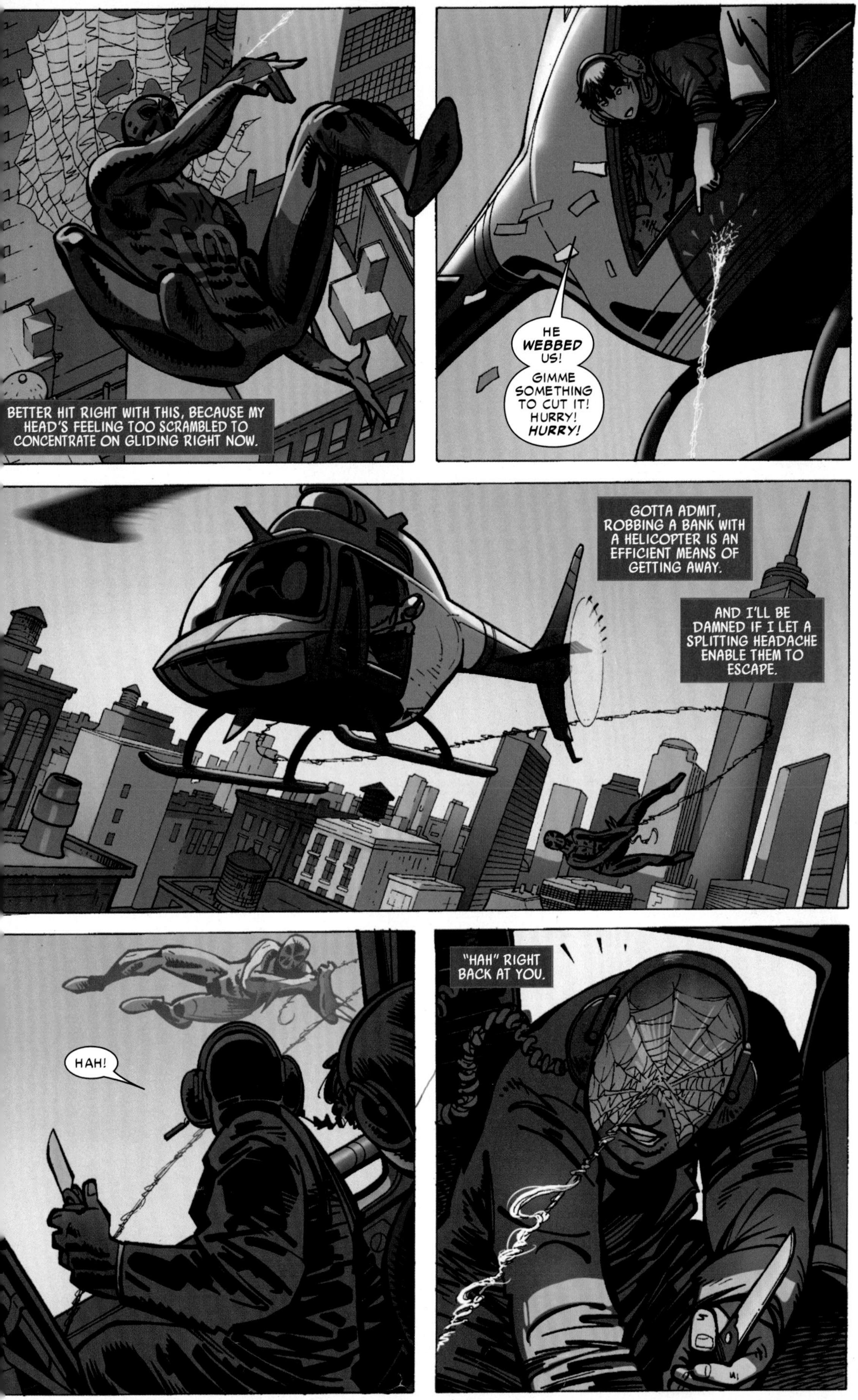
BETTER HIT RIGHT WITH THIS, BECAUSE MY HEAD'S FEELING TOO SCRAMBLED TO CONCENTRATE ON GLIDING RIGHT NOW.
HE WEBBED US! GIMME SOMETHING TO CUT IT! HURRY! HURRY!
GOTTA ADMIT, ROBBING A BANK WITH A HELICOPTER IS AN EFFICIENT MEANS OF GETTING AWAY.
AND I'LL BE DAMNED IF I LET A SPLITTING HEADACHE ENABLE THEM TO ESCAPE.
HAH!
"HAH" RIGHT BACK AT YOU.

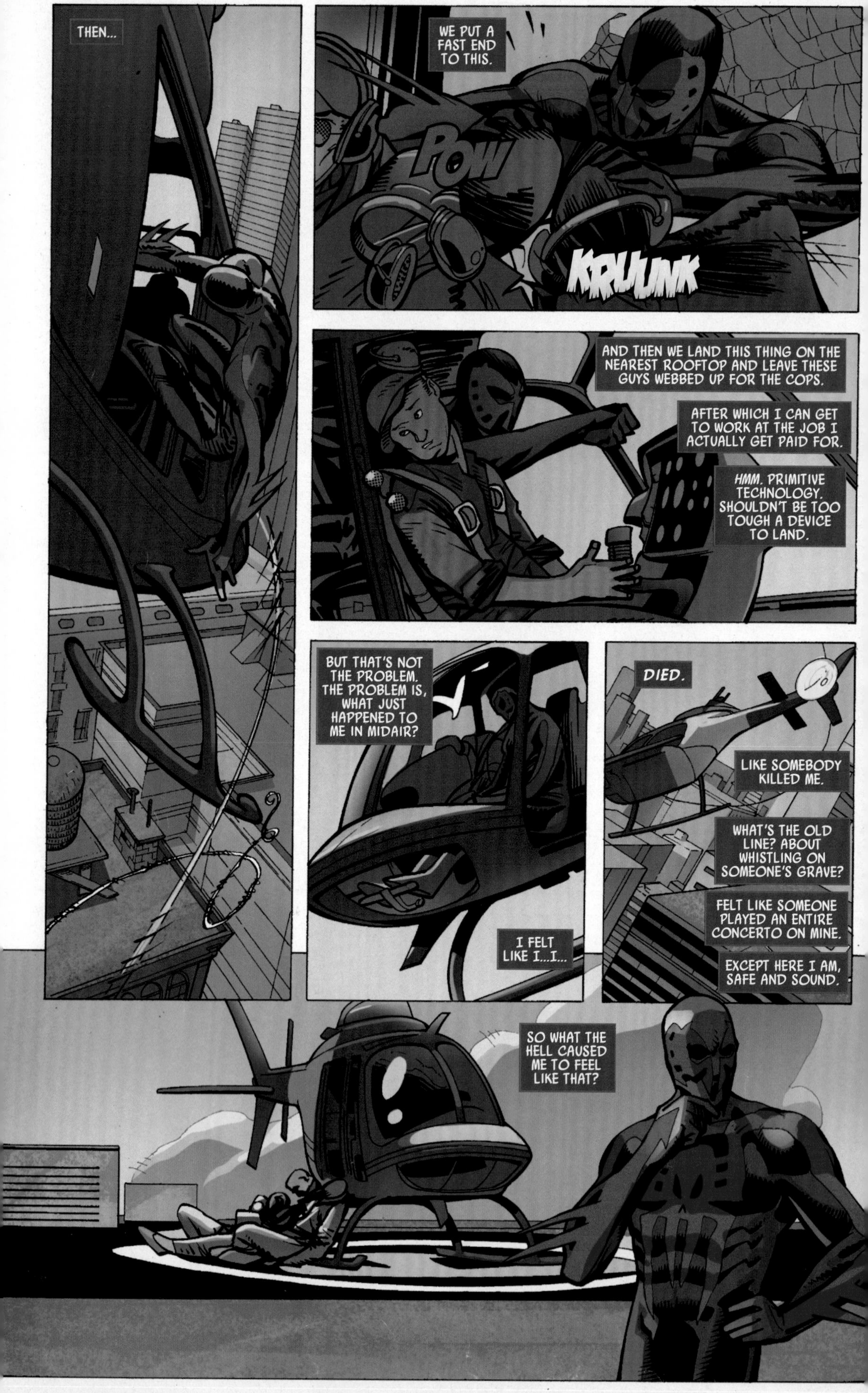
THEN...
WE PUT A FAST END TO THIS.
POW
KRUUNK
AND THEN WE LAND THIS THING ON THE NEAREST ROOFTOP AND LEAVE THESE GUYS WEBBED UP FOR THE COPS.
AFTER WHICH I CAN GET TO WORK AT THE JOB I ACTUALLY GET PAID FOR.
HMM. PRIMITIVE TECHNOLOGY. SHOULDN'T BE TOO TOUGH A DEVICE TO LAND.
BUT THAT'S NOT THE PROBLEM. THE PROBLEM IS, WHAT JUST HAPPENED TO ME IN MIDAIR?
I FELT LIKE I...I...
DIED.
LIKE SOMEBODY KILLED ME.
WHAT'S THE OLD LINE? ABOUT WHISTLING ON SOMEONE'S GRAVE?
FELT LIKE SOMEONE PLAYED AN ENTIRE CONCERTO ON MINE.
EXCEPT HERE I AM, SAFE AND SOUND.
SO WHAT THE HELL CAUSED ME TO FEEL LIKE THAT?

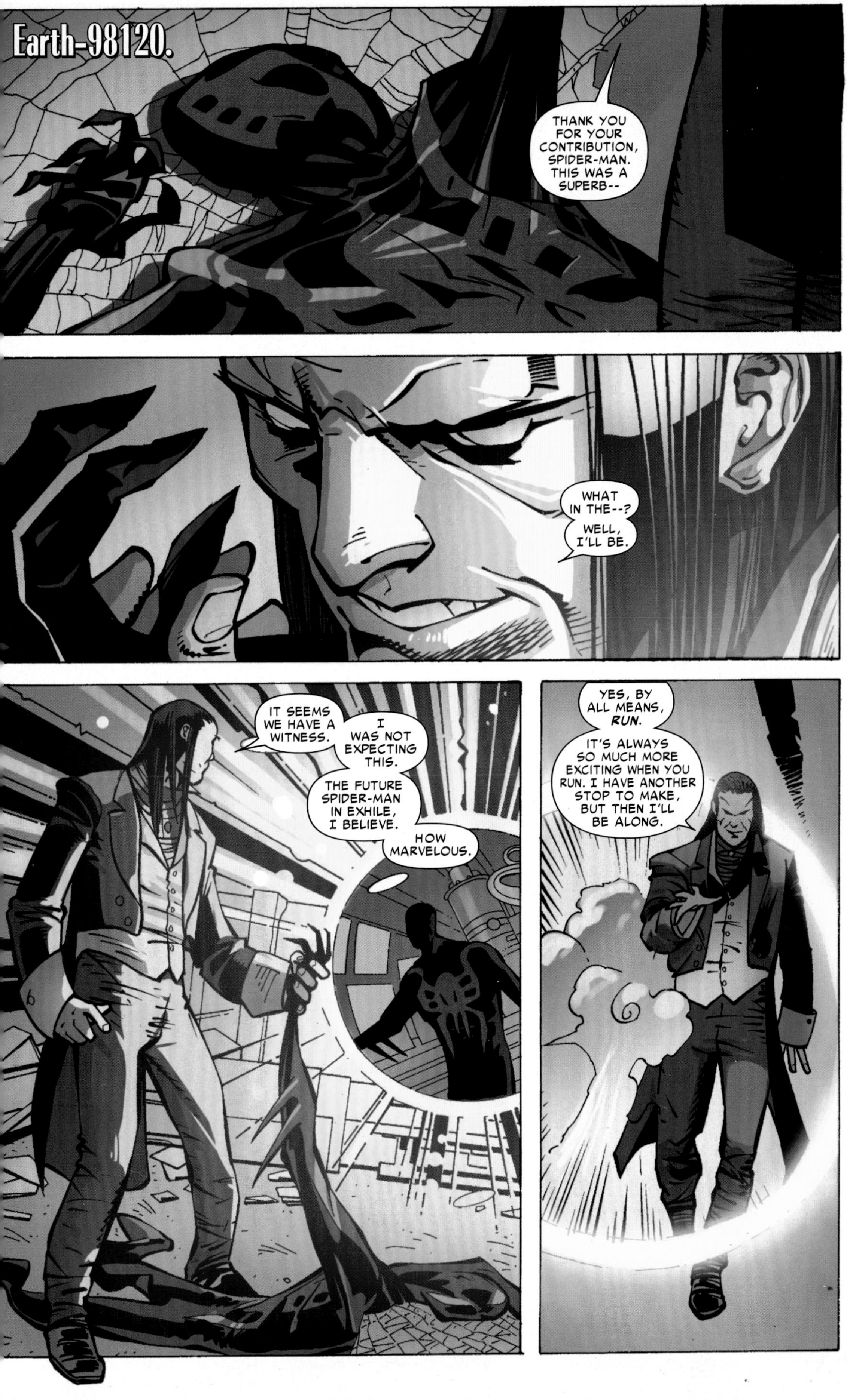
Earth-98120.
THANK YOU FOR YOUR CONTRIBUTION, SPIDER-MAN. THIS WAS A SUPERB--
WHAT IN THE--?
WELL, I'LL BE.
IT SEEMS WE HAVE A WITNESS.
I WAS NOT EXPECTING THIS.
THE FUTURE SPIDER-MAN IN EXHILE, I BELIEVE.
HOW MARVELOUS.
YES, BY ALL MEANS, ***RUN***.
IT'S ALWAYS SO MUCH MORE EXCITING WHEN YOU RUN. I HAVE ANOTHER STOP TO MAKE, BUT THEN I'LL BE ALONG.

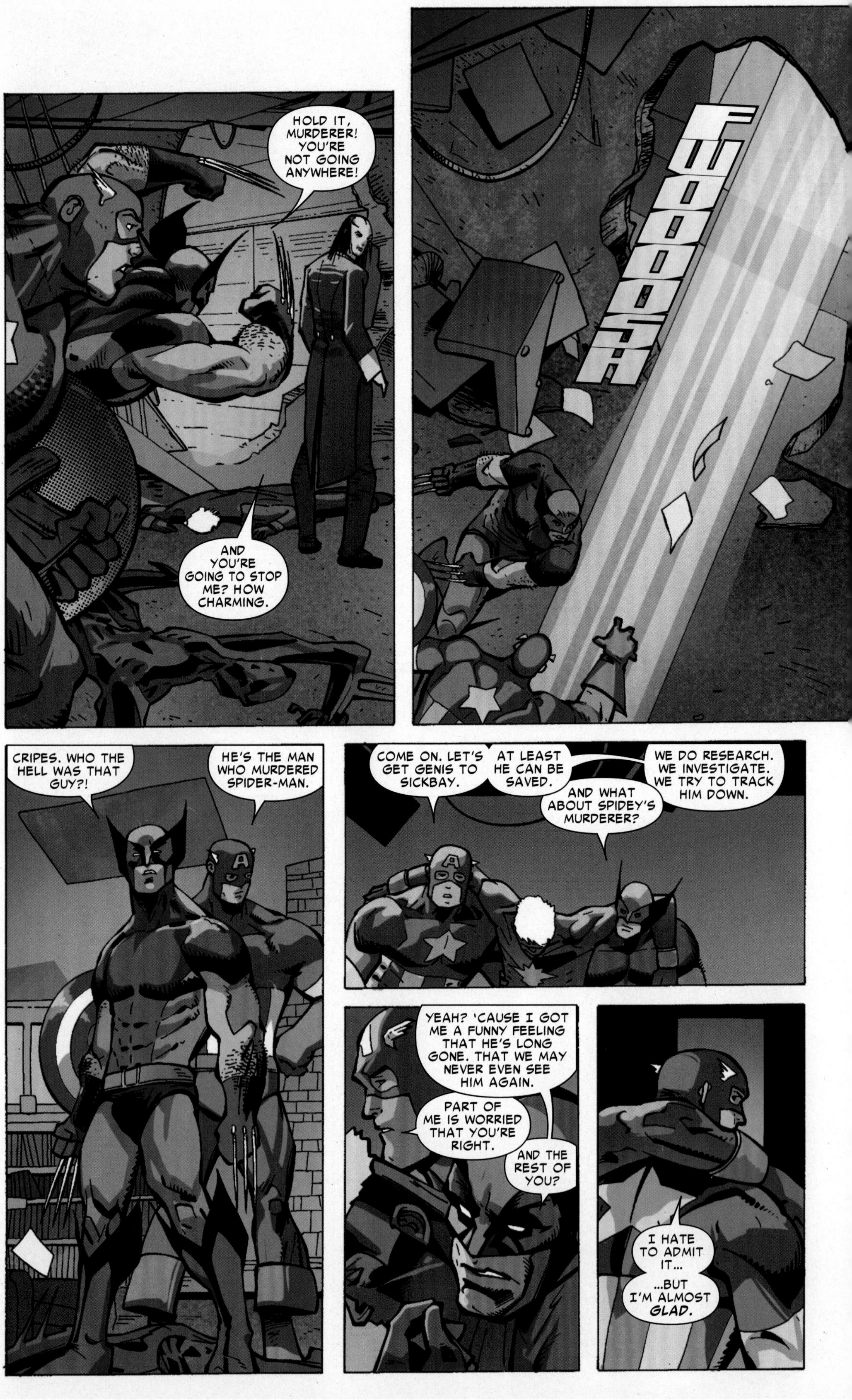
HOLD IT, MURDERER! YOU'RE NOT GOING ANYWHERE!
AND YOU'RE GOING TO STOP ME? HOW CHARMING.
FWOOOOSH
CRIPES. WHO THE HELL WAS THAT GUY?!
HE'S THE MAN WHO MURDERED SPIDER-MAN.
COME ON. LET'S GET GENIS TO SICKBAY.
AT LEAST HE CAN BE SAVED.
AND WHAT ABOUT SPIDEY'S MURDERER?
WE DO RESEARCH. WE INVESTIGATE. WE TRY TO TRACK HIM DOWN.
YEAH? 'CAUSE I GOT ME A FUNNY FEELING THAT HE'S LONG GONE. THAT WE MAY NEVER EVEN SEE HIM AGAIN.
PART OF ME IS WORRIED THAT YOU'RE RIGHT.
AND THE REST OF YOU?
I HATE TO ADMIT IT...
...BUT I'M ALMOST GLAD.

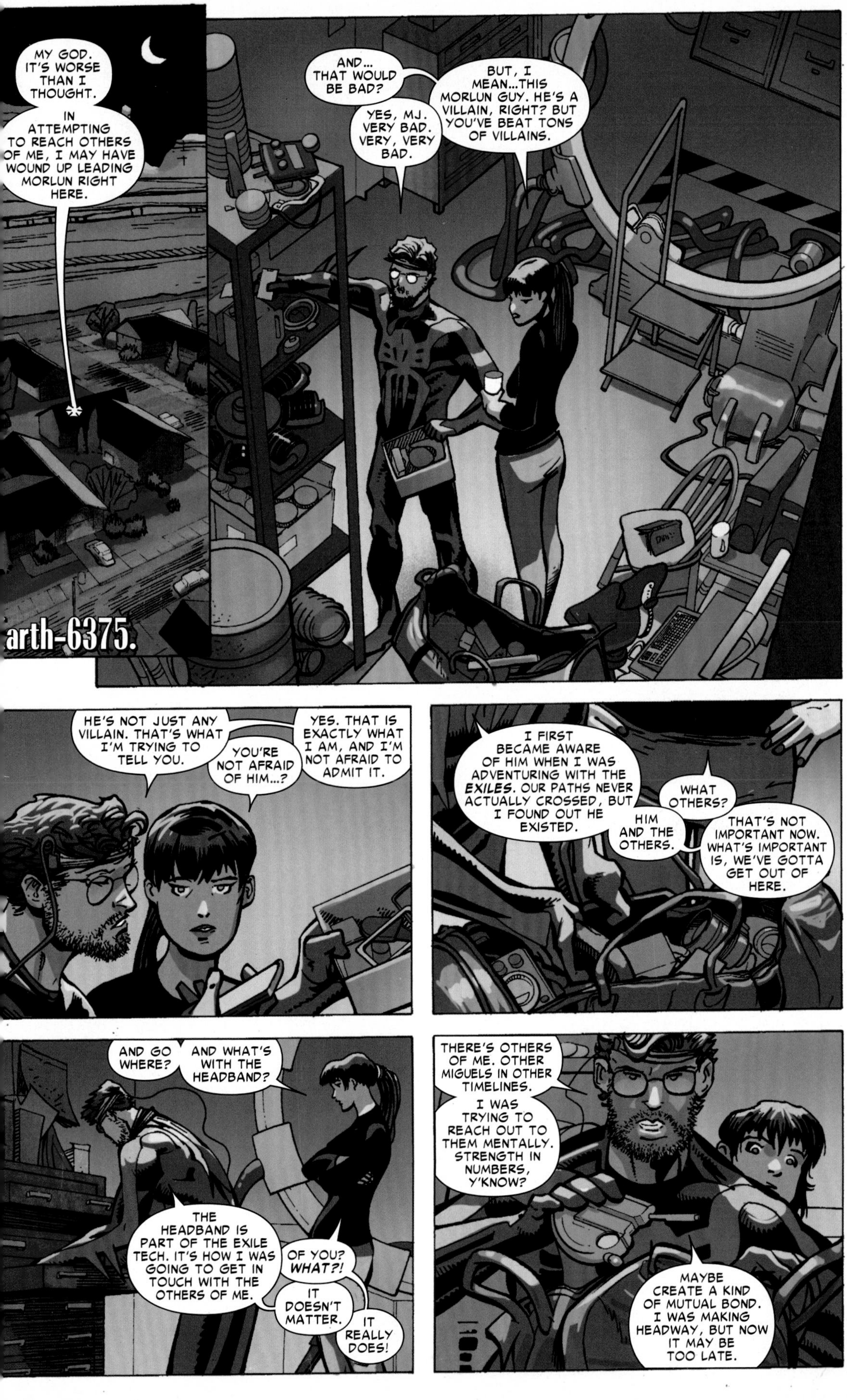
MY GOD. IT'S WORSE THAN I THOUGHT.
IN ATTEMPTING TO REACH OTHERS OF ME, I MAY HAVE WOUND UP LEADING MORLUN RIGHT HERE.
arth-6375.
AND... THAT WOULD BE BAD?
YES, MJ. VERY BAD. VERY, VERY BAD.
BUT, I MEAN...THIS MORLUN GUY. HE'S A VILLAIN, RIGHT? BUT YOU'VE BEAT TONS OF VILLAINS.
HE'S NOT JUST ANY VILLAIN. THAT'S WHAT I'M TRYING TO TELL YOU.
YOU'RE NOT AFRAID OF HIM...?
YES. THAT IS EXACTLY WHAT I AM, AND I'M NOT AFRAID TO ADMIT IT.
I FIRST BECAME AWARE OF HIM WHEN I WAS ADVENTURING WITH THE *EXILES*. OUR PATHS NEVER ACTUALLY CROSSED, BUT I FOUND OUT HE EXISTED.
HIM AND THE OTHERS.
WHAT OTHERS?
THAT'S NOT IMPORTANT NOW. WHAT'S IMPORTANT IS, WE'VE GOTTA GET OUT OF HERE.
AND GO WHERE?
AND WHAT'S WITH THE HEADBAND?
THE HEADBAND IS PART OF THE EXILE TECH. IT'S HOW I WAS GOING TO GET IN TOUCH WITH THE OTHERS OF ME.
OF YOU? *WHAT?!*
IT DOESN'T MATTER.
IT REALLY DOES!
THERE'S OTHERS OF ME. OTHER MIGUELS IN OTHER TIMELINES.
I WAS TRYING TO REACH OUT TO THEM MENTALLY. STRENGTH IN NUMBERS, Y'KNOW?
MAYBE CREATE A KIND OF MUTUAL BOND. I WAS MAKING HEADWAY, BUT NOW IT MAY BE TOO LATE.

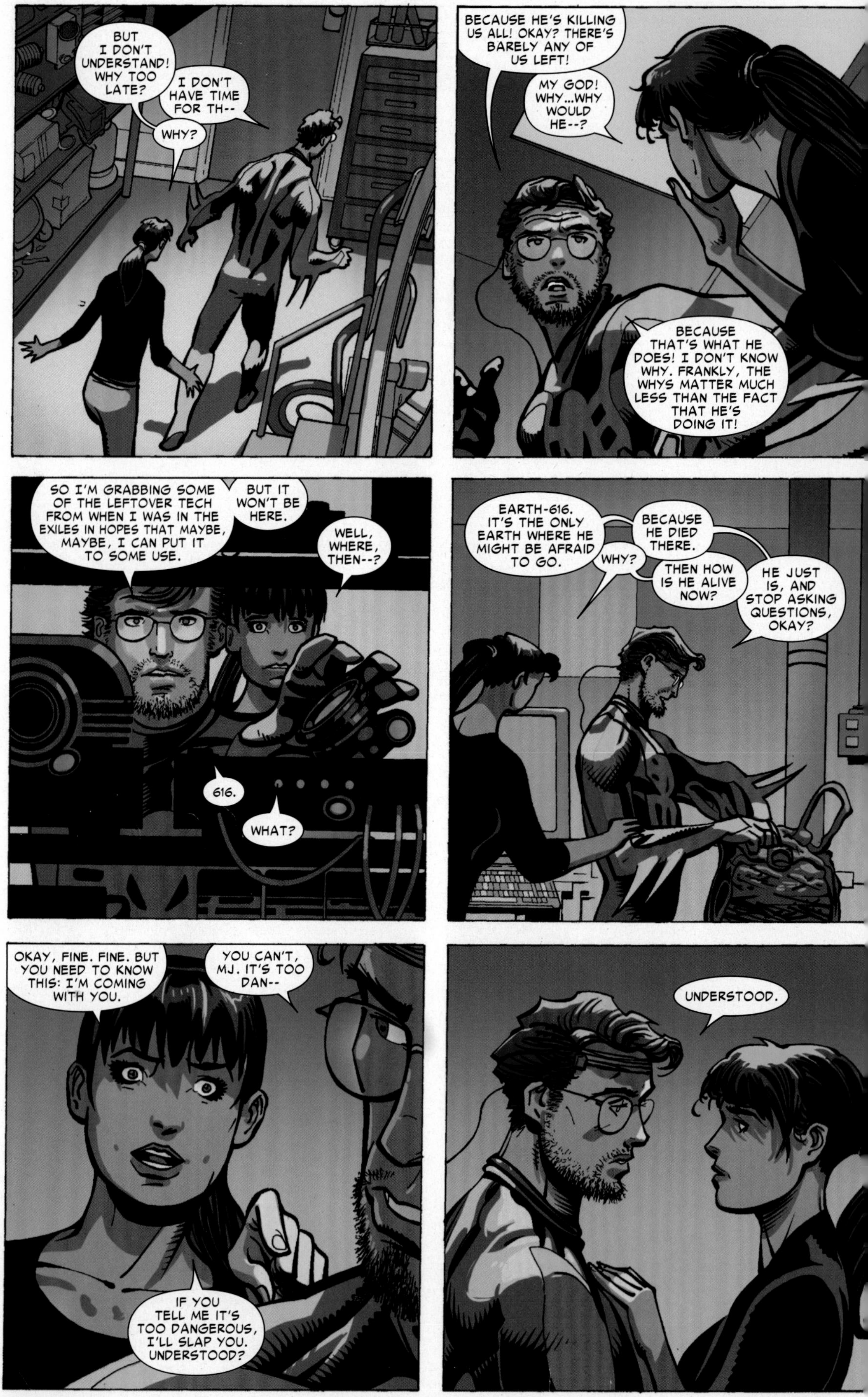
BUT I DON'T UNDERSTAND! WHY TOO LATE?
I DON'T HAVE TIME FOR TH--
WHY?
BECAUSE HE'S KILLING US ALL! OKAY? THERE'S BARELY ANY OF US LEFT!
MY GOD! WHY...WHY WOULD HE--?
BECAUSE THAT'S WHAT HE DOES! I DON'T KNOW WHY. FRANKLY, THE WHYS MATTER MUCH LESS THAN THE FACT THAT HE'S DOING IT!
SO I'M GRABBING SOME OF THE LEFTOVER TECH FROM WHEN I WAS IN THE EXILES IN HOPES THAT MAYBE, MAYBE, I CAN PUT IT TO SOME USE.
BUT IT WON'T BE HERE.
WELL, WHERE, THEN--?
616.
WHAT?
EARTH-616. IT'S THE ONLY EARTH WHERE HE MIGHT BE AFRAID TO GO.
WHY?
BECAUSE HE DIED THERE.
THEN HOW IS HE ALIVE NOW?
HE JUST IS, AND STOP ASKING QUESTIONS, OKAY?
OKAY, FINE. FINE. BUT YOU NEED TO KNOW THIS: I'M COMING WITH YOU.
YOU CAN'T, MJ. IT'S TOO DAN--
IF YOU TELL ME IT'S TOO DANGEROUS, I'LL SLAP YOU. UNDERSTOOD?
UNDERSTOOD.

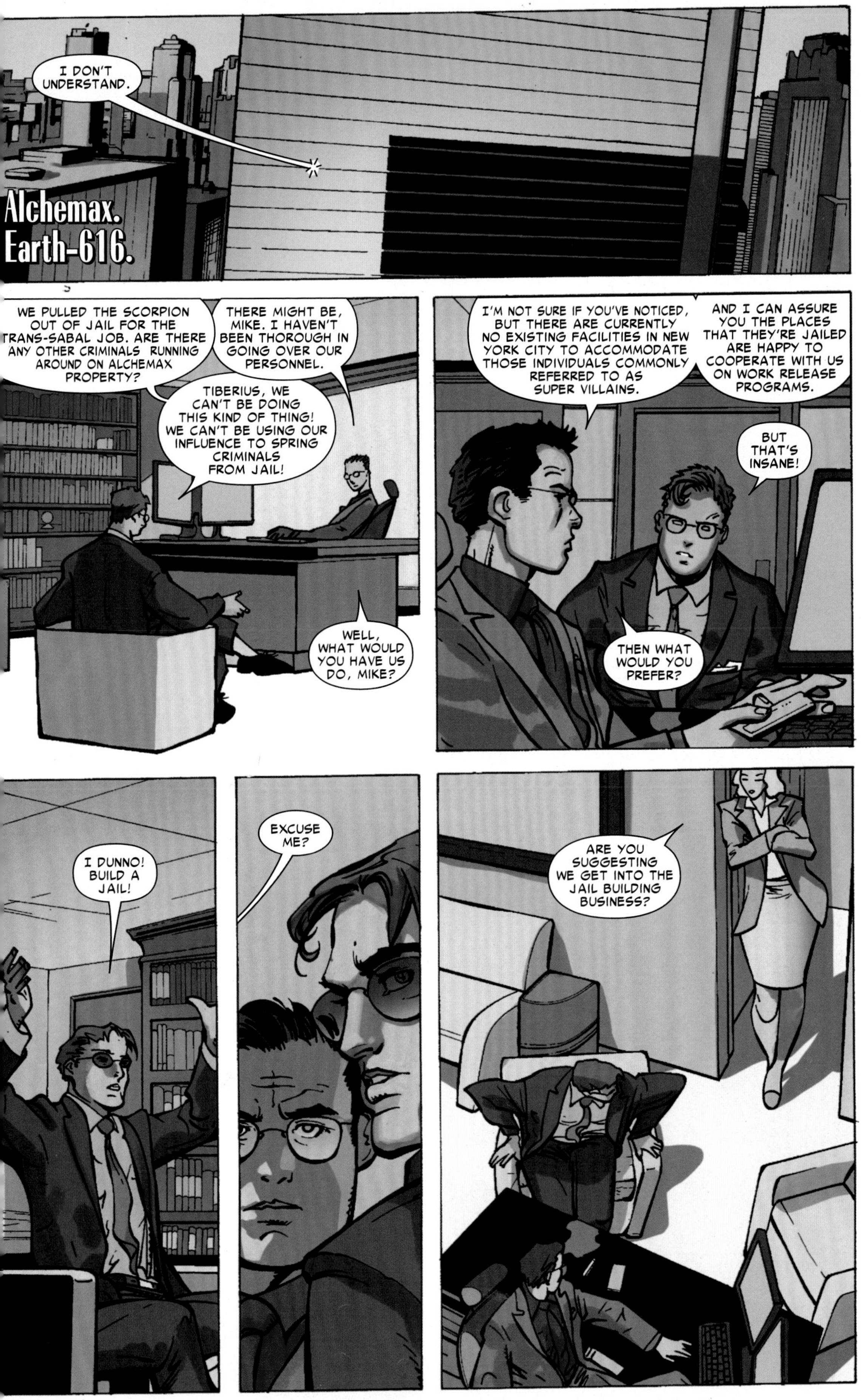
I DON'T UNDERSTAND.
Alchemax. Earth-616.
WE PULLED THE SCORPION OUT OF JAIL FOR THE TRANS-SABAL JOB. ARE THERE ANY OTHER CRIMINALS RUNNING AROUND ON ALCHEMAX PROPERTY?
THERE MIGHT BE, MIKE. I HAVEN'T BEEN THOROUGH IN GOING OVER OUR PERSONNEL.
TIBERIUS, WE CAN'T BE DOING THIS KIND OF THING! WE CAN'T BE USING OUR INFLUENCE TO SPRING CRIMINALS FROM JAIL!
WELL, WHAT WOULD YOU HAVE US DO, MIKE?
I'M NOT SURE IF YOU'VE NOTICED, BUT THERE ARE CURRENTLY NO EXISTING FACILITIES IN NEW YORK CITY TO ACCOMMODATE THOSE INDIVIDUALS COMMONLY REFERRED TO AS SUPER VILLAINS.
AND I CAN ASSURE YOU THE PLACES THAT THEY'RE JAILED ARE HAPPY TO COOPERATE WITH US ON WORK RELEASE PROGRAMS.
BUT THAT'S INSANE!
THEN WHAT WOULD YOU PREFER?
I DUNNO! BUILD A JAIL!
EXCUSE ME?
ARE YOU SUGGESTING WE GET INTO THE JAIL BUILDING BUSINESS?

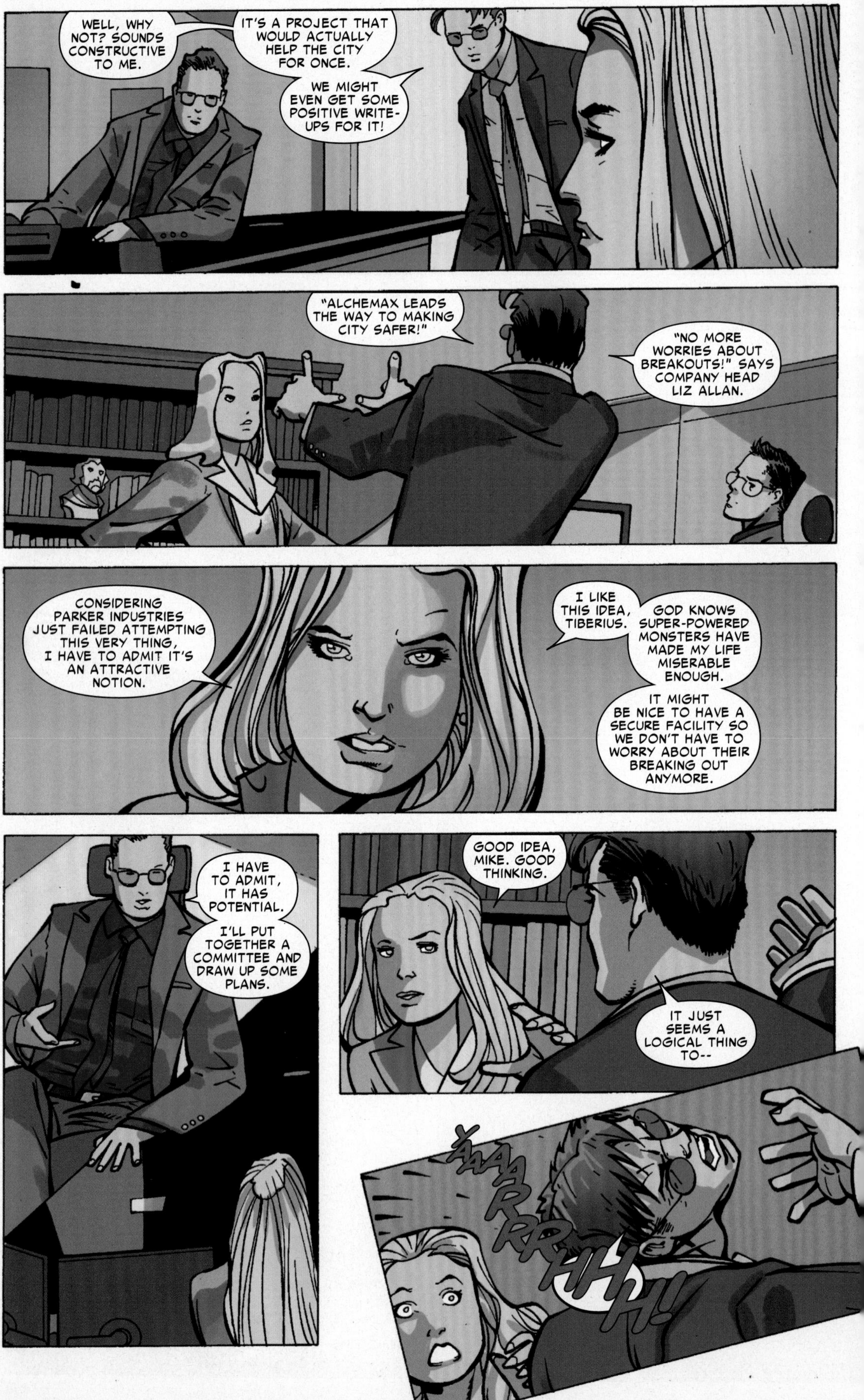
WELL, WHY NOT? SOUNDS CONSTRUCTIVE TO ME.
IT'S A PROJECT THAT WOULD ACTUALLY HELP THE CITY FOR ONCE.
WE MIGHT EVEN GET SOME POSITIVE WRITE-UPS FOR IT!
"ALCHEMAX LEADS THE WAY TO MAKING CITY SAFER!"
"NO MORE WORRIES ABOUT BREAKOUTS!" SAYS COMPANY HEAD LIZ ALLAN.
CONSIDERING PARKER INDUSTRIES JUST FAILED ATTEMPTING THIS VERY THING, I HAVE TO ADMIT IT'S AN ATTRACTIVE NOTION.
I LIKE THIS IDEA, TIBERIUS.
GOD KNOWS SUPER-POWERED MONSTERS HAVE MADE MY LIFE MISERABLE ENOUGH.
IT MIGHT BE NICE TO HAVE A SECURE FACILITY SO WE DON'T HAVE TO WORRY ABOUT THEIR BREAKING OUT ANYMORE.
I HAVE TO ADMIT, IT HAS POTENTIAL.
I'LL PUT TOGETHER A COMMITTEE AND DRAW UP SOME PLANS.
GOOD IDEA, MIKE. GOOD THINKING.
IT JUST SEEMS A LOGICAL THING TO--
YAAARRRHHH!

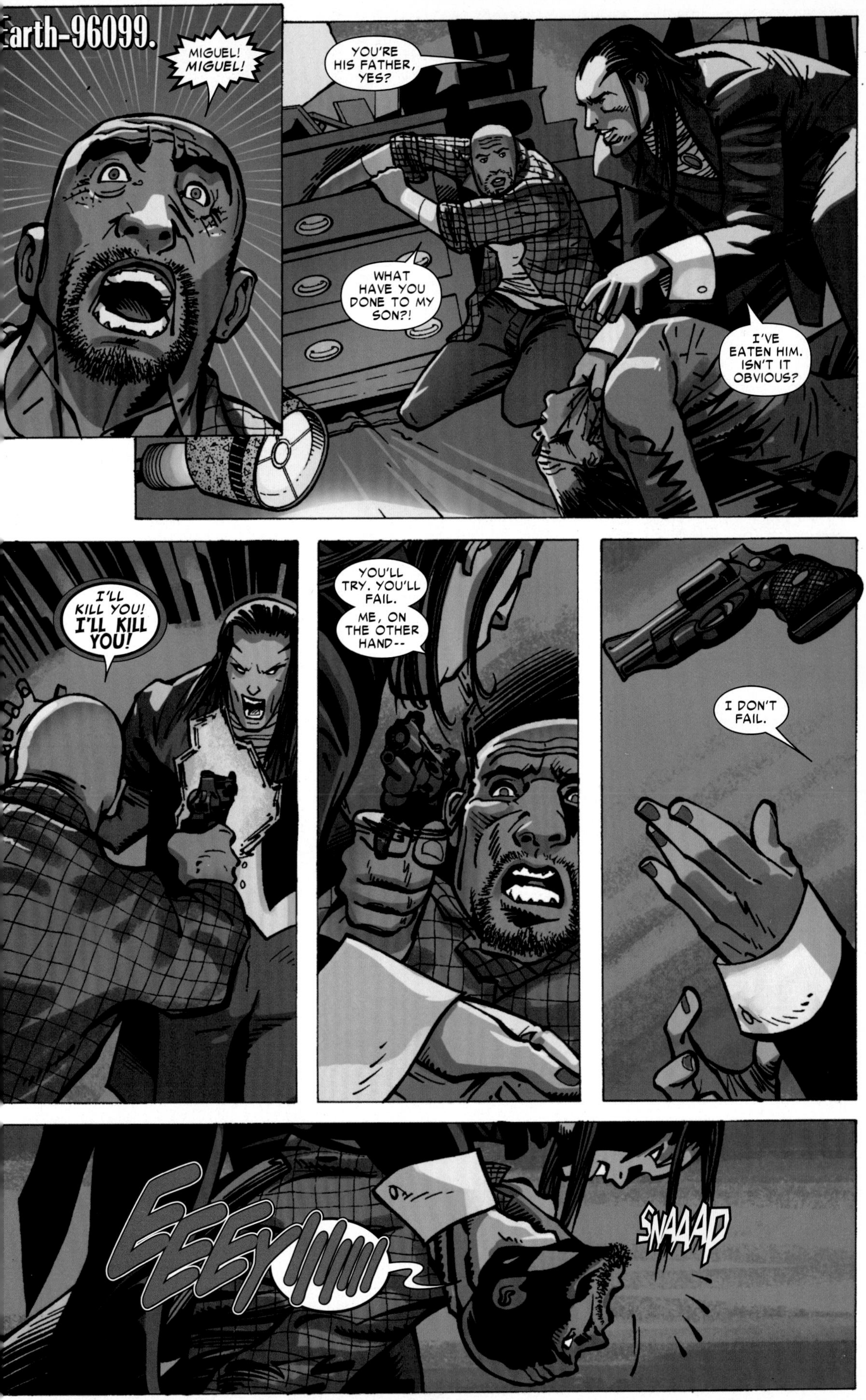
Earth-96099.
MIGUEL! MIGUEL!
YOU'RE HIS FATHER, YES?
WHAT HAVE YOU DONE TO MY SON?!
I'VE EATEN HIM. ISN'T IT OBVIOUS?
I'LL KILL YOU! I'LL KILL YOU!
YOU'LL TRY. YOU'LL FAIL.
ME, ON THE OTHER HAND--
I DON'T FAIL.
EEEYIIIIIII
SNAAAP

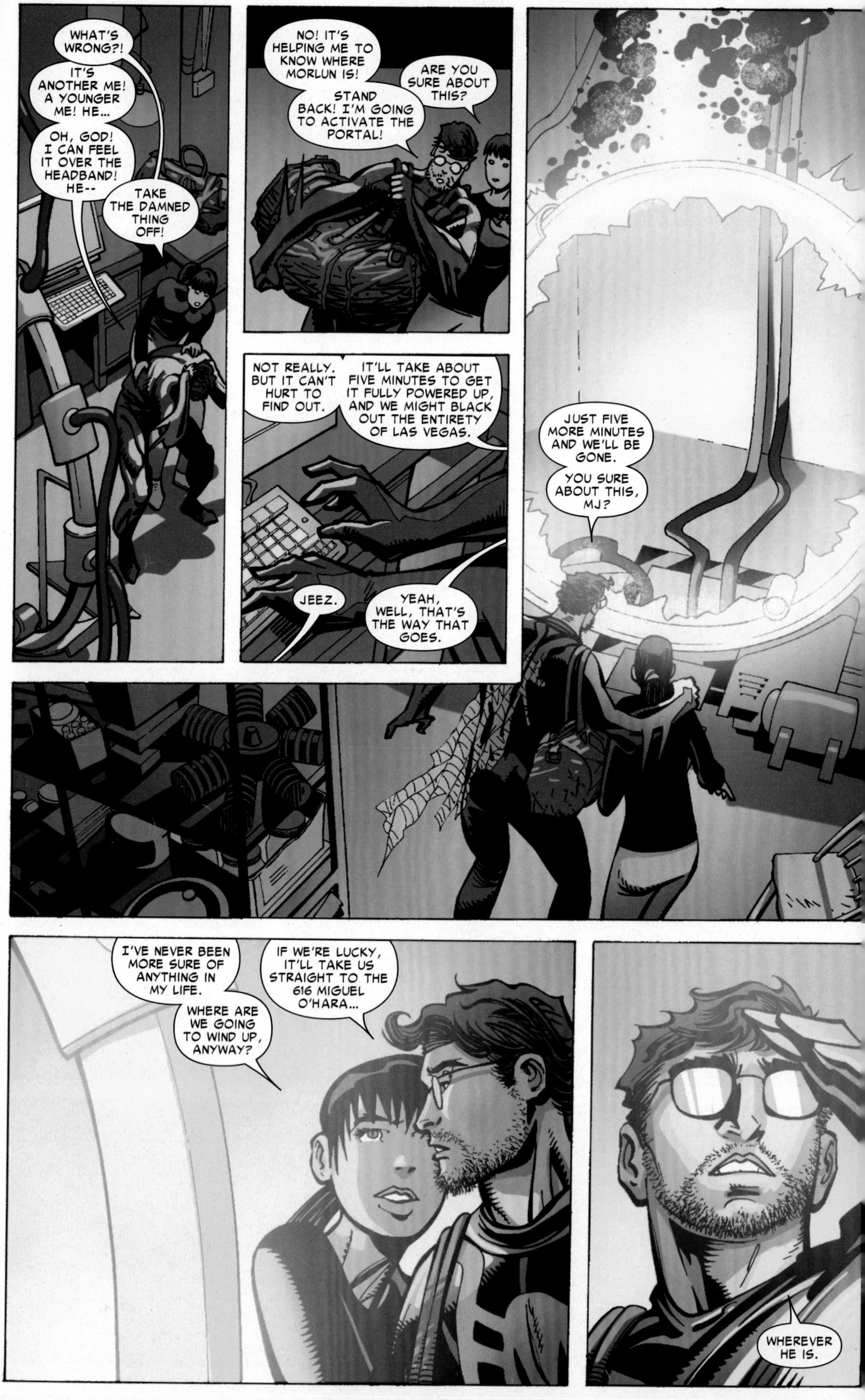
WHAT'S WRONG?!
IT'S ANOTHER ME! A YOUNGER ME! HE...
OH, GOD! I CAN FEEL IT OVER THE HEADBAND! HE--
TAKE THE DAMNED THING OFF!
NO! IT'S HELPING ME TO KNOW WHERE MORLUN IS!
ARE YOU SURE ABOUT THIS?
STAND BACK! I'M GOING TO ACTIVATE THE PORTAL!
NOT REALLY. BUT IT CAN'T HURT TO FIND OUT.
IT'LL TAKE ABOUT FIVE MINUTES TO GET IT FULLY POWERED UP, AND WE MIGHT BLACK OUT THE ENTIRETY OF LAS VEGAS.
JEEZ.
YEAH, WELL, THAT'S THE WAY THAT GOES.
JUST FIVE MORE MINUTES AND WE'LL BE GONE.
YOU SURE ABOUT THIS, MJ?
I'VE NEVER BEEN MORE SURE OF ANYTHING IN MY LIFE.
WHERE ARE WE GOING TO WIND UP, ANYWAY?
IF WE'RE LUCKY, IT'LL TAKE US STRAIGHT TO THE 616 MIGUEL O'HARA...
WHEREVER HE IS.

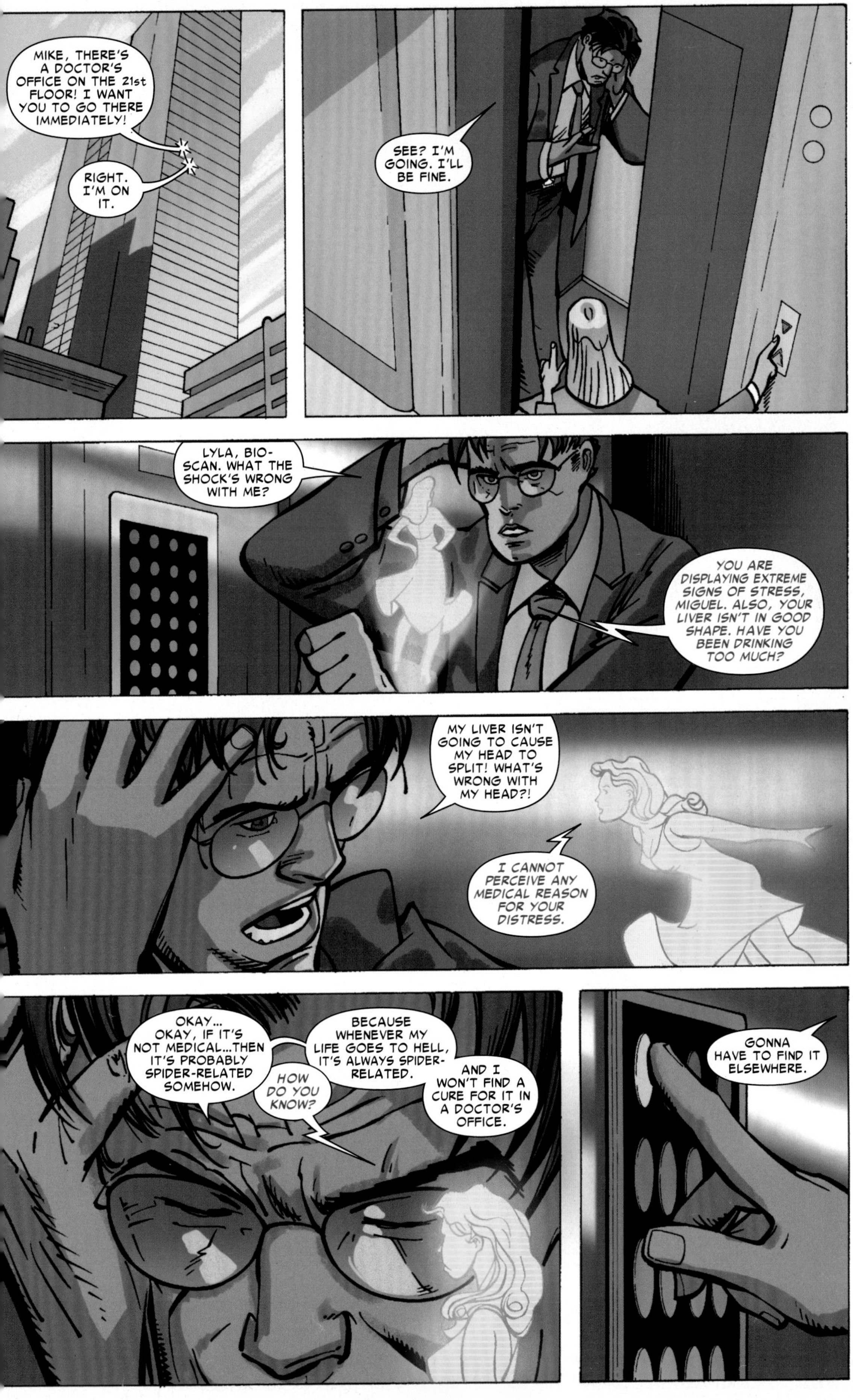
MIKE, THERE'S A DOCTOR'S OFFICE ON THE 21st FLOOR! I WANT YOU TO GO THERE IMMEDIATELY!
RIGHT. I'M ON IT.
SEE? I'M GOING. I'LL BE FINE.
LYLA, BIO-SCAN. WHAT THE SHOCK'S WRONG WITH ME?
YOU ARE DISPLAYING EXTREME SIGNS OF STRESS, MIGUEL. ALSO, YOUR LIVER ISN'T IN GOOD SHAPE. HAVE YOU BEEN DRINKING TOO MUCH?
MY LIVER ISN'T GOING TO CAUSE MY HEAD TO SPLIT! WHAT'S WRONG WITH MY HEAD?!
I CANNOT PERCEIVE ANY MEDICAL REASON FOR YOUR DISTRESS.
OKAY... OKAY, IF IT'S NOT MEDICAL...THEN IT'S PROBABLY SPIDER-RELATED SOMEHOW.
HOW DO YOU KNOW?
BECAUSE WHENEVER MY LIFE GOES TO HELL, IT'S ALWAYS SPIDER-RELATED.
AND I WON'T FIND A CURE FOR IT IN A DOCTOR'S OFFICE.
GONNA HAVE TO FIND IT ELSEWHERE.

LOSE THE CLOTHING HOLOGRAM.

YES, MIGUEL.

NOW WHAT?!

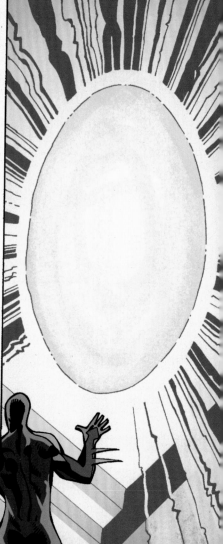

WHAT THE SHOCK IS THAT?!

IT APPEARS TO BE AN ENERGY APERTURE OF SOME SORT.

THEN WHY DID YOU ASK?

I KNOW THAT!

I WASN'T... OH, NEVER MIND.

IS THAT--? THAT'S--

IT'S ME! I DID IT! I--

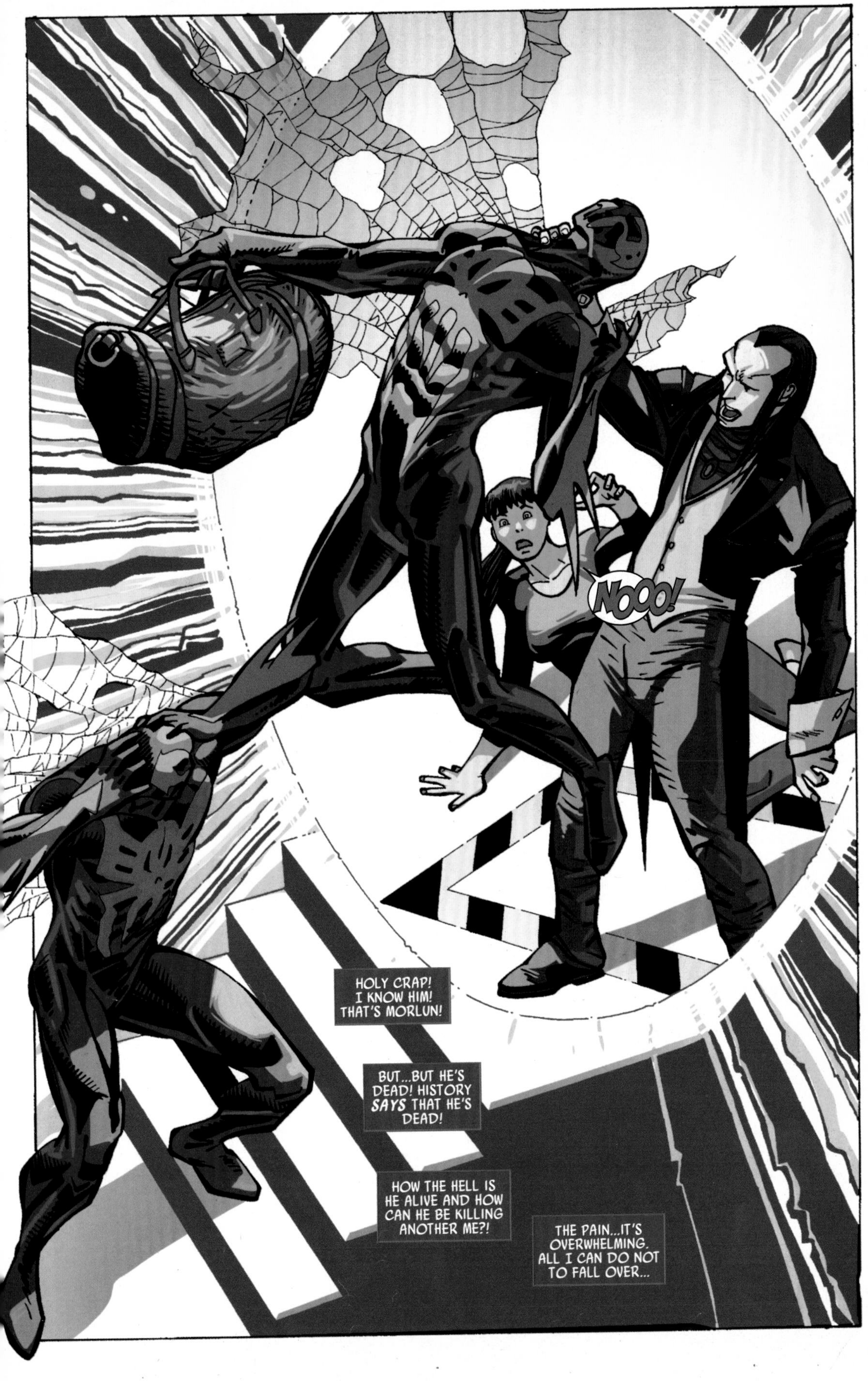
NOOO!
HOLY CRAP! I KNOW HIM! THAT'S MORLUN!
BUT...BUT HE'S DEAD! HISTORY *SAYS* THAT HE'S DEAD!
HOW THE HELL IS HE ALIVE AND HOW CAN HE BE KILLING ANOTHER ME?!
THE PAIN...IT'S OVERWHELMING. ALL I CAN DO NOT TO FALL OVER...

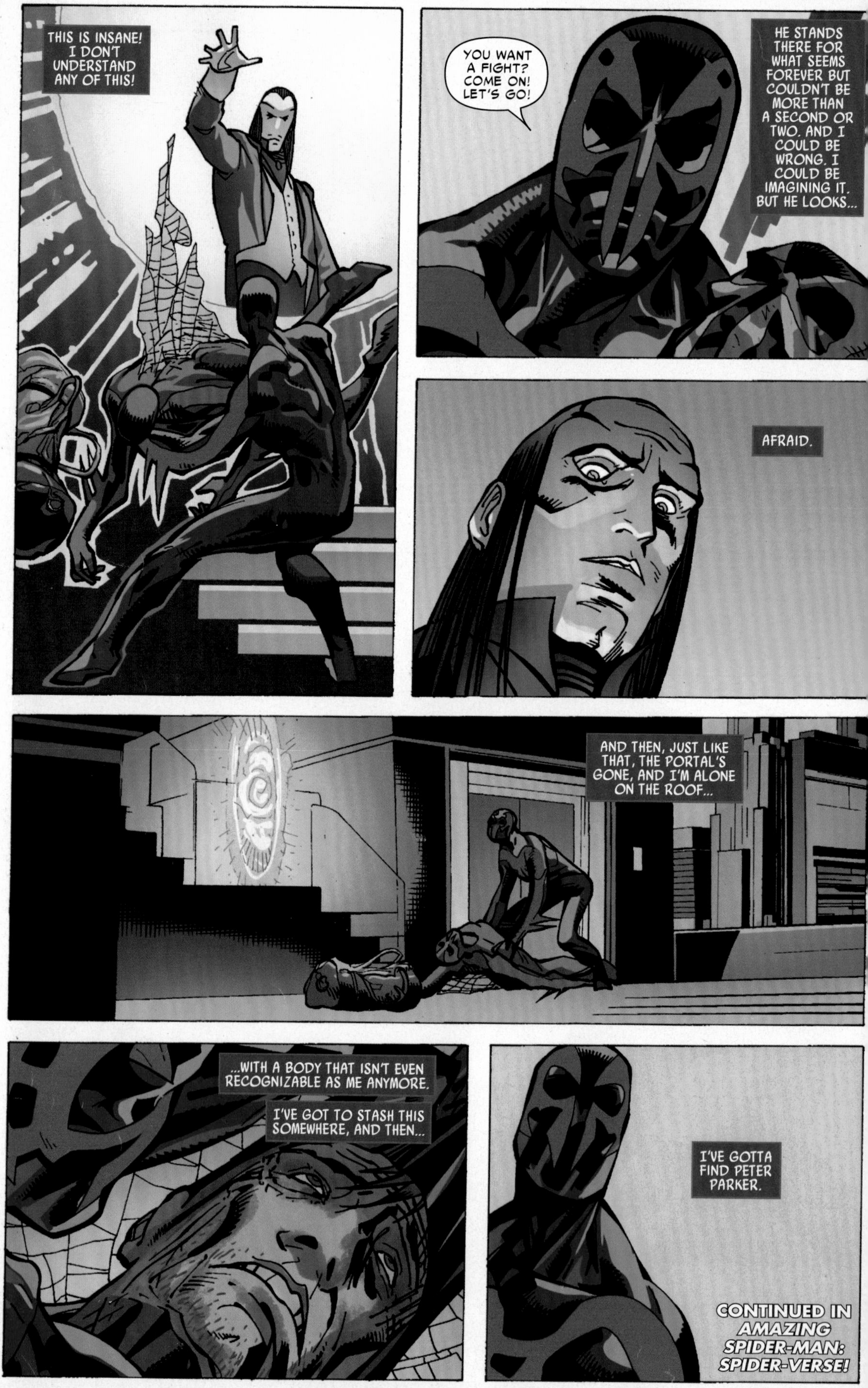
THIS IS INSANE! I DON'T UNDERSTAND ANY OF THIS!
YOU WANT A FIGHT? COME ON! LET'S GO!
HE STANDS THERE FOR WHAT SEEMS FOREVER BUT COULDN'T BE MORE THAN A SECOND OR TWO. AND I COULD BE WRONG. I COULD BE IMAGINING IT. BUT HE LOOKS...
AFRAID.
AND THEN, JUST LIKE THAT, THE PORTAL'S GONE, AND I'M ALONE ON THE ROOF...
...WITH A BODY THAT ISN'T EVEN RECOGNIZABLE AS ME ANYMORE.
I'VE GOT TO STASH THIS SOMEWHERE, AND THEN...
I'VE GOTTA FIND PETER PARKER.
CONTINUED IN AMAZING SPIDER-MAN: SPIDER-VERSE!

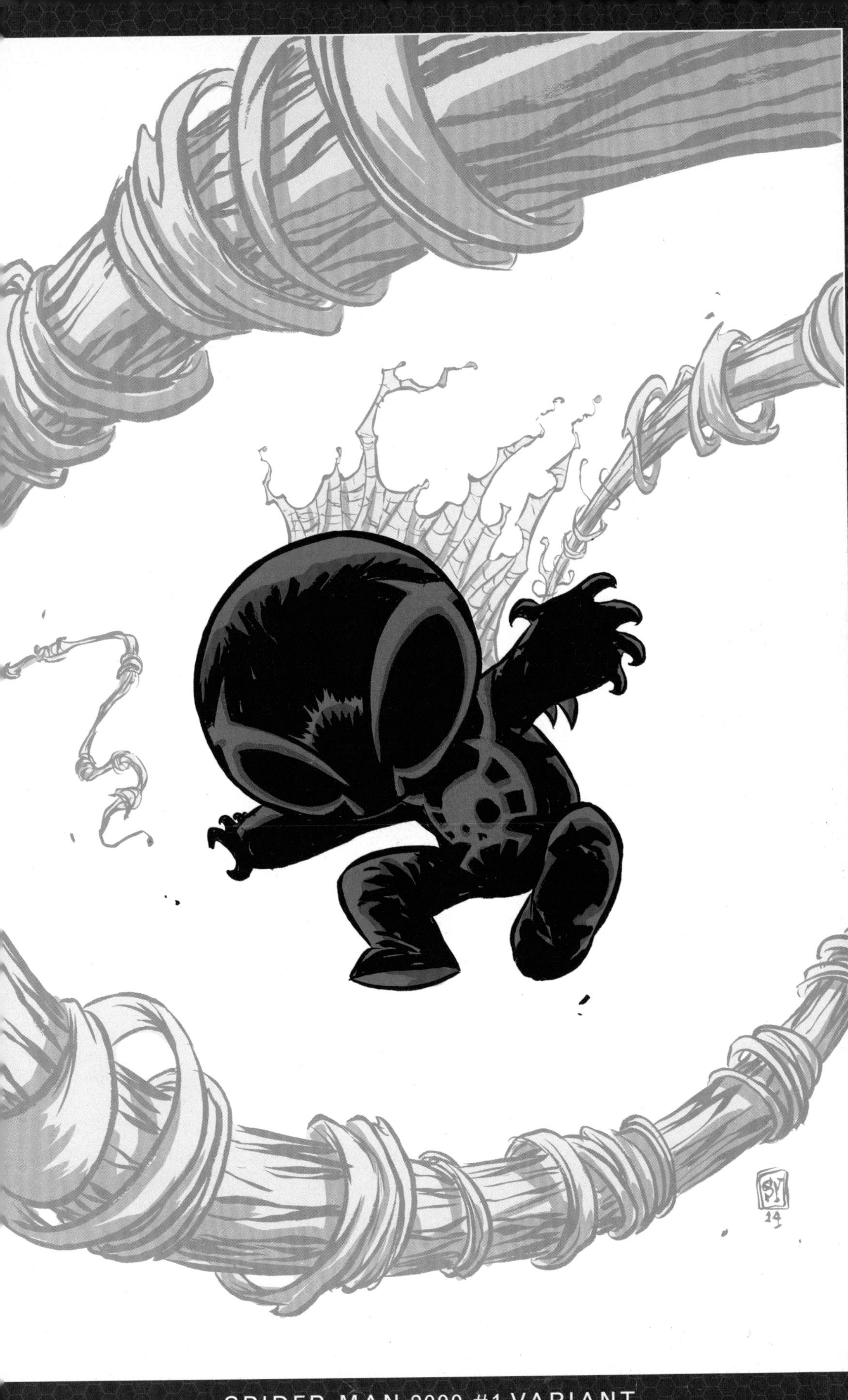

SPIDER-MAN 2099 #1 VARIANT
BY SKOTTIE YOUNG

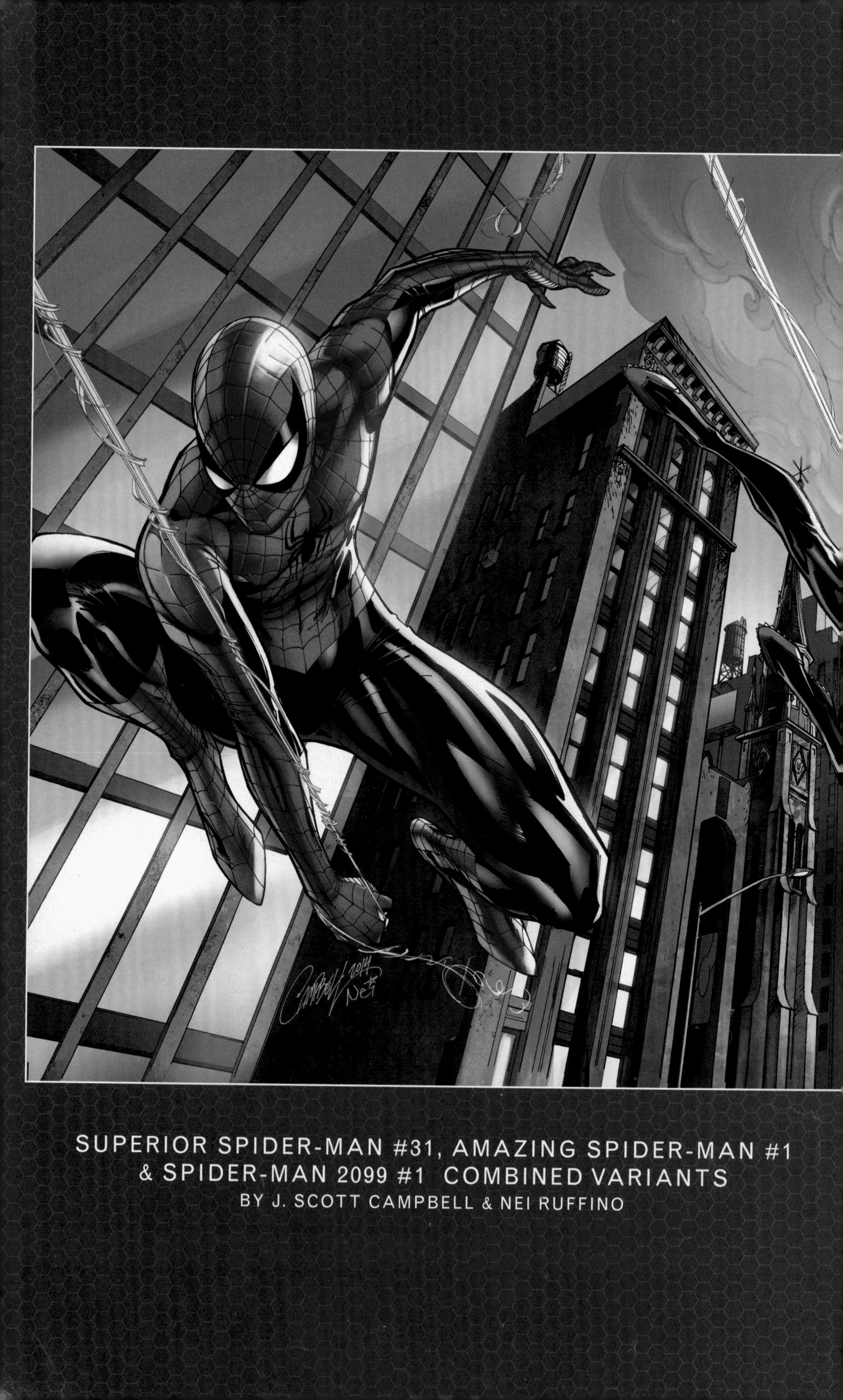

SUPERIOR SPIDER-MAN #31, AMAZING SPIDER-MAN #1
& SPIDER-MAN 2099 #1 COMBINED VARIANTS
BY J. SCOTT CAMPBELL & NEI RUFFINO

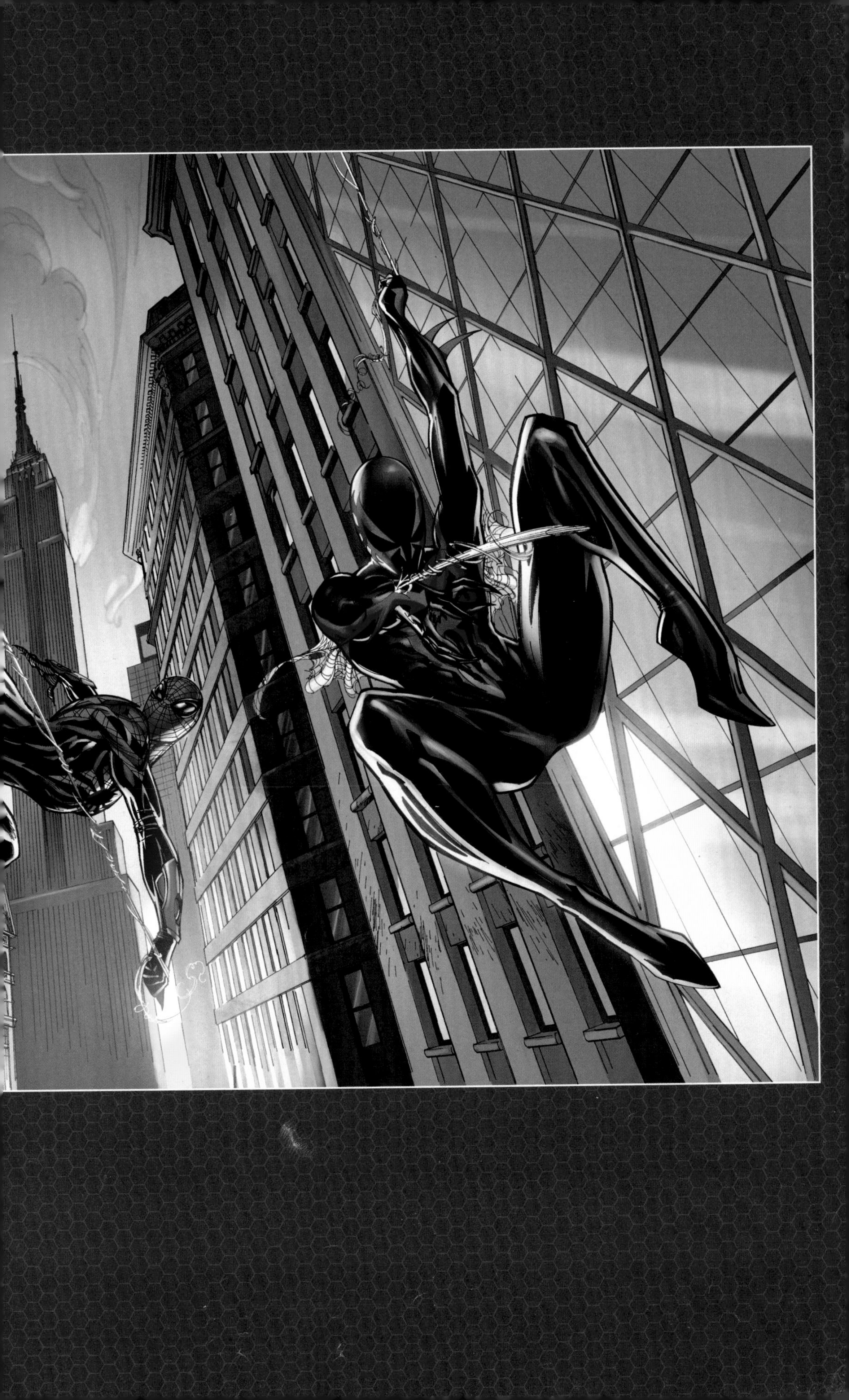

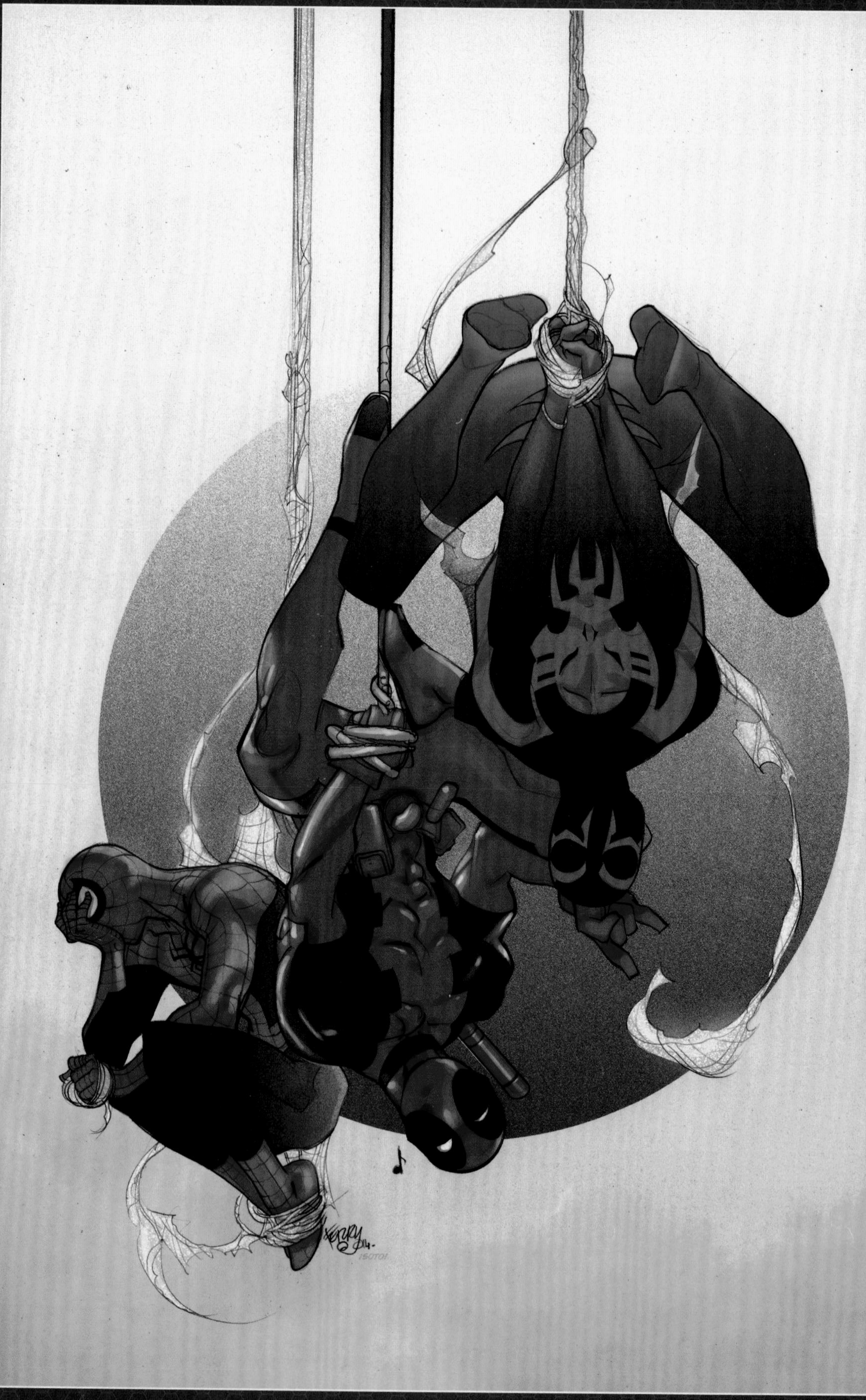

SPIDER-MAN 2099 #1 VARIANT
BY PASQUAL FERRY & SOTOCOLOR

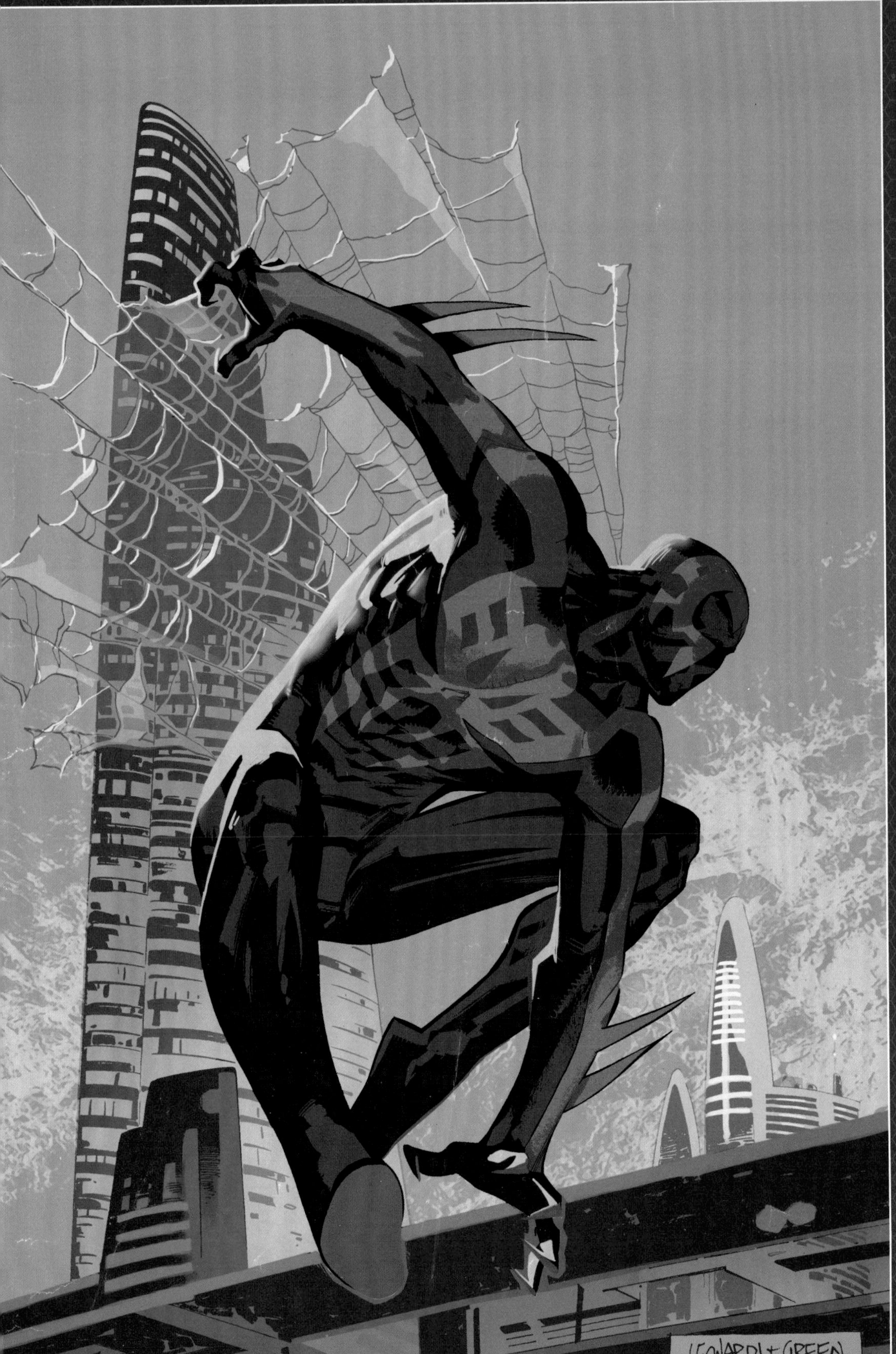
LEONARDI + GREEN
ANTONIO

SPIDER-MAN 2099 #1 VARIANT
BY RICK LEONARDI, DAN GREEN & ANTONIO FABELA

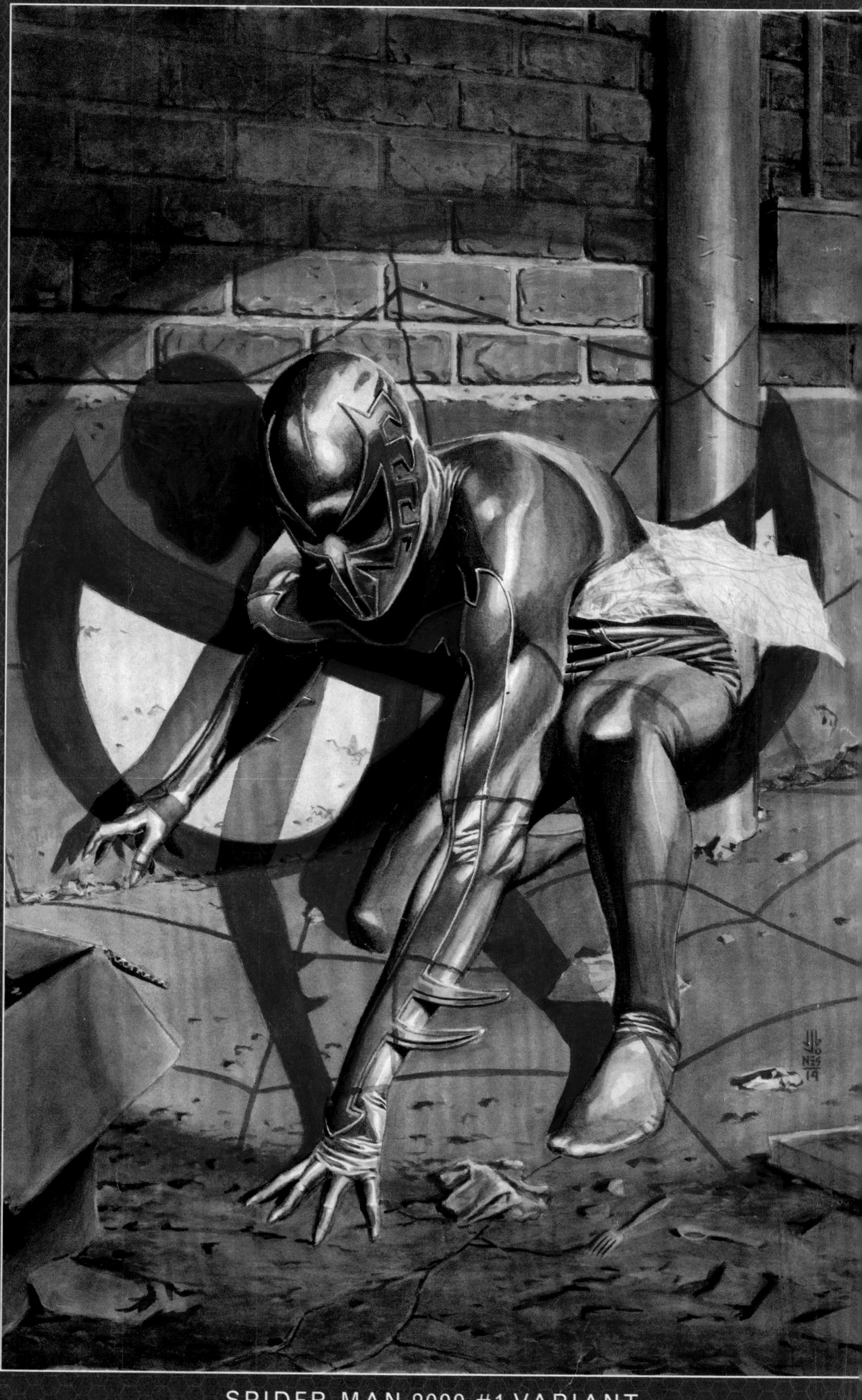

SPIDER-MAN 2099 #1 VARIANT
BY J.G. JONES

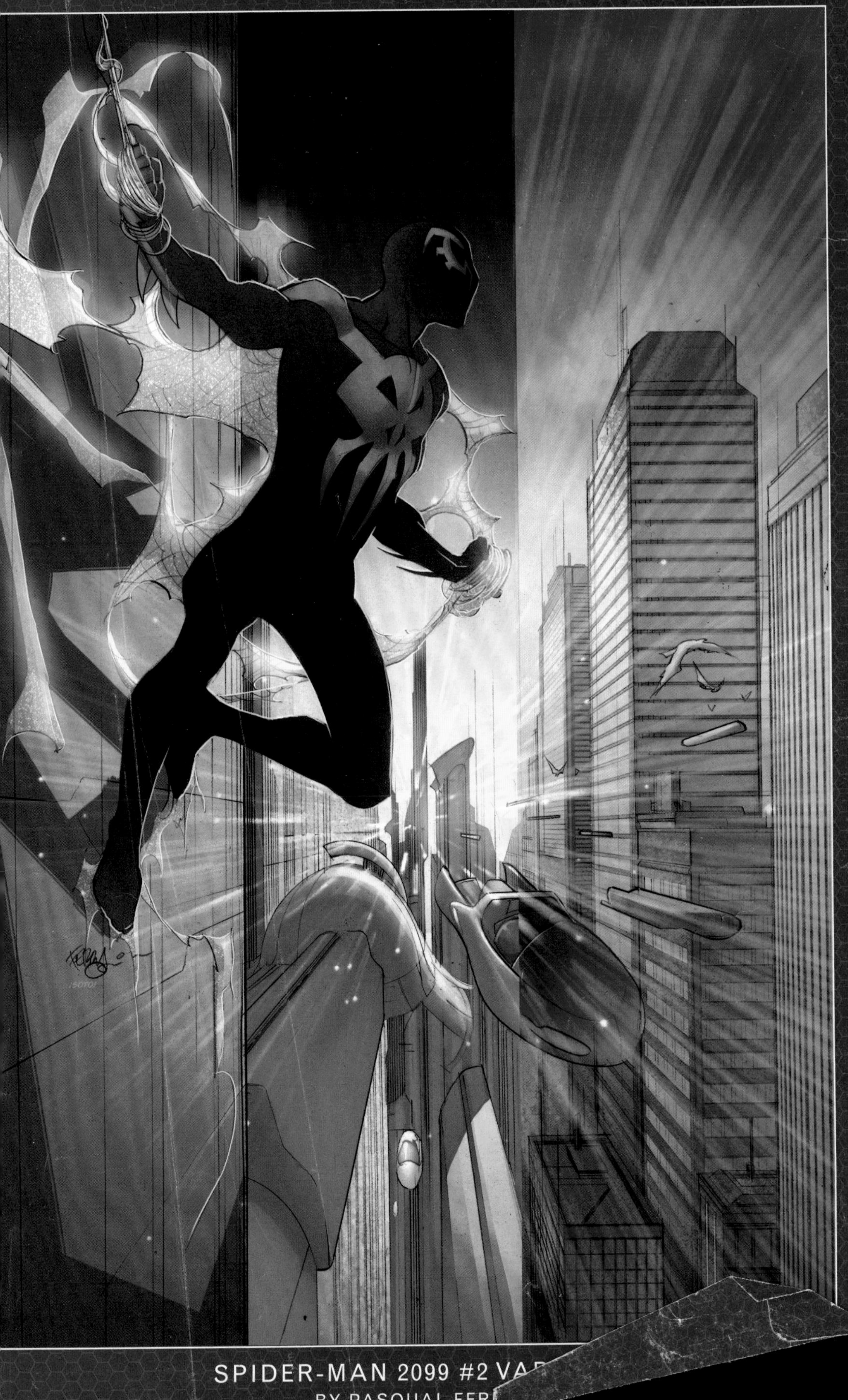

SPIDER-MAN 2099 #2 VA
BY PASQUAL FER

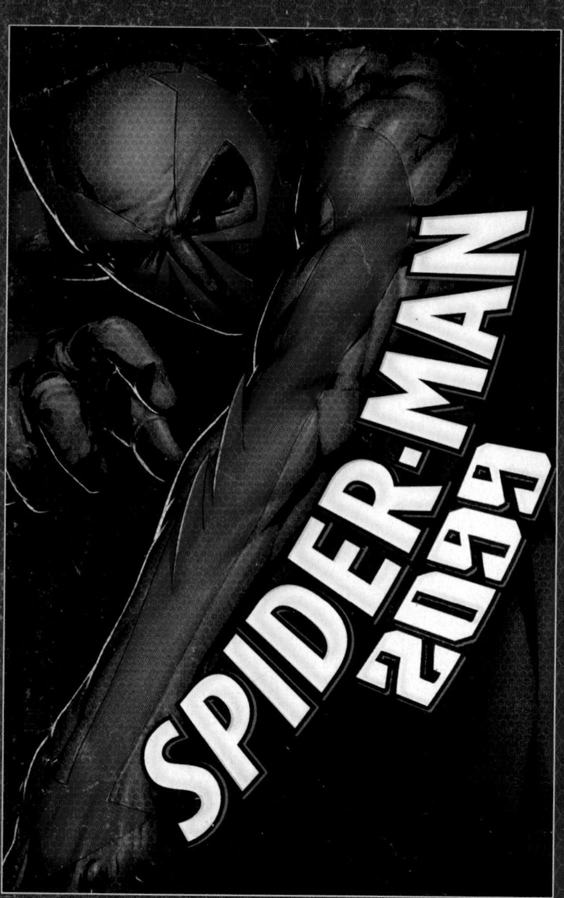
SPIDER-MAN
2099

SPIDER-MAN 2099 #3 VARIANT
BY JOHN TYLER CHRISTOPHER

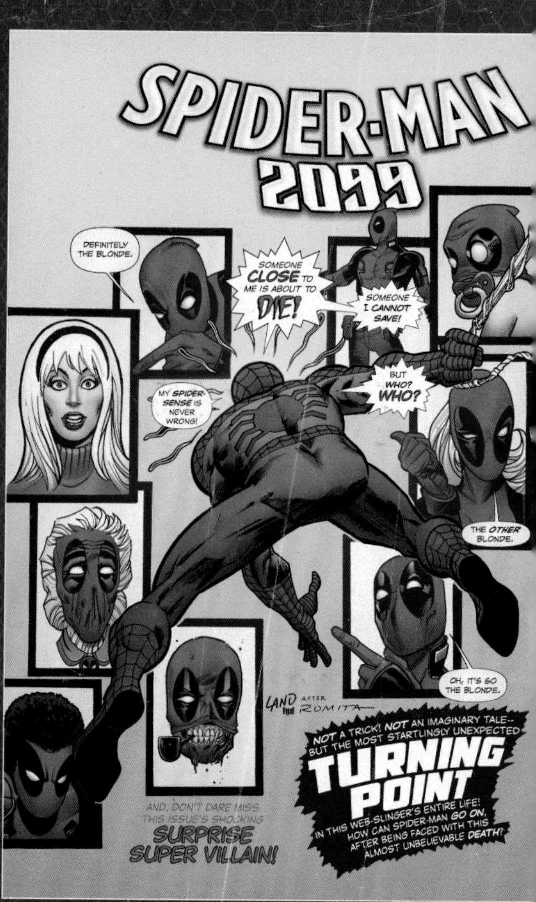
SPIDER-MAN
2099
DEFINITELY THE BLONDE.
SOMEONE CLOSE TO ME IS ABOUT TO DIE!
SOMEONE I CANNOT SAVE!
MY SPIDER-SENSE IS NEVER WRONG!
BUT WHO? WHO?
THE OTHER BLONDE.
OH, IT'S SO THE BLONDE.
LAND AFTER ROMITA
NOT A TRICK! NOT AN IMAGINARY TALE-- BUT THE MOST STARTLINGLY UNEXPECTED
TURNING POINT
IN THIS WEB-SLINGER'S ENTIRE LIFE! HOW CAN SPIDER-MAN GO ON, AFTER BEING FACED WITH THIS ALMOST UNBELIEVABLE DEATH?
AND, DON'T DARE MISS THIS ISSUE'S SHOCKING
SURPRISE SUPER VILLAIN!

SPIDER-MAN 2099 #4 VARIANT
BY GREG LAND & FRANK D'ARMATA

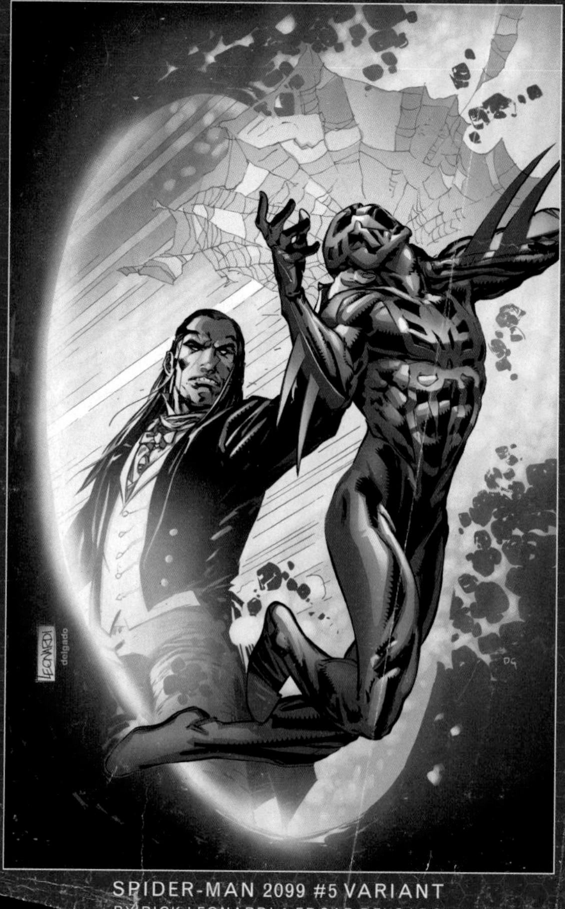
LEONARDI
delgado

SPIDER-MAN 2099 #5 VARIANT
BY RICK LEONARDI & EDGAR DELGADO